HISTORY OF INDIAN LITERATURE

HISTORY OF INDIAN LITERATURE

P. K. Sinha
Jagdish K. Ghosh

Commonwealth

History of Indian Literature

Edition : 2024

ISBN 978-81-311-0319-7

Published by :
COMMONWEALTH PUBLISHERS PVT. LTD.
4831/24, Prahlad Street,
Ansari Road, Darya Ganj,
New Delhi - 110002
Ph. : 23275511, 23257835
e-mail : commonwealthbooks@gmail.com

Laser Typesetting by :
Rishu Computers
Delhi

Printed at :
Roshan Offset Printers
Delhi

Preface

Indian literature, through its umpteen legends and folklore in prehistoric times, is today unanimously recognised and acknowledged as one of the oldest in the world. India possesses twenty-two officially accredited languages and a colossal variety of literature has been produced and reproduced in these languages over the graduating years. It thus becomes evident that history of Indian literature assimilates within itself an endless variety of untold stories and facts from ancient, medieval and comparatively modern times, which can be personified as a living entity.

History of Indian literature comes about in a wholesome domain through the Hindu epics like *Ramayana* and *Mahabharata*, treatises such as *Vaastu Shastra* in architecture and town planning and *Arthashastra* by Kautilya, making political science and involvement in politics household in ancient India. Prehistoric devotional Hindu play, poetry and songs sweep the subcontinent, with almost distinct imagery noticed in the gradual evolvement of literature in India.

The history of Indian literature is the historical development of writings in prose or poetry, which aim at providing education, entertainment and enlightenment to its readers, as well the development of the literary techniques employed in the communication of these pieces. This book is intended for advanced level students of English, who are taking exams or modules in English literature. It may also be suitable for teachers, researchers and the general reader who is interested in the history of literature.

Authors

Contents

1

Introduction to Indian Literature

Indian literature refers to the literature produced on the Indian subcontinent until 1947 and in the Republic of India thereafter. The Republic of India has 22 officially recognized languages.

The earliest works of Indian literature were orally transmitted. Sanskrit literature begins with the Rig Veda a collection of sacred hymns dating to the period 1500–1200 BCE. The Sanskrit epics *Ramayana* and *Mahabharata* appeared towards the end of the first millennium BCE. Classical Sanskrit literature flourished in the first few centuries of the first millennium CE, as did the Tamil Sangam literature, and the Pali Canon.

In the medieval period, literature in Kannada and Telugu appeared in the 9th and 11th centuries respectively. Later, literature in Marathi, Bengali, various dialects of Hindi, Persian and Urdu began to appear as well. Early in the 20th century, Bengali poet Rabindranath Tagore became India's first Nobel laureate. In contemporary Indian literature, there are two major literary awards; these are the Sahitya Akademi Fellowship and the Jnanpith Award. Seven Jnanpith awards each have been awarded in Hindi and

Kannada, followed by five in Bengali, four in Malayalam and three in Gujarati, Marathi and Indian literature in archaic Indian languages

Vedic Literature

Examples of early works written in Vedic Sanskrit include the holy Hindu texts, such as the core Vedas and the Upanishads. Other examples include the Sulba Sutras, which are some of the earliest texts on geometry.

Epic Sanskrit Literature

Ved Vyasa's *Mahabharata* and Valmiki's *Ramayana,* written in Epic Sanskrit, are regarded as the greatest Indian epics.

Classical Sanskrit Literature

The famous poet and playwright Kalidasa wrote two epics: *Raghuvamsha* (*Dynasty of Raghu*) and *Kumarasambhava (Birth of Kumar Kartikeya)*; they were written in Classical Sanskrit rather than Epic Sanskrit. Other examples of works written in Classical Sanskrit include the Pânini's *Ashtadhyayi* which standardized the grammar and phonetics of Classical Sanskrit. The *Laws of Manu* is an important text in Hinduism. Kalidasa is often considered to be the greatest playwright in Sanskrit literature, and one of the greatest poets in Sanskrit literature, whose *Recognition of Shakuntala* and *Meghaduuta* are the most famous Sanskrit plays. He occupies the same position in Sanskrit literature that Shakespeare occupies in English literature. Some other famous plays were *Mricchakatika* by Shudraka, *Svapna Vasavadattam* by Bhasa, and *Ratnavali* by Sri Harsha. Later poetic works include

Geeta Govinda by Jayadeva. Some other famous works are Chanakya's *Arthashastra* and Vatsyayana's *Kamasutra*.

Prakrit Literature

The most notable Prakrit languages were Ardhamagadhi, Pali and Sauraseni Prakrit. Many of Ashvaghosha's plays were written in Shauraseni Prakrit. Another major work in Sauraseni was *Karpuramanjari*. Kalidasa, Harsha and Haal used Maharashtrian Prakrit in some of their plays and poetry. Many Shwetambar Jain works are also written in the Maharashtri Prakrit. Many plays (like those of Ashvaghosha) and Jain works were written in the Ardha Magadhi Prakrit. Canto 13 of the Bhattikavya (Bhatti's Poem) is written in what is called "like the vernacular" *bhasasama*, that is, it can be read in two languages simultaneously: Prakrit and Sanskrit.

Pali Literature

The Pali Canon is mostly of Indian origin. Later Pali literature however was mostly produced outside of the mainland Indian subcontinent, particularly in Sri Lanka and Southeast Asia. Pali literature includes Buddhist philosophical works, poetry and some grammatical works. Major works in Pali are *Jataka tales, Dhammapada, Atthakatha,* and *Mahavamsa*. Some of the major Pali grammarians were Kaccayana, Moggallana and Vararuci.

Literature in Regional Languages

Assamese Literature

The Charyapadas are often cited as the earliest

example of Assamese literature. The Charyapadas are Buddhist songs composed in 8th-12th century. These writings bear similarities to Oriya and Bengali languages as well. The phonological and morphological traits of these songs bear very strong resemblance to Assamese some of which are extant.

After the Charyapadas, the period may again be split into Pre-Vaishnavite and Vaishnative sub-periods. The earliest known Assamese writer is Hema Saraswati, who wrote a small poem "Prahlada Charita". In the time of the King Indranarayana (1350-1365) of Kamatapur the two poets Harihara Vipra and Kaviratna Saraswati composed Asvamedha Parva and Jayadratha Vadha respectively. Another poet named Rudra Kandali translated Drona Parva into Assamese. But the most well-known poet of the Pre-Vaishnavite sub period is Madhav Kandali, who rendered Valmiki's Ramayana into Assamese verse (Kotha Ramayana, 11th century) under the patronage of Mahamanikya, a Kachari king of Jayantapura.

The most famous modern Assamese writers are Indira Goswami, Nirupama Bargohain, Birendra Kumar Bhattacharya, Homen Borgohain, Bhabendra Nath Saikia, Amulya Barua, Nabakanta Barua, Atul Chandra Hazarika, Nalini Bala Devi, Nirmal Prabha Bordoloi, Mahim Bora, Arupa Patangia Kalita, Bhabananda Deka, Purobi Bormudoi, Arun Sharma, Anuradha Sharma Pujari, Atulananda Deva Goswami, etc.

Bengali Literature

The first evidence of Bengali literature is known as Charyapada or Charyageeti, which were Buddhist hymns from the 8th century. Charyapada is in the oldest known written form of Bengali. The famous Bengali linguist Harprashad Shastri discovered the palm leaf Charyapada manuscript in the Nepal Royal Court Library in 1907. The most internationally famous Bengali writer is Nobel laureate Rabindranath Tagore, who received the Nobel Prize for Literature in 1913 for his work "Gitanjali". He wrote the national anthem of India and Bangladesh namely, "Jana Gana Mana" and "Amar Sonar Bangla", respectively. He was the first Asian who won the Nobel Prize. Rabindranath has written enormous amount of Poems, Songs, Essays, Novels, Plays and Short-stories. His songs remain popular and are still widely sung in Bengal.

Another poet, one generation younger is equally popular, valuable, and influential in his country, though virtually unknown in foreign countries: Kazi Nazrul Islam. Other famous Indian Bengali writers were Sharat Chandra Chattopadhyay, Bankim Chandra Chattopadhyay, and Michael Madhusudan Dutt. Bengali is the second most commonly spoken language in India (after Hindi). As a result of the Bengal Renaissance in the 19th and 20th centuries, many of India's most famous, and relatively recent, literature, poetry, and songs are in Bengali. In the history of Bengali literature there has been only one path-breaking literary movement by a group of poets and artists who called themselves Hungryalists.

Hindi Literature

Hindi literature started as religious and philosophical poetry in medieval periods in dialects like Avadhi and Brij. The most famous figures from this period are Kabir and Tulsidas. In modern times, the *Khadi* dialect became more prominent and Sanskrit.

Chandrakanta, written by Devaki Nandan Khatri, is considered to be the first work of prose in Hindi. Munshi Premchand was the most famous Hindi novelist. The *chhayavadi* poets include Suryakant Tripathi 'Nirala', Jaishankar Prasad, Sumitranandan Pant, and Mahadevi Varma. Other renowned poets include Ramdhari Singh 'Dinkar', Maithili Sharan Gupt, Agyeya, Harivansh Rai Bachchan, and Dharmveer Bharti.

Kannada Literature

Kannada writer and Jnanpith Award winner for the year 1994, U. R. Ananthamurthy.

The oldest existing record of Kannada poetry in *tripadi* metre is the Kappe Arabhatta record of 700 CE. *Kavirajamarga* by King Nripatunga Amoghavarsha I (850 CE) is the earliest existing literary work in Kannada. It is a writing on literary criticism and poetics meant to standardize various written Kannada dialects used in literature in previous centuries. The book makes reference to Kannada works by early writers such as King Durvinita of the sixth century and Ravikirti, the author of the Aihole record of 636 CE. An early extant prose work, the *Vaddaradhane* by Shivakotiacharya of 900 CE provides an elaborate description of the life of Bhadrabahu of Shravanabelagola. Since the earliest available Kannada work is one on grammar and a guide of sorts to unify existing variants of Kannada grammar and literary styles, it can be safely assumed that literature in Kannada must have started several centuries earlier. The works of the midieval period are based on Jain and Hindu principles. The Vachana Sahitya tradition of the twelfth century is purely native and unique in world literature. It is the sum of contributions by all sections of society. Vachanas were pithy comments on that period's social, religious and economic conditions. More importantly, they held a mirror to the seed of social revolution, which caused a radical re-examination of the ideas of caste, creed and religion. Some of the important writers of Vachana literature include Basavanna, Allama Prabhu and Akka Mahadevi. Kumara Vyasa, who wrote the *Karnata Bharata Katamanjari,* has arguably been the most famous and most influential Kannada writer of the fifteenth century. The Bhakti movement gave rise to Dasa Sahitya around the fifteenth century which significantly contributed to the evolution of Carnatic music in its present form. This period witnessed great Haridasas like Purandara Dasa who has been aptly called the *Pioneer of Carnatic music,* Kanaka Dasa, Vyasathirtha and Vijaya Dasa. Modern Kannada in the twentieth century has been influenced by many movements, notably *Navodaya, Navya, Navyottara, Dalita* and *Bandaya.* Contemporary Kannada literature has been highly successful in reaching people of all classes in society. Works of Kannada literature have received seven Jnanpith awards, which is the highest number awarded for the literature in any Indian language. It has also received forty-seven Sahitya Academy awards.

Malayalam Literature

Even up to 500 years since the start of the Malayalam calendar which commenced in 825 AD, Malayalam literature remained in preliminary stage. During this time, Malayalam literature consisted mainly of various genres of songs. *Ramacharitham* written by *Cheeramakavi* is a collection of poems written at the end of preliminary stage in Malayalam literaure's evolution, and is the oldest Malayalam book available. Thunchaththu Ramanujan Ezhuthachan (17th century) is considered as the Father of the Malayalam language, because of his influence on the acceptance of the Malayalam alphabet and his extremely popular poetic works like Adhyathmaramayanam. Several noted works were written during the 19th century, but it was in the 20th century the Malayalam literary movement came to prominence. Malayalam literature flourished under various genres and today it is a fully developed part of Indian literature.

Manipuri Literature

Manipuri literature is the literature written in the Manipuri Language (Meeteilon), including literature composed in Manipuri Language by writers from Manipur, Assam, Tripura, Myanmar and Bangladesh .The history of Manipuri literature trace back to thousands of years with flourish of its civilization.

The survival of Manipuri literature after passing through the massive devastation, the terror event of history, by burning of Meetei Scriptures, which is known as Puya Meithaba, was a miracle. The resilience that Meeteis could acquire in the event of devastation proved her ability to survive in history. Most of the early literary works found in Manipuri Literature were in Poetry and Prose. Some of the books were written with combination of both the Prose and Poetry.

Marathi Literature

Marathi literature began with saint-poets like Dnyaneshwar, Tukaram, Ramdas, and Eknath. Modern Marathi literature was marked by a theme of social reform. Well-known figures from this phase include

Mahatma Jyotiba Phule, Lokhitwadi, and others. Prominent modern literary figures include Vishnu Sakharam Khandekar, P.L. Deshpande, Vijay Tendulkar, Indira Sant and Vishnu Vaman Shirvadakar (*Kavi Kusumagraj*).

Oriya Literature

Oriya has a rich literary heritage dating back to the thirteenth century. Sarala Dasa who lived in the fourteenth century is known as the Vyasa of Orissa. He translated the Mahabharata into Oriya. In fact the language was initially standardised through a process of translation of classical Sanskrit texts like the Mahabharata, the Ramayana and the Srimad Bhagabatam. Jagannatha Das translated the Srimad Bhagabatam into Oriya and his translation standardized the written form of the language. Oriya has had a strong tradition of poetry, especially that of devotional poetry. Some other eminent ancient Oriya Poets include Kabi Samrat Upendra Bhanja and Kabi Surya Bala Dev Ratha.

In nineteenth Century, Fakir Mohan Senapati (1843-1918), Gouri Shankar Ray, Gopal Chandra Praharaj, Pandit Nilmani Vidyaratna, Kabibar Radhanath Ray were prominent figure in prose and poetry writinga of Oriya Literature. In twentieth century Godabarish Mohapatra, Kalindi Charana Panigrahi, Kanhu Charan Mohanty (1906-1994), Gopinath Mohanty, Sachchidananda Routray, Surendra Mohanty, Manoj Das, Kishori Charan Das, Sitakanta Mohapatra, Ramakanta Rath, Binapani Mohanty, Jagadish Mohanty, Sarojini Sahoo, Rajendra Kishore Panda, Padmaj Pal, Ramchandra Behera, Pratibha Satpathy are few names who made the Oriya Literature and Oriya language worthy.

Punjabi Literature

The history of Punjabi literature starts with advent of Aryan in Punjab. Punjab provided them the perfect environment in which to compose the ancient texts. The Rig-Veda is first example in which references are made to the rivers, flora and fauna of Punjab.

Tamil Literature

Tamil literature has a rich and long literary tradition spanning more than 2000 years. Tolkaappiyam has been credited as the oldest work in Tamil available today. The history of Tamil literature follows the history of Tamil Nadu, closely following the social and political trends of various periods.

The secular nature of the early Sangam poetry gave way to works of religious and didactic nature during the Middle Ages. Tirukkural is a fine example of such work on human behaviour and political morals. A wave of religious revival helped generate a great volume of literary output by Saivite and Vaishnavite authors. Jain and Buddhist authors during the medieval period and Muslim and European authors later also contributed to the growth of Tamil literature.

A revival of Tamil literature took place from the late nineteenth century when works of religious and philosophical nature were written in a style that made it easier for the common people to enjoy. Nationalist poets began to utilise the power of poetry in influencing the masses. Short stories and novels began to appear. The popularity of Tamil Cinema has also provided opportunities for modern Tamil poets to emerge.

Telugu Literature

Telugu, the second largest language (after Hindi) spoken in India, is rich in literary traditions. The earliest written literature dates back to the seventh century. The epic literary tradition started with Nannayya who is acclaimed as Telugu's *Aadikavi* meaning the first poet. He belongs to the tenth or eleventh century.

Vemana who lived in the fourteenth century (a prince called Pedakomati. Vemaa Reddy) wrote in the language of the common man. He wrote poems in a simple style. He questioned the prevailing pseudo values and conventions and religious practices in his poems. His philosophy made him a unique poet of the masses.

Viswanadha Satyanarayana (*Veyipadagalu*), a doyen of conventional yet creative literature, was the first to receive the Jnanpith Award for Telugu followed by C. Narayana Reddy.

Srirangam Srinivasarao or Sri Sri was a popular modern poet and lyricist. Srisri took the "Telugu literary band wagon that travelled in roads of kings and queens in to that of muddy roads of common man".

Literary Movements

Telugu literature has been enriched by many literary movements like Veera Shaiva movement which gave birth sto dwipada kavitvam (couplets). Bhakti movement which gave us immortal compilations by Annamayya, Kshetrayya and Tyagaraja and kancharla Gopanna (Ramadasu). The renaissance movement heralded by Vemana stand for the old Telugu literary movements.

Romantic Movemnet (led by Krishnasashtri, Rayaprolu, Vedula), Progressive Writers Movement, Digambara Kavitvam (Nagnamuni, Cherabanda Raju, Jwalamukhi, Nikhileswar, Bhairavayya and Mahaswapna Revolutionary Writers' Movement, Streevada Kavitvam and Dalita Kavitvam all flourished in Telugu Literature and in fact, Telugu Literature has been the standard bearer of Indian Literature in these respects.

Kadukuri Veeresalingam, is said to be the father of Modern Telugu fiction. Kodavatiganti Kutumba Rao laid foundation for the realistic modern Telugu Novel and Short Story, Rachakonda and Kalipatnam carried the flag in to excellency. Annamaya, Gurajada Appa Rao, Kandukuri, Devulapalli, Jashuva, Unnava Laxminarayana, Bucchi Babu, Tripuraneni Gopichand and many more had a profound impact on Telugu literature.

Urdu Literature

Among other traditions, Urdu poetry is a fine example of linguistic and cultural synthesis. Arab and Persian vocabulary based on the Hindi language resulted in a vast and extremely beloved class of ghazal literature, usually written by Muslims in contexts ranging from romance and society to philosophy and devotion to Allah. Urdu soon became the court language of the Mughals and in its higher forms was once called the "Kohinoor" of Indian languages.

Indian literature in Foreign Languages

Indian Persian Literature

During the early Muslim period, Persian became the

lingua franca of the subcontinent, used by most of the educated and the government. Although Persian literature from Persia itself was popular, several Indians became major Persian poets, the most notable being Amir Khusro and in more modern times Allama Iqbal. Much of the older Sanskrit literature was also translated into Persian.

For a time, it remained the court language of the Mughals, soon to be replaced by Urdu. Persian still held its status, despite the spread of Urdu, well into the early years of the British rule in India. Most British officials had to learn Persian on coming to India and concluded their conversations in Persian. In 1837, however, the British, in an effort to expand their influence, made a government ruling to discontinue the use of Persian and commence the use of English instead.

Thus started the decline of Persian as the subcontinent's lingua franca, a position to be taken up by the new language of the British Raj, English. Many modern Indian languages still show signs of heavy Persian influence, most notably Urdu and Hindi.

Indian English Literature

In the last century, several Indian writers have distinguished themselves not only in traditional Indian languages but also in English. India's only Nobel laureate in literature was the Bengali writer Rabindranath Tagore, who wrote some of his work originally in English, and did some of his own English translations from Bengali. More recent major writers in English who are either Indian or of Indian origin and derive much inspiration from Indian themes are R. K. Narayan, Vikram Seth, Salman Rushdie, Arundhati

Roy, Raja Rao, Amitav Ghosh, Rohinton Mistry, Vikram Chandra, Vijay Singh, Mukul Kesavan, Raj Kamal Jha, Vikas Swarup, Khushwant Singh, Shashi Tharoor, Nayantara Sehgal, Anita Desai, Kiran Desai, Ashok Banker, Shashi Deshpande, Anurag Mathur,Jhumpa Lahiri, Kamala Markandaya, Gita Mehta, Manil Suri, Ruskin Bond and Bharati Mukherjee.

In the 1950s, the Writers Workshop collective in Calcutta was founded by the poet and essayist P. Lal to advocate and publish Indian writing in English. The press was the first to publish Pritish Nandy, Sasthi Brata, and others; it continues to this day to provide a forum for English writing in India. In recent years, English-language writers of Indian origin are being published in the West at an increasing rate.

2

Vedic Literature

The Vedas are a large body of texts originating in Ancient India. Composed in Vedic Sanskrit, the texts constitute the oldest layer of Sanskrit literature and the oldest scriptures of Hinduism.

The class of "Vedic texts" is aggregated around the four canonical *Samhitas* or Vedas proper (*turiya*), of which three (*traya*) are related to the performance of yajna (sacrifice) in historical (Iron Age) Vedic religion:

1. The Rigveda, containing hymns to be recited by the hotr or chief priest;
2. The Yajurveda, containing formulas to be recited by the adhvaryu or officiating priest;
3. The Samaveda, containing formulas to be chanted by the udgatr.

The fourth is the Atharvaveda, a collection of spells and incantations, stories, predictions, apotropaic charms and some speculative hymns.

According to Hindu tradition, the Vedas are *apauruseya* "not of human agency", are supposed to have been directly revealed, and thus are called *Sruti* ("what is heard"). The four *Samhitas* are metrical (with the exception of prose commentary interspersed in the

Black Yajurveda). The term *samhita* literally means "composition, complation". The individual verses contained in these compilations are known as *mantras*. Some selected Vedic mantras are still recited at prayers, religious functions and other auspicious occasions in contemporary Hinduism.

The various Indian philosophies and sects have taken differing positions on the Vedas. Schools of Indian philosophy which cite the Vedas as their scriptural authority are classified as "orthodox" (astika). Other traditions, notably Buddhism and Jainism, which did not regard the Vedas as authorities are referred to by traditional Hindu texts as "heterodox" or "non-orthodox" (nastika) schools. In addition to Buddhism and Jainism, Sikhism and Brahmoism do not accept the authority of the Vedas.

The Sanskrit word *Veda* "knowledge, wisdom" is derived from the root *vid-* "to know". This is reconstructed as being derived from the Proto-Indo-

In English, the term *Veda* is mostly used to refer to the *Samhitas* (collection of *mantras*, or chants) of the four canonical Vedas (*Rigveda, Yajurveda, Samaveda* and *Atharvaveda*). The Sanskrit term *veda* as a common noun means "knowledge", but can also be used to refer to fields of study unrelated to liturgy or ritual, e.g. in *agada-veda* "medical science", *sasya-veda* "science of agriculture" or *sarpa-veda* "science of snakes" (already found in the early Upanishads); *durveda* means "with evil knowledge, ignorant".

The Vedas are among the oldest sacred texts. The Samhitas date to roughly 1500–1000 BCE, and the "circum-Vedic" texts, as well as the redaction of the Samhitas, date to c. 1000-500 BCE, resulting in a Vedic period, spanning the mid 2nd to mid 1st millennium

BCE, spanning the Late Bronze Age and the Iron Age. Gavin Flood sums up mainstream estimates, according to which the Rigveda was compiled from as early as 1500 BCE over a period of several centuries. The Vedic period reaches its peak only after the composition of the mantra texts, with the establishment of the various shakhas all over Northern India which annotated the mantra samhitas with Brahmana discussions of their meaning, and reaches its end in the age of Buddha and Panini and the rise of the Mahajanapadas (archaeologically, Northern Black Polished Ware). Michael Witzel gives a time span of c. 1500 BCE to c. 500-400 BCE. Witzel makes special reference to the Near Eastern Mitanni material of the 14th c. BCE the only epigraphic record of Indo-Aryan contemporary to the Rigvedic period. He gives 150 BCE (Patanjali) as a terminus ante quem for all Vedic Sanskrit literature, and 1200 BCE (the early Iron Age) as terminus post quem for the Atharvaveda. The general accepted historical chronology of the Vedas ranks the Rig Veda as the first, followed by the Yajur Veda, Sama Veda and finally the Atharva Veda.

Transmission of texts in the Vedic period was by oral tradition alone, preserved with precision with the help of elaborate mnemonic techniques.

A literary tradition set in only in post-Vedic times, after the rise of Buddhism in the Maurya period, perhaps earliest in the Kanva recension of the Yajurveda about the 1st century BCE; however oral tradition predominated until c. 1000 CE. Due to the ephemeral nature of the manuscript material (birch bark or palm leaves), surviving manuscripts rarely surpass an age of a few hundred years. The Benares Sanskrit University has a Rigveda manuscript of the mid-14th century; however, there are a number of older Veda manuscripts in Nepal belonging to the Vajasaneyi tradition that are dated from the 11th century onwards.

Categories of Vedic Texts

The term "Vedic texts" is used in two distinct meanings:

1. Texts composed in Vedic Sanskrit during the Vedic period (Iron Age India)
2. Any text considered as "connected to the Vedas" or a "corollary of the Vedas"

Vedic Sanskrit Corpus

a) The Samhita (Sanskrit *samhita,* "collection"), are collections of metric texts ("mantras"). There are four "Vedic" Samhitas: the Rig-Veda, Sama-Veda, Yajur-Veda, and Atharva-Veda, most of which are available in several recensions (*Sakha*). In some contexts, the term *Veda* is used to refer to these Samhitas. This is the oldest layer of Vedic texts, apart from the Rigvedic hymns, which were probably essentially complete by 1200 BC, dating to ca. the 12th to 10th centuries BC. The complete corpus of Vedic mantras as collected in Bloomfield's *Vedic Concordance* (1907) consists of some 89,000 padas (metric feet), of which 72,000 occur in the four Samhitas.

b) The Brahmanas are prose texts that discuss, in technical fashion, the solemn sacrificial rituals as well as comment on their meaning and many connected themes. Each of the Brahmanas is associated with one of the Samhitas or its recensions. The Brahmanas may either form separate texts or can be partly integrated into the text of the Samhitas. They may also include the Aranyakas and Upanishads.

c) The Aranyakas , "wilderness texts" or "forest treaties", were composed by people who meditated in the woods as recluses and are the third part of the Vedas. The texts contain discussions and interpretations of dangerous rituals (to be studied outside the settlement) and various sorts of additional materials. It is frequently read in secondary literature.

d) Some of the older Mukhya Upanishads (Brhadaranyaka, Chandogya, Katha).

e) Certain Sutra literature, i.e. the Shrautasutras and the Grhyasutras.

The Shrauta Sutras, regarded as belonging to the smriti, are late Vedic in language and content, thus forming part of the Vedic Sanskrit corpus. The composition of the Shrauta and Grhya Sutras (ca. 6th century BC) marks the end of the Vedic period , and at the same time the beginning of the flourishing of the "circum-Vedic" scholarship of Vedanga, introducing the early flowering of classical Sanskrit literature in the Mauryan and Gupta periods.

While production of Brahmanas and Aranyakas ceases with the end of the Vedic period, there is a large number of Upanishads composed after the end of the Vedic period. While most of the ten mukhya Upanishads can be considered to date to the Vedic or Mahajanapada period, most of the 108 Upanishads of the full Muktika canon date to the Common Era.

The Brahmanas, Aranyakas, and Upanishads often interpret the polytheistic and ritualistic Samhitas in philosophical and metaphorical ways to explore abstract concepts such as the Absolute (Brahman), and the soul or the self (Atman), introducing Vedanta philosophy, one of the major trends of later Hinduism.

The Vedic Sanskrit corpus is the scope of *A Vedic Word Concordance* (*Vaidika-Padanukrama-Kosa*) prepared from 1930 under Vishva Bandhu, and published in five volumes in 1935-1965. Its scope extends to about 400 texts, including the entire Vedic Sanskrit corpus besides some "sub-Vedic" texts.

Volume I: Samhitas

Volume II: Brahmanas and Aranyakas

Volume III: Upanishads

Volume IV: Vedangas

A revised edition, extending to about 1800 pages, was published in 1973-1976.

Shruti Literature

The texts considered "Vedic" in the sense of "corollaries of the Vedas" is less clearly defined, and may include numerous post-Vedic texts such as Upanishads or Sutra literature.

The latter group of texts is called *Shruti* (Sanskrit: *Shruuti*; "the heard"). Since post-Vedic times it has been considered to be revealed wisdom, as distinct from other texts, collectively known as *Smriti* (Sanskrit: *Smriti*; "the remembered"), that is texts that are considered to be of human origin. This indigenous system of categorization was adopted by Max Muller and, while it is subject to some debate, it is still widely used. As Axel Michaels explains:

These classifications are often not tenable for linguistic and formal reasons: There is not only *one* collection at any one time, but rather several handed down in separate Vedic schools; Upanishads ... are sometimes not to be distinguished from Aranyakas...; Brahman as contain older strata of language attributed to the Samhitas; there are various dialects and locally prominent traditions of the Vedic schools. Nevertheless, it is advisable to stick to the division adopted by Max Müller because it follows the Indian tradition, conveys the historical sequence fairly accurately, and underlies the current editions, translations, and monographs on Vedic literature.

The Upanishads are largely philosophical works in dialog form. They discuss questions of nature philosophy and the fate of the soul, and contain some mystic and spiritual interpretations of the Vedas. For long, they have been regarded as their putative end and essence, and are thus known as Vedânta ("the end of the Vedas"). Taken together, they are the basis of the Vedanta school.

Other texts such as the Bhagavad Gita or the Vedanta Sutras are considered *shruti* or "Vedic" by some Hindu denominations but not universally within Hinduism. The Bhakti movement, and Gaudiya Vaishnavism in particular extended the term to include the Sanskrit Epics and Vaishnavite devotional texts such as the Pancaratra.

Vedic Schools or Recensions

Study of the extensive body of Vedic texts has been organized into a number of different schools or branches (Sanskrit *sakha,* literally "branch" or "limb") each of which specialized in learning certain texts.

Multiple recensions are known for each of the Vedas, and each Vedic text may have a number of schools associated with it. Elaborate methods for preserving the text were based on memorizing by heart instead of writing. Specific techniques for parsing and reciting the texts were used to assist in the memorization process.

Prodigous energy was expended by ancient Indian culture in ensuring that these texts were transmitted from generation to generation with inordinate fidelity. For example, memorization of the sacred *Vedas* included up to eleven forms of recitation of the same text. The texts were subsequently "proof-read" by comparing the different recited versions. Forms of recitation included the *jata-patha* (literally "mesh recitation") in which every two adjacent words in the text were first recited in their original order, then repeated in the reverse order, and finally repeated again in the original order.

That these methods have been effective is testified to by the preservation of the most ancient Indian religious text, the *Rgveda,* as a redacted into single text during the *Brahmana* period, without any variant readings.

The Four Vedas

Rigveda (padapatha) manuscript in Devanagari, early 19th century. The canonical division of the Vedas is fourfold (*turiya*) viz.,

1. Rigveda (RV)
2. Yajurveda (YV, with the main division TS *vs.* VS)
3. Sama-Veda (SV)
4. Atharva-Veda (AV)

Of these, the first three were the principal original division, also called *"trayi vidya"*, that is, "the triple sacred science" of reciting hymns (RV), performing sacrifices (YV), and chanting (SV). This triplicity is so introduced in the Brahmanas (ShB, ABr and others), but the Rigveda is the older work of the three from which the other two borrow, next to their own independent Yajus, sorcery and speculative mantras.

Thus, the Mantras are properly of three forms:

1. *Ric*, which are verses of praise in metre, and intended for loud recitation;
2. *Yajus*, which are in prose, and intended for recitation in lower voice at sacrifices;
3. *Saman*, which are in metre, and intended for singing at the Soma ceremonies.

The Yajurveda, Samaveda and Atharvaveda are independent collections of mantras and hymns intended as manuals for the Adhvaryu, Udgatr and Brahman priests respectively.

The Atharvaveda is the fourth Veda. Its status has occasionally been ambiguous, probably due to its use in sorcery and healing. However, it contains very old materials in early Vedic language. Manusmrti, which often speaks of the three Vedas, calling them *trayam-brahma-sanatanam*, "the triple eternal Veda".

The Atharvaveda like the Rigveda, is a collection of original incantations, and other materials borrowing relatively little from the Rigveda. It has no direct relation to the solemn Srauta sacrifices, except for the fact that the mostly silent Brahmán priest observes the procedures and uses Atharvaveda mantras to 'heal' it when mistakes have been made. Its recitation also produces long life, cures diseases, or effects the ruin of enemies.

Each of the four Vedas consists of the metrical Mantra or Samhita and the prose Brahmana part, giving discussions and directions for the detail of the ceremonies at which the Mantras were to be used and explanations of the legends connected with the Mantras and rituals. Both these portions are termed shruti (which tradition says to have been heard but not composed or written down by men). Each of the four Vedas seems to have passed to numerous Shakhas or schools, giving rise to various recensions of the text. They each have an Index or Anukramani, the principal work of this kind being the general Index or *Sarvanukramani*.

Rigveda

The Rigveda Samhita is the oldest extant Indic text. It is a collection of 1,028 Vedic Sanskrit hymns and 10,600 verses in all, organized into ten books (Sanskrit: *mandalas*). The hymns are dedicated to Rigvedic deities.

The books were composed by poets from different priestly groups over a period of several centuries, commonly dated to the period of roughly the second half of the 2nd millennium BCE (the early Vedic period) in the Punjab (Sapta Sindhu) region of the Indian subcontinent.

There are strong linguistic and cultural similarities between the Rigveda and the early Iranian Avesta, deriving from the Proto-Indo-Iranian times, often associated with the Andronovo culture; the earliest horse-drawn chariots were found at Andronovo sites in the Sintashta-Petrovka cultural area near the Ural Mountains and date to ca. 2000 BCE.

Yajurveda

The Yajurveda Samhita consists of archaic prose mantras and also in part of verses borrowed and adapted from the Rigveda. Its purpose was practical, in that each mantra must accompany an action in sacrifice but, unlike the Samaveda, it was compiled to apply to all sacrificial rites, not merely the Somayajna. There are two major groups of recensions of this Veda, known as the "Black" (Krishna) and "White" (Shukla) Yajurveda. While White Yajurveda separates the Samhita from its Brahmana (the Shatapatha Brahmana), the e Black Yajurveda intersperses the Samhita with Brahmana commentary. Of the Black Yajurveda four major recensions survive (Maitrayani, Katha, Kapisthala-Katha, Taittiriya).

Samaveda

The Samaveda Samhita (from *Saman,* the term for a melody applied to metrical hymn or song of praise) consists of 1549 stanzas, taken almost entirely (except for 78 stanzas) from the Rigveda. Like the Rigvedic stanzas in the Yajurveda, the Samans have been changed and adapted for use in singing. Some of the Rigvedic verses are repeated more than once. Including repetitions, there are a total of 1875 verses numbered in the Samaveda recension translated by Griffith. Two major recensions remain today, the Kauthuma/Ranayaniya and the Jaiminiya. Its purpose was liturgical, as the repertoire of the *udgatr* or "singer" priests who took part in the sacrifice.

Atharvaveda

The Artharvaveda Samhita is the text 'belonging to the Atharvan and Angirasa poets. It has 760 hymns, and about 160 of the hymns are in common with the Rigveda. Most of the verses are metrical, but some sections are in prose. It was compiled around 900 BCE, although some of its material may go back to the time of the Rigveda, and some parts of the Atharva-Veda are older than the Rig-Veda though not in linguistic form.

The Atharvanaveda is preserved in two recensions, the Paippalada and Saunaka. According to Apte it had nine schools (*shakhas*). The Paippalada text, which exists in a Kashmir and an Orissa version, is longer than the Saunaka one; it is only partially printed in its two versions and remains largely untranslated.

Unlike the other three Vedas, the Atharvanaveda has less connection with sacrifice. Its first part consists chiefly of spells and incantations, concerned with protection against demons and disaster, spells for the healing of diseases, for long life and for various desires or aims in life.

The second part of the text contains speculative and philosophical hymns.

The Atharvaveda is a comparatively late extension of the "Three Vedas" connected to priestly sacrifice to a canon of "Four Vedas". This may be connected to an extension of the sacrificial rite from involving three types of priest to the inclusion of the Brahman overseeing the ritual.

Brahmanas

The mystical notions surrounding the concept of the one "Veda" that would flower in Vedantic philosophy have their roots already in Brahmana literature, for example in the Shatapatha Brahmana. The Vedas are identified with Brahman, the universal principle. Vac "speech" is called the "mother of the Vedas". The knowledge of the Vedas is endless, compared to them, human knowledge is like mere handfuls of dirt. The universe itself was originally encapsulated in the three Vedas.

Vedanta

While contemporary traditions continued to maintain Vedic ritualism, Vedanta renounced all ritualism and radically re-interpreted the notion of "Veda" in purely philosophical terms. The association of the three Vedas with the *bhur bhuvah svah* mantra is found in the Aitareya Aranyaka: "*Bhuh* is the Rigveda, *bhuvah* is the Yajurveda, *svah* is the Samaveda". The Upanishads reduce the "essence of the Vedas" further, to the syllable Aum (ॐ). Thus, the Katha Upanishad has:

> "The goal, which all Vedas declare, which all austerities aim at, and which humans desire when they live a life of continence, I will tell you briefly it is *Aum*"

Post-Vedic Literature

Six technical subjects related to the Vedas are traditionally known as *vedariga* "limbs of the Veda". V. S. Apte defines this group of works as:

> "N. of a certain class of works regarded as auxiliary to the Vedas and designed to aid in the correct pronunciation and interpretation of the text and the right employment of the *Mantras* in ceremonials."

These subjects are treated in Sutra literature dating from the end of the Vedic period to Mauryan times, seeing the transition from late Vedic Sanskrit to Classical Sanskrit.

The six subjects of Vedanga are:

a) Phonetics (Siksa)
b) Ritual (Kalpa)
c) Grammar (Vyakarana)
d) Etymology (Nirukta)
e) Meter (Chandas)

Parisista

Parisista "supplement, appendix" is the term applied to various ancillary works of Vedic literature, dealing mainly with details of ritual and elaborations of the texts logically and chronologically prior to them: the Samhitas, Brahmanas, Aranyakas and Sutras. Naturally classified with the Veda to which each pertains, Parisista works exist for each of the four Vedas. However, only the literature associated with the Atharvaveda is extensive.

i) The *Asvalayana Grhya Parisista* is a very late text associated with the Rigveda canon.
ii) The *Gobhila Grhya Parisista* is a short metrical text of two chapters, with 113 and 95 verses respectively.
iii) The Katiya Parisistas, ascribed to Katyayana, consist of 18 works enumerated self-referentially in the fifth of the series (the Caranavyuha)
iv) The Krsna Yajurveda has 3 parisistas The Apastamba Hautra Parisista, which is also found as the second *prasna* of the *Satyasadha Srauta Sutra', the Varaha Srauta Sutra Parisista and the Katyayana Srauta Sutra Parisista.*
v) For the Atharvaveda, there are 79 works, **collected** as 72 distinctly named parisistas.

Puranas

A traditional view given in the Vishnu Purana (likely dating to the Gupta period) attributes the current arrangement of four Vedas to the mythical sage Vedavyasa. Puranic tradition also postulates a single original Veda that, in varying accounts, was divided into three or four parts. According to the Vishnu Purana the original Veda was divided into four parts, and further fragmented into numerous shakhas, by Lord Vishnu in the form of Vyasa, in the Dvapara Yuga; the Vayu Purana recounts a similar division by Vyasa, at the urging of Brahma. The Bhagavata Purana traces the origin of the primeval Veda to the syllable aum, and says that it was divided into four at the start of *Dvapara Yuga*, because men had declined in age, virtue and understanding. In a differing account Bhagavata Purana attributes the division of the primeval veda (*aum*) into three parts to the monarch Pururavas at the beginning of Treta Yuga. The Mahabharata also mentions the division of the Veda into three in *Treta Yuga*.

Upaveda

The term upaveda ("applied knowledge") is used in traditional literature to designate the subjects of certain technical works. Lists of what subjects are included in this class differ among sources. The Charanavyuha mentions four Upavedas:

a) Medicine (Ayurveda), associated with the Rigveda

b) Archery (Dhanurveda), associated with the Yajurveda

c) Music and sacred dance (Gandharvaveda), associated with the Samaveda

d) Military science (Shastrashastra), associated with the Atharvaveda

But Sushruta and Bhavaprakasha mention Ayurveda as an upaveda of the Atharvaveda. Sthapatyaveda (architecture), Shilpa Shastras (arts and crafts) are mentioned as fourth upaveda according to later sources.

Fifth Veda

Some post-Vedic texts, including the Mahabharata, the Natyasastra and certain Puranas, refer to themselves as the "fifth Veda". The earliest reference to such a "fifth Veda" is found in the Chandogya Upanishad. "Dravida Veda" is a term for canonical Tamil Bhakti texts.

3

Indian Epic Poetry

Indian epic poetry is the epic poetry written in the Indian subcontinent. Originally composed in Sanskrit and translated thereafter into Kannada, Tamil, Telugu and Hindi, it includes some of the oldest epic poetry ever created and some works form the basis of Hindu scripture.

Sanskrit Epics

The ancient Sanskrit epics, the *Ramayana* and *Mahabharata*, also termed *Itihasa* (History) or *Mahakavya* (Great Compositions), refer to epic poems that form a canon of Hindu scripture. Indeed, the epic form prevailed and verse was and remained until very recently the preferred form of Hindu literary works. Hero-worship was and is a central aspect of Indian culture, and thus readily lent itself to a literary tradition that abounded in epic poetry and literature. The Puranas, a massive collection of verse-form histories of India's many Hindu gods and goddesses, followed in this tradition. Itihasas and Puranas are mentioned already in Atharva Veda and referred to as the *fifth Veda*.

The language of these texts, termed "Epic Sanskrit", constitutes the earliest phase of Classical Sanskrit, following the latest stage of Vedic Sanskrit found in the Shrauta Sutras.

The famous poet and playwright Kalidasa also wrote two epics: *Raghuvamsha* (*Dynasty of Raghu*) and *Kumarasambhava* (*Birth of Kumar Kartikeya*), though they were written in Classical Sanskrit rather than Epic Sanskrit.

The Ramayana

The *Ramayana* is attributed to the Hindu sage Valmiki and forms an important part of the Hindu canon. The *Ramayana* is one of the two great epics of India, the other being the *Mahabharata*. It depicts the duties of relationships, portraying ideal characters like the ideal servant, the ideal brother, the ideal wife and the ideal king.

The name *Ramayana* is a tatpurusha compound of Rama and ayana ("going, advancing"), translating to "Rama's Journey". The *Ramayana* consists of 24,000 verses in seven books and 500 cantos (sargas), and tells the story of Rama, whose wife Sita is abducted by the demon king of Lanka, Ravana. Thematically, the epic explores the tenets of human existence and the concept of dharma.

Verses in the *Ramayana* are written in a 32-syllable meter called anustubh. The epic was an important influence on later Sanskrit poetry and Indian life and culture, particularly through its establishment of the shloka meter. Like its epic cousin the *Mahabharata*, the *Ramayana* is not just an ordinary story: it contains the teachings of ancient Hindu sages and presents them in narrative allegory with philosophical and the devotional elements interspersed. The characters Rama, Sita, Lakshmana, Bharata, Hanuman and Ravana are all fundamental to the cultural consciousness of India.

There are other versions of the *Ramayana,* notably Buddhist and Jain in India, and also Thai, Laos and Malaysian versions of the tale.

Textuality

Traditionally, the *Ramayana* is ascribed to Valmiki, regarded as India's first poet. The Indian tradition is unanimous in its agreement that the poem is the work of a single poet, the sage Valmiki, a contemporary of Rama and a peripheral actor in the epic drama. The story's original version in Sanskrit is known as Valmiki *Ramayana,* dating to approximately the 4th century B.C. According to Hindu tradition, the *Ramayana* takes place during a period of time known as Treta Yuga.

In its extant form, Valmiki's *Ramayana* is an epic poem of some 50,000 lines. The text survives in several thousand partial and complete manuscripts, the oldest of which appears to date from the 11th century A.D. The text has several regional renderings, recensions and subrecensions. Textual scholar Robert P. Goldman differentiates two major regional recensions: the northern (N) and the southern (S). Famous recensions include the *Ramayanam* of Kamban in Tamil (ca. 11th-12th century), Shri Rama Panchali or Krittivasi Ramayan by Krittibas Ojha in Bengali (ca. 15th Century), and Ramacharitamanas by Tulasidas in Awadhi which is a dialect of Hindi (c. 16th century). Scholar Romesh Chunder Dutt writes that "the *Ramayana,* like the *Mahabharata,* is a growth of centuries, but the main story is more distinctly the creation of one mind."

There has been speculation as to whether the first and the last chapters of Valmiki's *Ramayana* were written by the original author. Raghunathan writes that many experts believe they are integral parts of the book in spite of some style differences and narrative contradictions between these two chapters and the rest of the book.

Period

According to literary scholarship, the main body of the *Ramayana* first appeared as an oral composition somewhere between 750 and 500 BCE. Cultural evidence (the presence of sati in the *Mahabharata* but not in the main body of the *Ramayana*) suggests that the *Ramayana* predates the *Mahabharata*. By tradition, the epic belongs to the Treta Yuga, one of the four eons (yuga) of Hindu chronology; thus, it is held to date back 880,000 years. Rama is said to have been born in the Treta Yuga to King Dasaratha in Ikshuaku vansh (clan).

The core events of the epic may be of even greater age, as the names of the characters (Rama, Sita, Dasaratha, Janaka, Vasishta, Vishwamitra) are all known in Vedic literature such as the Brahmanas which are older than the Valmiki *Ramayana*. However, nowhere in the surviving Vedic poetry is a story similar to the *Ramayana* of Valmiki. According to the modern academic view, Brahma, one of the main characters of *Ramayana*, and Vishnu, who according to Bala Kanda was incarnated as Rama, are not Vedic deities, and come first into prominence with the epics themselves and further during the 'Puranic' period of the later 1st millennium CE. There is also a version of *Ramayana*, known as Ramopakhyana, found in the epic

Mahabharata. This version, depicted as a narration to Yudhishtra, does not accord divine characteristics to Rama.

There is general consensus that books two to six form the oldest portion of the epic while the first book Bala Kanda and the last the Uttara Kanda are later additions. The author or authors of Bala Kanda and Ayodhya Kanda appear to be familiar with the eastern Gangetic basin region of northern India and the Kosala and Magadha region during the period of the sixteen janapadas as the geographical and geopolitical data is in keeping with what is known about the region. However, when the story moves to the Aranya Kanda and beyond, it seems to turn abruptly into fantasy with its demon-slaying hero and fantastic creatures. The geography of central and South India is increasingly vaguely described. The knowledge of the location of the island of Sri Lanka also lacks detail. Basing his assumption on these features, the historian H.D. Sankalia has proposed a date of the 4th century BC for the composition of the text. A. L. Basham, however, is of the opinion that Rama may have been a minor chief who lived in the 8th or the 7th century BC.

Characters

Rama seated with Sita, fanned by Lakshmana, while Hanuman pays his respects.Rama is the hero of the tale. Portrayed as the seventh incarnation of the god Vishnu, he is the eldest and favorite son of the King of Ayodhya, Dasharatha, and his wife Kousalya. He is portrayed as the epitome of virtue. Dasharatha is forced by Kaikeyi, one of his wives, to command Rama to relinquish his right to the throne for fourteen years and go into exile.

Sita is the beloved wife of Rama and the daughter of king Janaka. Sita is also known as Janaki. She is the incarnation of goddess Lakshmi, the consort of Vishnu. Sita is portrayed as the epitome of female purity and virtue. She follows her husband into exile and is abducted by Ravana. She is imprisoned on the island of Lanka until Rama rescues her by defeating the demon king Ravana. Later, she gives birth to Lava and Kusha, the heirs of Rama.

Hanuman is a vanara belonging to the kingdom of Kishkindha. He is portrayed as an incarnation of the god Shiva (the Eleventh Rudra) and an ideal bhakta of Rama. He is born as the son of Kesari, a vanara king, and the goddess Anjana. He plays an important part in locating Sita and in the ensuing battle.

Lakshmana, the younger brother of Rama, who chose to go into exile with him. He is portrayed as an incarnation of the Shesha, the naga associated with the god Vishnu. He spends his time protecting Sita and Rama. He is forced to leave Sita, who was deceived by the demon Maricha into believing that Rama was in trouble. Sita is abducted by Ravana upon him leaving her.

Ravana, a rakshasa, is the king of Lanka. After performing severe penance for ten thousand years he received a boon from the creator-god Brahma that he could not be killed by gods, demons or spirits. He is portrayed as a powerful demon king, who disturbs the penances of Rishis. Vishnu incarnates as the human Rama to defeat him, thus circumventing the boon given by Brahma.

Dasharatha is the king of Ayodhya and the father of Rama. He has three queens, Kousalya, Sumitra and

Kaikeyi, and three other sons: Bharata, Lakshmana and Shatrughna. Kaikeyi, Dasharatha's favourite queen, forces him to make his son Bharata crown prince and send Rama into exile. Dasharatha dies heartbroken after Rama goes into exile.

Bharata is the son of Dasharatha. When he learns that his mother Kaikeyi had forced Rama into exile and caused Dasharatha to die brokenhearted, he storms out of the palace and goes in search of Rama in the forest. When Rama refuses to return from his exile to assume the throne, Bharata obtains Rama's sandals and places them on the throne as a gesture that Rama is the true king. Bharata then rules Ayodhya as the regent of Rama for the next fourteen years.

Shatrughna is the son of Dasharatha and his third wife Queen Sumitra. He is the youngest brother of Rama and also the twin brother of Lakshmana.

Synopsis

The poem is traditionally divided into several major kandas or books, that deal chronologically with the major events in the life of Rama—Bala kanda, Ayodhya Kanda, Aranya Kanda, Kishkinda Kanda, Sundara Kanda, Yuddha Kanda, and Uttara Kanda. The Bala Kanda describes the birth of Rama, his childhood and marriage to Sita. The Ayodhya Kanda describes the preparations for Rama's coronation and his exile into the forest. The third part, Aranya Kanda, describes the forest life of Rama and the kidnapping of Sita by the demon king Ravana. The fourth book, Kishkinda Kanda, describes the meeting of Hanuman with Rama, the destruction of the vanara king Vali and the coronation of his younger brother Sugriva to the throne of the kingdom of Kishkindha. The fifth book is

Sundara Kanda, which narrates the heroism of Hanuman, his flight to Lanka and meeting with Sita. The sixth book, Yuddha Kanda, describes the battle between Rama's and Ravana's armies. The last book, Uttara Kanda, describes the birth of Lava and Kusha to Sita, their coronation to the throne of Ayodhya, and Rama's final departure from the world.

Influence on Culture

One of the most important literary works of ancient India, the *Ramayana* has had a profound impact on art and culture in the Indian subcontinent and Southeast Asia. The story ushered in the tradition of the next thousand years of massive-scale works in the rich diction of regal courts and Brahminical temples. It has also inspired much secondary literature in various languages, notably the Kamba*Ramayana*m by the Tamil poet Kambar of the 13th century, the Telugu-language Molla *Ramayana,* 14th century Kannada poet Narahari Kavi's Torave Ramayan, and 15th century Bengali poet Krittibas Ojha's Krittivasi Ramayan, as well as the 16th century Awadhi version, Ramacharitamanas, written by Tulsidas. The *Ramayana* became popular in Southeast Asia during the 8th century and was represented in literature, temple architecture, dance and theatre. Today, dramatic enactments of the story of *Ramayana,* known as Ramlila, take place all across India and in many places across the globe within the Indian diaspora.

Variant Versions

The epic story of *Ramayana* was adopted by several cultures across Asia. Shown here is a Thai historic artwork depicting the battle which took place between Rama and Ravana.As in many oral epics, multiple versions of the *Ramayana* survive. In particular, the *Ramayana* related in North India differs in important respects from that preserved in South India and the rest of South-East Asia. There is an extensive tradition of oral storytelling based on the *Ramayana* in Thailand, Cambodia, Malaysia, Laos, Vietnam, Indonesia and Maldives. Father Kamil Bulke, author of Ramakatha, has identified over 300 variants of *Ramayana*.

There are diverse regional versions of the *Ramayana* written by various authors in India. Some of them differ significantly from each other. During the 12th century AD, Kamban wrote Ramavatharam, known popularly as Kamba*Ramayana*m in Tamil. Valmiki's *Ramayana* inspired the Sri Ramacharit Manas by Tulasidas in 1576, an epic Awadhi (a dialect of Hindi) version with a slant more grounded in a different realm of Hindu literature, that of bhakti. It is an acknowledged masterpiece of India, popularly known as Tulsi-krita *Ramayana*. Gujarati poet Premanand wrote a version of *Ramayana* in the 17th century. Other versions include a Bengali version by Krittivas in the 14th century, in Oriya by Balarama Das in the 16th century, in Marathi by Sridhara in the 18th century, a Telugu version by Ranganatha in the 15th century, a Torave *Ramayana* in Kannada by the 16th century poet Narahari and in 20th century Rashtrakavi Kuvempu's Sri *Ramayana* Darshnam, Kotha *Ramayana* in Assamese by the 14th century poet Madhava Kandali and Adhyathma *Ramayana*m Kilippattu, a Malayalam version by Thunchaththu Ezhuthachan in the 16th century.

There is a sub-plot to *Ramayana*, prevalent in some parts of India, relating the adventures of Ahi Ravana and Mahi Ravana, the evil brother of Ravana, which enhances the role of Hanuman in the story. Hanuman rescues Rama and Lakshmana after they are kidnapped by the Ahi-mahi Ravana at the behest of Ravana and held prisoner in a subterranean cave, to be sacrificed to the goddess Kali.

Two versions of *Ramayana* are present in Nepal. One is written by Mahakabhi Siddhidas Mahaju in Nepal Bhasa. The other one is written by Aadikavi Bhanubhakta Acharya. The Nepal Bhasa version by Siddhidas Mahaju marks a great point in the renaissance of Nepal Bhasa whereas the one of Bhanubhakta Acharya is the first epic of Nepali.

Many other Asian cultures have adapted the *Ramayana,* resulting in other national epics. Kakawin *Ramayana* is an old Javanese rendering; Yogesvara *Ramayana* is attributed to the scribe Yogesvara circa 9th century CE, who was employed in the court of the Sriwijaya. It has 2774 stanzas in manipravala style, a mixture of Sanskrit and Archaic prose Javanese language. The most influential version of the *Ramayana* is the Ravanavadham of Bhatti, popularly known as Bhattikavya. The Javanese *Ramayana* differs markedly from the original Hindu prototype.

Phra Lak Phra Lam is a Lao language version, whose title comes from Lakshmana and Rama. The story of Lakshmana and Rama is told as the previous life of the Buddha. In Hikayat Seri Rama of Malaysia, Dasharatha is the great-grandson of the Prophet Adam. Ravana receives boons from Allah instead of Brahma. In many Malay language versions, Lakshmana is given greater importance than Rama, whose character is considered somewhat weak.

The Khmer retelling of the tale, the Reamker, is popularly expressed in traditional regional dance theatre.The Cambodian version of *Ramayana,* the Reamker, is the most famous story of Khmer Literature since the Funan era. It adapts the Hindu concepts to Buddhist themes and shows the balance of good and evil in the world. The Reamker has several differences from the original *Ramayana,* including scenes not included in the original and emphasis on Hanuman and Sovanna Maccha, a retelling which influences the Thai and Lao versions. Reamker in Cambodia is not confined to the realm of literature but extends to all Cambodian art forms, such as sculpture, Khmer classical dance, theatre known as Lakhorn Luang (the foundation of the royal ballet), poetry and the mural and bas reliefs seen at the Silver Pagoda and Angkor wat.

Thailand's popular national epic Ramakien is derived from the Hindu epic. In Ramakien, Sita is the daughter of Ravana and Mandodari (T'os'akanth (=Dasakanth) and Mont'o). Vibhisana (P'ip'ek), the astrologer brother of Ravana, predicts calamity from the horoscope of Sita. So Ravana has her thrown into the waters, who, later, is picked by Janaka (Janok). While the main story is identical to that of the *Ramayana,* many other aspects were transposed into a Thai context, such as the clothes, weapons, topography, and elements of nature, which are described as being Thai in style. It has an expanded role for Hanuman and he is portrayed as a lascivious character. Ramakien can be seen in an elaborate illustration at the Wat Phra Kaew temple in Bangkok.

Other Southeast Asian adaptations include Ramakavaca of Bali (Indonesia), Maharadya Lawana and Darangen of Mindanao (Philippines), and the Yama Zatdaw of Myanmar. Aspects of the Chinese epic Journey to the West were also inspired by the *Ramayana,* particularly the character Sun Wukong, who is believed to have been based on Hanuman.

Theological Significance

Rama, the hero of the *Ramayana,* is a popular deity worshiped in the Hindu religion. Each year, many devout pilgrims trace his journey through India, halting at each of the holy sites along the way. The poem is not seen as just a literary monument, but serves as an integral part of Hinduism, and is held in such reverence that the mere reading or hearing of it, or certain passages of it, is believed by Hindus to free them from sin and bless the reader or listener.

According to Hindu tradition, Rama is an incarnation (Avatar) of the god Vishnu. The main purpose of this incarnation is to demonstrate the righteous path (dharma) for all living creatures on earth.

The Mahabharata

The *Mahabharata* is a major Sanskrit epic and is part of the Hindu itihasa. A major text of Hinduism and a cornerstone of Hindu mythology, it is of immense importance to the culture of the Indian subcontinent. Its consideration of human goals (dharma or duty, artha or purpose, kama, pleasure or desire and moksha or liberation) is part of a long-standing tradition which seeks to explain the relationship of the individual to society and the world (the nature of the 'Self') and the workings of karma.

Traditionally, the authorship of the *Mahabharata* is attributed to Vyasa. There have been many attempts to unravel its historical growth and compositional layers, the earliest of which probably date back to the late Vedic period (ca. 8th c. BCE). The text probably reached its final form by the early Gupta period (ca. 4th c. CE). The title may be translated as "the great tale of the Bharata dynasty". According to the *Mahabharata* itself, the tale is extended from a shorter version of 24,000 verses, called simply Bharata'.

With about one hundred thousand verses, long prose passages, and about 1.8 million words in total, the *Mahabharata* is the longest epic poem in the world. It is roughly ten times the length of the Iliad and Odyssey combined, roughly five times longer than Dante's Divine Comedy, and about four times the length of the Ramayana. The *Mahabharata* has a total length of more than 90,000 verses.

Besides its epic narrative of the Kurukshetra War and the fates of the Kauravas and the Pandavas, the *Mahabharata* contains much philosophical and devotional material, such as the Shrimad Bhagavad Gita (6.25-42) which has a very high level of philosophical and religious content, or a discussion of the four "goals of life" or purusharthas (12.161). The latter are enumerated as dharma (right action), artha (purpose), kama (pleasure), and moksha (liberation).

Among the principal works and stories that are a part of the *Mahabharata* are the following (often considered as works in their own right):

- the Bhagavad Gita in book 6 (Bhishmaparva): Krishna advises and teaches Arjuna when he is ridden with doubt.
- the story of Damayanti, sometimes called (Nala and Damayanti) in book 3 (Aranyakaparva), a love story.

- An abbreviated version of the Ramayana, in book 3 (Aranyakaparva)
- Rishyasringa, the horned boy and rishi, in book 3 (Aranyakaparva)

Arshia Sattar states that the central theme of the *Mahabharata*, as well as the Ramayana, is respectively Krishna's and Ram's hidden divinity and its progressive revelation.

Textual Structure

The epic is traditionally ascribed to Vyasa, who is also a major character in the epic. The first section of the *Mahabharata* states that it was Ganesha who, at the request of Vyasa, wrote down the text to Vyasa's dictation. Ganesha is said to have agreed to write it only on condition that Vyasa never pause in his recitation. Vyasa agreed, provided Ganesha took the time to understand what was said before writing it down.

The epic employs the story within a story structure, otherwise known as frametales, popular in many Indian religious and secular works. It is recited to the King Janamejaya who is the great-grandson of Arjuna, by Vaisampayana, a disciple of Vyasa. The recitation of Vaisampayana to Janamejaya is then recited again by a professional storyteller named Ugrasrava Sauti, many years later, to an assemblage of sages.

It is usually thought that the full length of the *Mahabharata* has accreted over a long period. Research on the *Mahabharata* has put an enormous effort into recognizing and dating various layers within the text. The *Mahabharata* itself (1.1.61) distinguishes a core portion of 24,000 verses, the Bharata proper, as opposed to additional secondary material, while the Ashvalayana Grhyasutra (3.4.4) makes a similar distinction. According to the Adi-parva of the *Mahabharata* (shlokas 81, 101-102), the text was originally 8,800 verses when it was composed by Vyasa and was known as the Jaya (Victory), which later became 24,000 verses in the Bharata recited by Vaisampayana, and finally over 90,000 verses in the *Mahabharata* recited by Ugrasrava Sauti.

The state of the text has been described by some early 20th century Indologists as unstructured and chaotic. Hermann Oldenberg supposed that the original poem must once have carried an immense "tragic force", but dismissed the full text as a "horrible chaos."

The earliest known references to the *Mahabharata* and its core Bharata date back to the Ashtadhyayi (sutra 6.2.38) of Pa?ini (fl. 4th century BCE), and in the Ashvalayana Grhyasutra (3.4.4). This may suggest that the core 24,000 verses, known as the Bharata, as well as an early version of the extended *Mahabharata,* were composed by the 4th century BCE. Parts of the Jaya's original 8,800 verses possibly may date back as far as the 9th-8th century BCE.

The *Mahabharata* is presumed to predate the Greek epic Iliad, and some episodes of the *Mahabharata* are syncretistically said to identify with the story of the Iliad. Christian Lassen, in his Indische Alterthumskunde, supposed that the reference is ultimately to Dhritarashtra's sorrows, the laments of Gandhari and Draupadi, and the valor of Arjuna and Duryodhana or Karna. This interpretation, endorsed in such standard references as Albrecht Weber's History of Indian Literature, has often been repeated.

Later, the copper-plate inscription of the Maharaja Sharvanatha (533-534) from Khoh (Satna District, Madhya Pradesh) describes the *Mahabharata* as a "collection of 100,000 verses" (shatasahasri samhita). The redaction of this large body of text was carried out after formal principles, emphasizing the numbers 18 and 12. The addition of the latest parts may be dated by the absence of the Anushasana-parva from MS Spitzer, the oldest surviving Sanskrit philosophical manuscript dated to the first century, that contains among other things a list of the books in the *Mahabharata*. From this evidence, it is likely that the redaction into 18 books took place in the first century. An alternative division into 20 parvas appears to have co-existed for some time. The division into 100 sub-parvas (mentioned in Mbh. 1.2.70) is older, and most parvas are named after one of their constituent sub-parvas. The Harivamsa consists of the final two of the 100 sub-parvas, and was considered an appendix (khila) to the *Mahabharata* proper by the redactors of the 18 parvas.

The 18 parvas

The division into 18 parvas is as follows:

1. *Adi Parva (The Book of the Beginning).* How the *Mahabharata* came to be narrated by Sauti to the assembled rishis at Naimisharanya. The recital of the *Mahabharata* at the sarpasattra of Janamejaya by Vaishampayana at Tak?asila. The history of the Bharata race is told in detail and the parva also traces history of the Bhrigu race. The birth and early life of the Kuru princes. (adi means first)
2. *Sabha Parva (The Book of the Assembly Hall).* Maya

Indraprastha. Life at the court, Yudhishthira's Rajasuya Yajna, the game of dice, and the eventual exile of the Pandavas.

3. *Vana Parva also Aranyaka-parva, Aranya-parva (The Book of the Forest).* The twelve years of exile in the forest (aranya).
4. *Virata Parva (The Book of Virata).* The year in incognito spent at the court of Virata.
5. *Udyoga Parva (The Book of the Effort).* Preparations for war and efforts to bring about peace between the Kurus and the Pandavas which eventually fail (udyoga means effort or work).
6. *Bhishma Parva (The Book of Bhishma).* The first part of the great battle, with Bhishma as commander for the Kauravas and his fall on the bed of arrows.
7. *Drona Parva (The Book of Drona).* The battle continues, with Drona as commander. This is the major book of the war. Most of the great warriors on both sides are dead by the end of this book.
8. *Karna Parva (The Book of Karna).* The battle again, with Karna as commander.
9. *Shalya Parva (The Book of Shalya).* The last day of the battle, with Shalya as commander. Also told in detail is the pilgrimage of Balarama to the fords of the river Saraswati and the mace fight between Bhima and Duryodhana which ends the war, since Bima kills Duryodhana by smashing him on the thighs with a mace.
10. *Sauptika Parva (The Book of the Sleeping Warriors).* Ashvattama, Kripa and Kritavarma kill the remaining Pandava army in their sleep. Only 7 warriors remain on the Pandava side and 3 on the Kaurava side.

11. *Stri Parva (The Book of the Women).* Gandhari, Kunti and the women (stri) of the Kurus and Pandavas lament the dead.
12. *Shanti Parva (The Book of Peace).* The crowning of Yudhisthira as king of Hastinapura, and instructions from Bhishma for the newly anointed king on society, economics and politics. This is the longest book of the *Mahabharata* (shanti means peace).
13. *Anushasana Parva (The Book of the Instructions).* The final instructions (anushasana) from Bhishma.
14. *Ashvamedhika Parva (The Book of the Horse Sacrifice).* The royal ceremony of the Ashvamedha (Horse sacrifice) conducted by Yudhisthira. The world conquest by Arjuna. The Anugita is told by Krishna to Arjuna.
15. *Ashramavasika Parva (The Book of the Hermitage).* The eventual deaths of Dhritarashtra, Gandhari and Kunti in a forest fire when they are living in a hermitage in the Himalayas. Vidura predeceases them and Sanjaya on Dhritarashtra's bidding goes to live in the higher Himalayas.
16. *Mausala Parva (The Book of the Clubs).* The infighting between the Yadavas with maces and the eventual destruction of the Yadavas.
17. *Mahaprasthanika Parva (The Book of the Great Journey).* The great journey of Yudhisthira and his brothers across the whole country and finally their ascent of the great Himalayas where each Pandava falls except for Yudhisthira.
18. *Svargarohana Parva (The Book of the Ascent to Heaven)* Yudhisthira's final test and the return of the Pandavas to the spiritual world (svarga).

There is one more Parva —Khila Harivamsa Parva (The Book of the Genealogy of Hari)—Life of Krishna which is not covered in the 18 parvas of the *Mahabharata*.

The Adi-parva includes the snake sacrifice (sarpasattra) of Janamejaya, explaining its motivation, detailing why all snakes in existence were intended to be destroyed, and why in spite of this, there are still snakes in existence. This sarpasattra material was often considered an independent tale added to a version of the *Mahabharata* by "thematic attraction", and considered to have particularly close connection to Vedic (Brahmana) literature, in particular the Panchavimsha Brahmana which describes the sarpasattra as originally performed by snakes, among which are snakes named Dhrtarashtra and Janamejaya, two main characters of the *Mahabharata*'s sarpasattra, and Takshaka, the name of a snake also in the *Mahabharata*. The Shatapatha Brahmana gives an account of an Ashvamedha performed by Janamejaya Parikshit.

According to what one character says at Mbh. 1.1.50, there were three versions of the epic, beginning with Manu, Astik or Vasu, respectively. These versions would correspond to the addition of one and then another 'frame' settings of dialogues. The Vasu version would omit the frame settings and begin with the account of the birth of Vyasa. The astika version would add the sarpasattra and ashvamedha material from Brahmanical literature, introduce the name *Mahabharata*, and identify Vyasa as the work's author. The redactors of these additions were probably Pancharatrin scholars who according to Oberlies likely retained control over the text until its final redaction.

Mention of the Huna in the Bhishma-parva however appears to imply that this parva may have been edited around the 4th century.

Historical Context

English language map of "Bharatvarsha" (Kingdom of India) during the era of the *Mahabharata* and Ramayana.The historicity of the Kurukshetra War is unclear. Some historians like A L Basham estimate the date of the Kurukshetra war to Iron Age India of the 10th century BCE.

Other historians like M Witzel have corroborated that the general setting of the epic has a historical precedent in Iron Age (Vedic) India, where the Kuru kingdom was the center of political power during roughly 1200 to 800 BCE. A dynastic conflict of the period could have been the inspiration for the Jaya, the foundation on which the *Mahabharata* corpus was built, with a climactic battle eventually coming to be viewed as an epochal event.

Puranic literature presents genealogical lists associated with the *Mahabharata* narrative. The evidence of the Puranas is of two kinds. Of the first kind, there is the direct statement that there were 1015 (or 1050) years between the birth of Parikshit (Arjuna's grandson) and the accession of Mahapadma Nanda, commonly dated to 382 BCE, which would yield an estimate of about 1400 BCE for the Bharata battle. However, this would imply improbably long reigns on average for the kings listed in the genealogies. Of the second kind are analyses of parallel genealogies in the Puranas between the times of Adhisimakrishna (Parikshit's great-grandson) and Mahapadma Nanda. Pargiter accordingly estimated 26 generations by averaging 10 different dynastic lists and, assuming 18 years for the average duration of a reign, arrived at an estimate of 850 BCE for Adhisimakrishna, and thus approximately 950 BCE for the Bharata battle.

B. B. Lal used the same approach with a more conservative assumption of the average reign to estimate a date of 836 BCE, and correlated this with archaeological evidence from Painted Grey Ware sites, the association being strong between PGW artifacts and places mentioned in the epic.

Attempts to date the events using methods of archaeoastronomy have produced, depending on which passages are chosen and how they are interpreted, estimates ranging from the late 4th to the mid 2nd millennium BCE. The late 4th millennium date has a precedent in the calculation of the Kaliyuga epoch, based on planetary conjunctions, by Aryabhata (6th century). His date of February 18 3102 BCE has become widespread in Indian tradition (for example, the Aihole inscription of Pulikeshi II, dated to Saka 556 = 634 CE, claims that 3735 years have elapsed since the Bharata battle.) Another traditional school of astronomers and historians, represented by Vriddha-Garga, Varahamihira (author of the Brhatsamhita) and Kalhana (author of the Rajatarangini), place the Bharata war 653 years after the Kaliyuga epoch, corresponding to 2449 BCE.

Other evidence exists for estimating the date of the *Mahabharata* war. These include: Aihole inscriptions, Hisse Borala inscriptions of Deva Sena and records from the Greek ambassador Megasthenes. P.V. Vartak provides an extensive summary of the different evidences available based for dating the *Mahabharata* war.

Synopsis

The core story of the work is that of a dynastic struggle for the throne of Hastinapura, the kingdom ruled by the Kuru clan. The two collateral branches of the family that participate in the struggle are the Kaurava and the Pandava. Although the Kaurava is the senior branch of the family, Duryodhana, the eldest Kaurava, is younger than Yudhisthira, the eldest Pandava. Both Duryodhana and Yudhisthira claim to be first in line to inherit the throne.

The struggle culminates in the great battle of Kurukshetra, in which the Pandavas are ultimately victorious. The battle produces complex conflicts of kinship and friendship, instances of family loyalty and duty taking precedence over what is right, as well as the converse.

The *Mahabharata* itself ends with the death of Krishna, and the subsequent end of his dynasty and ascent of the Pandava brothers to heaven. It also marks the beginning of the Hindu age of Kali (Kali Yuga), the fourth and final age of mankind, in which great values and noble ideas have crumbled, and man is heading toward the complete dissolution of right action, morality and virtue.

Versions, Translations, and Derivative Works

Many regional versions of the work developed over time, mostly differing only in minor details, or with verses or subsidiary stories being added. These include some versions from outside the Indian subcontinent, such as the Kakawin Bharatayuddha from Java. The plays of the Tamil street theatre, terukkuttu, use themes from the Tamil language versions of *Mahabharata*, focusing on Draupadi.

Between 1919 and 1966, scholars at the Bhandarkar Oriental Research Institute, Pune, compared the various manuscripts of the epic from India and abroad and produced the Critical Edition of the *Mahabharata*, on 13,000 pages in 19 volumes, followed by the Harivamsha in another two volumes and six index volumes. This is the text that is usually used in current *Mahabharata* studies for reference. This work is sometimes called the 'Pune' or 'Poona' edition of the *Mahabharata.*

The Kannada novelist S.L. Bhyrappa wrote a novel in Kannada (now translated to most Indian languages and English) titled Parva, giving a new interpretation to the story of *Mahabharata.* He tried to understand the social and ethical practices in these regions and correlate them with the story of *Mahabharata.*

Malayalam writer M. T. Vasudevan Nair's novel Randamoozham tells the *Mahabharata* from Bhima's point of View. Mrityunjay (English: Triumph Over Death) written by Shivaji Sawant is a Novel with Karna as the central character of *Mahabharata.*

In Indian cinema, several film versions of the epic exist, dating back from 1920. The internationally-acclaimed parallel Bengali film director Satyajit Ray also intended to direct a theatrical adaptation of the epic, but the project was never realized during his lifetime.

In the late 1980s, the Mahabharat TV series, directed by Ravi Chopra, was televised and shown on India's national television (Doordarshan). In the Western world, a well-known presentation of the epic is Peter Brook's nine-hour play, which premiered in Avignon in 1985, and its five-hour movie version The *Mahabharata* (1989).

Among literary reinterpretations of the *Mahabharata* the most famous is arguably Sashi Tharoor's major work entitled "The Great Indian Novel", an involved literary, philosophical, and political novel which superimposes the major moments of post-independence India in the 20th century onto the driving events of the *Mahabharata* epic.

Mahabharata was also reinterpreted by Shyam Benegal in Kalyug. Kalyug is a modern-day replaying of the *Mahabharata.*

Western interpretations of the *Mahabharata* include William Buck's *Mahabharata* and Elizabeth Seeger's Five Sons of King Pandu.

The first complete English translation was the Victorian prose version by Kisari Mohan Ganguli, published between 1883 and 1896 (Munshiram Manoharlal Publishers) and by M. N. Dutt (Motilal Banarsidass Publishers). Most critics consider the translation by Ganguli to be faithful to the original text. The complete text of Ganguli's translation is in the public domain and is available online.

Another English prose translation of the full epic, based on the Critical Edition, is also in progress, published by University Of Chicago Press, initiated by Chicago Indologist J. A. B. van Buitenen (books 1-5) and, following a 20-year hiatus caused by the death of van Buitenen, is being continued by D. Gitomer of DePaul University (book 6), J. L. Fitzgerald of Brown University (books 11-13) and W. Doniger of the University of Chicago (books 14-18).

A poetic translation of the full epic into English, done by the poet P. Lal is complete, and in 2005 began being published by Writers Workshop, Calcutta. The P.

Lal translation is a non-rhyming verse-by-verse rendering, and is the only edition in any language to include all slokas in all recensions of the work (not just those in the Critical Edition). The completion of the publishing project is scheduled for 2010. Sixteen of the eighteen volumes are now available:

Many condensed versions, abridgements and novelistic prose retellings of the complete epic have been published in English, including work by William Buck, R.K. Narayan, C. Rajagopalachari, Krishna Dharma, Romesh C. Dutt, and Bharadvaja Sarma.

A Kawi version is found on the Indonesian island of Bali and was translated by Dr. I. Gusti Putu Phalgunadi. Of the eighteen parvas, only eight Kawi manuscripts remain.

In the Bhagavd Gita, Krishna explains to Arjuna his duties as a warrior and prince and elaborates on different Yogic and Vedantic philosophies, with examples and analogies. This has led to the Gita often being described as a concise guide to Hindu philosophy and a practical, self-contained guide to life. In modern times, Swami Vivekananda, Bal Gangadhar Tilak, Mahatma Gandhi and many others used the text to help inspire the Indian independence movement.

Kannada Epic Poetry

Kannada epic poetry mainly consists of Jain religious literature. Asaga wrote *Vardhaman Charitra* (Life of Vardhman Mahavir), an epic which runs in 18 cantos, in 853 CE, the first Sanskrit language biography of 24th and last Thirthankara of Jainism, Mahavira, though his Kannada language version of Kalidasa's epic poem, Kumârasambhava, *Karnataka Kumarasambhava Kavya* is lost. The most famous poet from this period is Adikavi

Pampa (902-975 CE), one of the most famous writers in the Kannada language. His *Vikramarjuna Vijaya* (also called *pampa bharatha*) is hailed as a classic even to this day. With this and his other important work Adipurana he set a trend of poetic excellence for the Kannada poets of the future. The former work is an adaptation of the celebrated *Mahabharata*, and is the first such adaptation in Kannada. Noted for the strong human bent and the dignified style in his writing, Pampa has been one of the most influential writers in Kannada. He is identified as *Adi kavi*. (First poet). It is only in Kannada that we have a *Ramayana* and a *Mahabharata* based on the Jaina tradition in addition to those based on Brahmanical tradition.

Shivakotiacharya was the first writer in prose style. His work Vaddaradhane is dated to 900 CE. *Sri Ponna* (939-966 CE) is also an important writer from the same period, with *Shanti Purana* as his magnum opus. Another major writer of the period is *Ranna* (949-? CE). His most famous works are the Jain religious work *Ajita Tirthankara Purana* and the *Gada Yuddha* (The Mace fight), a birds' eye view of the *Mahabharata*, set in the last day of the Battle of Kurukshetra and relating the story of the *Mahabharata* through a series of flashbacks. Structurally, the poetry in this period is in the *Champu* style, essentially poetry interspersed with lyrical prose.

Tamil Epics

The post-sangam period (2nd century-6th century) saw many great Tamil epics being written, including *Cilappatikaram* (or *Silappadhikaram*), *Manimegalai*, *Jeevaga-chintamani*, *Valayapati* and *Kundalakesi*. Later, during the Chola period, Kamban (12th century) wrote what is considered one of the greatest Tamil epics — the Kamba *Ramayanam* of Kamban, based on the *Ramayana*.

Hindi Epics

The first epic to appear in Hindi was Tulsidas' (1543-1623) *Ramacharitamanasa,* also based on the *Ramayana*. It is considered a great classic of Hindi epic poetry and literature, and shows the author Tulsidas in complete command over all the important styles of composition — narrative, epic, lyrical and dialectic. He has given a human character to Rama, the Hindu avatar of Vishnu, portraying him as an ideal son, husband, brother and king.

In modern Hindi literature, Kamayani by Jaishankar Prasad has attained the status of an epic. The narrative of Kamayani is based on a popular mythological story, first mentioned in Satapatha Brahmana. It is a story of the great flood and the central characters of the epic poem are Manu (a male) and Shraddha (a female). Manu is representative of the human psyche and Shradha represents love. Another female character is Ida, who represents rationality. Some critics surmise that the three lead characters of Kamayani symbolize a synthesis of knowledge, action and desires in human life.

Apart from Kamayani; *Kurukshetra* (1946), *Rashmirathi* (1952) and *Urvashi* (1961) by Ramdhari Singh 'Dinkar' have attained the status of epic poetry.

4

Sanskrit Literature

India is a land of rich classical heritage. The land of many great thinkers and writers, our collection of literature in Sanskrit is priceless. Known as the mother of many languages, Sanskrit is abundant in the treasure of literature. Many people think of Sanskrit in terms of chants, hymns and verses. Not many know the vast collection of poetry, drama, stories and even epics in Sanskrit literature. Sanskrit language literature is a very broad category that requires elaborate understanding of this varied language. In our related sections, you shall find information about various Sanskrit epics, plays and major Sanskrit pioneers of India.

With time, the definition of classical Sanskrit literature has also changed. It used to be primarily a source of gaining knowledge and was used a lot during religious rituals. Now, Sanskrit has become a language that is solely seen upon as an entity for entertainment. People follow Sanskrit to amuse themselves rather than gain knowledge. People may go to see plays or listen to legendary folklores in Sanskrit with the sole aim of entertaining themselves. Priests who perform religious rituals use pure Sanskrit in

India. Though attempts are being made to revive this ancient language in India, it will be a long time before people realize the value of this ancient language in the contemporary world.

As we progress by leaps and bounds in the 21st Century, we fail to value some of the most important things of life. More often than not, they form the backbone of our progress and give us our own identity in this era of globalization. This ancient classical language is a plethora of knowledge that is useful even in this century. We only need to use it judiciously in the right way and it is never too late to learn.

Ancient Sanskrit Literature

Literature in Sanskrit begins with the Vedas, and continues with the Sanskrit Epics of Iron Age India; the golden age of Classical Sanskrit literature dates to late Antiquity (roughly the 3rd to 8th centuries AD). Literary production saw a late bloom in the 11th century before declining after 1100 AD. There are contemporary efforts towards revival, with events like the "All-India Sanskrit Festival" (since 2002) holding composition contests.

The Vedas

Composed between approximately 1500 BC and 600 BC (the Late Bronze Age to Early Iron Age) in pre-classical Sanskrit , Vedic literature forms the basis for the further development of Hinduism. There are four Vedas - *Rig, Yajur, Sâma and Atharva,* each with a main Samhita and a number of circum-vedic genres, including Brahmanas, Aranyakas,Vedang i.e. Grhyasutras and Shrautasutras and Dharmasutras. The main period of Vedic literary activity falls into ca. the

9th to 7th centuries when the various shakhas (schools) compiled and memorized their respective corpora.

The older Upanishads (BAU, ChU, JUB, KathU, MaitrU) belong to the Vedic period, but the larger part of the Muktika canon is post-Vedic. The Aranyakas form part of both the Brahmana and Upanishad corpus.

Sutras

Continuing the tradition of the late Vedic Shrautasutra literature, Late Iron Age scholarship (ca. 500 to 100 BCE) organized knowledge into Sutra treatises, including the Vedanga and the religious or philosophical Brahma Sutras, Yoga Sutras, Nyaya Sutras.

In the Vedanga disciplines of grammar and phonetics, no author had greater influence than Panini with his Astadhyayi (ca. 5th century BC). In the tradition of Sutra literature exposing the full grammar of Sanskrit in extreme brevity, Panini's brilliance lies in the nature of his work of a prescriptive generative grammar, involving metarules, transformations and recursion. Being prescriptive for all later grammatical works, such as Patanjali's Mahabhasya, Panini's grammar effectively fixed the grammar of Classical Sanskrit. The Backus-Naur Form or BNF grammars used to describe modern programming languages have significant similarities with Panini's grammar rules.

Epics

The period between approximately the 6th to 1st centuries BC saw the composition and redaction of the two great epics, the *Mahabharata* and the *Ramayana*, with subsequent redaction progressing down to the 4th century AD. They are known as itihasa, or *"that which occurred"*.

Classical Sanskrit Literature

Sanskrit literature came into being with the making of Vedas and left a rich legacy of literary knowledge for the times to come. However, the language of the Vedas differs from the language used in poetry and drama. Classical Sanskrit literature is found to be in vogue when it comes to writing poetry and dance dramas. This form of classic literature in Sanskrit is a huge contribution in the field of literary knowledge. Sanskrit poetry is different from Vedic poetry. Read on further about literature in classical Sanskrit and check our related sections on Sanskrit plays and Sanskrit poetry.

Sanskrit drama evolved as early as 2nd century B.C. Shudraka, the great Sanskrit writer wrote the earliest play in Sanskrit Mricchakatika around this time. The central theme of these dramas and plays used to be based on heroic tales of the protagonist. The Natya Shastra, which was written by Bharata, literally means the Science of Theater. It contained all the essential elements that go into making a successful dance drama. Other famous dramatists are Kalidasa, Bhasa, Asvaghosa, etc. Check our related sections for further information on their works.

Classical Sanskrit poetry is a varied genre and has many forms of poetry in it. The most famous examples of epic poetry are Ramayana and Mahabharata, the two epics that are held in high reverence by Indians. Romantic poetry was given a boost during the time of Kalidasa, the great poet of India. The epics poems can be recited as well as sung. Thus, one can say that classical music also started from classical Sanskrit literature. Classic literature in Sanskrit is indeed a valuable treasure of Indian cultural heritage.

The classical period of Sanskrit literature dates to the Gupta period and the successive pre-Islamic Middle kingdoms of India, spanning roughly the 3rd to 8th centuries CE.

Dramas

The combination of different genres of drama and Sanskrit resulted in a unique amalgamation that gave us the literary treasure of Sanskrit dramas and Sanskrit plays. The famous dramatists of Sanskrit literature were Kalidasa, Bhasa, Shudraka and Asvaghosa who gave us many famous Sanskrit plays. With the revival of Sanskrit theater in modern times, these Sanskrit plays are gaining much popularity again among Sanskrit scholars and theater enthusiasts. Given here are some famous Sanskrit plays that are worth a read.

Abhijnanasakuntalam

Abhijnanasakuntalam is a beautiful tale of love and romance and how one moment can make or break a relation. Written by one of the greatest poets of India, Shakuntalam Kalidasa is synonymous to its author, Kalidasa.

Malavikagnimitram

The first play composed by the great poet Kalidasa is Malavikagnimitram. Often it is called Kalidasa Malavikagnimitram, as an honor to Kalidasa. This beautiful play of intrigue grips its readers and keeps them glued till the very end. The plot of the play is cleverly constructed and it revolves around the King's love interest who is a maid in the royal palace.

Ritusamhara

India has always believed in the harmonious relation between man and forces of nature and the importance of each season has been beautifully brought into light by the great poet Kalidasa in Ritu Samhaara, a poem written by him. It can be called the "Medley of Seasons" or "Garland of Seasons". The Ritusamharam has been divided into six main chapters, each chapter describing vividly, the seasons of India.

Vikramorvasiyam

Written by the most famous poet Kalidasa, Vikramorvasiyam is a play that tells the tale of a mortal king Vikramaditya who is in love with a heavenly damsel, Urvashi. It tells the story of his effort and determination and how he wins the love of the divine nymph, who is supposed to be the most gorgeous heavenly fairy. Out of desperation, the king wanders through dense forests in search of his love. A truly intriguing tale of love and possessiveness, it contains beautiful verses that describe true love.

Mrichakatika

Regarded as one of the earliest Indian plays written in Sanskrit, Mrichakatika is a beautiful play by Shudraka. The play is a comedy set in the royal backdrop in which love and mistaken identity play a part. Translated in English, the name means little clay cart. It was written around the Gupta Period in Sanskrit.

Natya Shastra

Written by the sage Bharata Muni, this beautiful text was written in Sanskrit around 400 B.C. The text contains information on the minutest details that should be taken care of during dance. Thus, it can be said that Natya Shastra is set of rules and regulations that are implemented in fine arts in India. The Natya Shastra is the first known text on dance and it has had a strong impact on classical dance forms in both olden and modern times.

Bhasa's Plays

Bhasa's plays are generally shorter as compared to other epic poems and plays. This great Sanskrit dramatist lived before Kalidasa and wrote many short plays that are staged even today. Most of his plays were based on the two major epics, Ramayana and Mahabharata. Most of his plays have graphic depictions of violence, something that was frowned upon by the Natya Shastras. Some of his famous plays are Madhyamavyayogam, Urubhangam, Karnabharam, Pancaratram, among others.

Scholarly Treatises

The earliest surviving treatise on astrology is the Yavanajataka "sayings of the Greeks" (3rd century). Classical Hindu astrology is based on early medieval compilations, notably the Brhat Parasara Horasastra and Saravali (7th to 8th century). The earliest surviving treatise on (non-divinatory) Indian astronomy predates the Yavanajataka: the Vedanga Jyotisha of Ladaga documents the state of in the Maurya period. The astronomy of the classical Gupta period, the centuries following Indo-Greek contact, is documented in treatises known as Siddhantas (which means "established conclusions"). Varahamihira in his *Pancha-Siddhantika* contrasts five of these: The Surya Siddhanta besides the Paitamaha Siddhantas (which is more similar to the "classical" Vedanga Jyotisha), the

Paulisha and Romaka Siddhantas (directly based on Hellenistic astronomy) and the Vasishta Siddhanta.

The earliest treatise in Indian mathematics is the *Aryabhatiya* (written ca. 500 CE), a work on astronomy and mathematics. The mathematical portion of the *Aryabhatiya* was composed of 33 *Sutras* (in verse form) consisting of mathematical statements or rules, but without any proofs. However, according to (Hayashi 2003, p. 123), "this does not necessarily mean that their authors did not prove them. It was probably a matter of style of exposition." From the time of Bhaskara I (600 CE onwards), prose commentaries increasingly began to include some derivations (*upapatti*).

"Tantra" is a general term for a scientific, magical or mystical treatise and mystical texts both Hindu and Buddhist said to concern themselves with five subjects:

1. the creation,
2. the destruction of the world,
3. the worship of the gods,
4. the attainment of all objects,
5. the four modes of union with the supreme spirit by meditation.

These texts date to the entire lifespan of Classical Sanskrit literature.

Fairy Tales and Fables

Sanskrit fairy tales and fables are chiefly characterised by ethical reflections and proverbial philosophy. A peculiar style, marked by the insertion of a number of different stories within the framework of a single narrative, made its way to Persian and Arabic literatures, exerting a major influence on works such as *One Thousand and One Nights*.

The two most important collections are Panchatantra and Hitopadesha; originally intended as manuals for the instruction of kings in domestic and foreign policy, they belong to the class of literature which the Hindus call *niti-sastra,* or "Science of Political Ethics".

Other notable prose works include a collection of pretty and ingenious fairy tales, with a highly Oriental colouring, the *Vetala-panchavimsati* or "Twenty-five Tales of the Vetala" (a demon supposed to occupy corpses), the *Simhasana-dvatrimçika* or "Thirty-two Stories of the Lion-seat" (i.e. throne), which also goes by the name of *Vikrama-charita,* or "Adventures of Vikrama" and the *Suka-saptati,* or "Seventy Stories of a Parrot". These three collections of fairy tales are all written in prose and are comparatively short.

Somadeva's Katha-sarit-sagara or "Ocean of Rivers of Stories" is a work of special importance: composed in verse and is of very considerable length. It contains more than 22,000 shlokas, equal to nearly one-fourth of the Mahabharata. Fable collections, originally serving as the handbooks of practical moral philosophy, provided an abundant reservoir of ethical maxims that become so popular that works consisting exclusively of poetical aphorisms started to appear. The most important are the two collections by the highly-gifted Bhartrhari, entitled respectively *Niti-sataka,* or "Century of Conduct," and *Vairagya-sataka,* or "Century of Renunciation." The keynote prevailing in this new ethical poetry style is the doctrine of the vanity of human life, which was developed before the rise of Buddhism in the sixth century B.C., and has dominated Indian

Classical Poetry

This refers to the poetry produced from the approximately the 3rd to 8th centuries. Kalidasa is the foremost example of a classical poet.

But a striking characteristic of Indian literary tradition is that sometimes poets show off their technical dexterity with highly Oulipian word-games, like stanzas that read the same backwards and forwards, words that can be split in different ways to produce different meanings, sophisticated metaphors, and so on. This style is referred to as Kavya. A classic example is the poet Bharavi and his magnum opus, the Kiratarjuniya (6th-7th century). Magh is noted for his epic poem (mahAkAvya) Shishupala Vadha, the 20 cantos of which are based on the Mahabharata episode where the defiant king Shishupala is beheaded by Krishna's chakra (disc)

Sanskrit poetry is a vast treasure of knowledge that gives us immense information about ancient thoughts and principles. Some of the best works in ancient Sanskrit literature are in the form of Sanskrit poems. Some of the most famous and respected poets have given us the treasure of poetry in Sanskrit. These poets are synonymous with Sanskrit poetry and most poems are followed by the name of the poet. We are covering some great works of these poets in our related sections. Read on further to know more about these Sanskrit poems.

Kumarasambhavam

Anyone interested in the Sanskrit language is sure to know the story of Kumarasambhavam. One of the gems of Sanskrit literature, Kumarasambhava poem is one of the greatest epic poems written by the famous poet Kalidasa. Both the names go hand in hand and the poem is often called Kumarasambhavam Kalidasa.

Meghadutam

A beautiful piece of literary treasure, the Meghadutam Kalidasa is a short poem of a little over 100 verses. The stanzas are uniform in length of four sentences each. This convenient length makes it a favorite among scholars and translators. The Meghaduta poem is a beautiful work of literary art and the descriptions given in it are so vivid that one visualizes what the poet wants to convey.

Ritusamhara

India has always believed in the harmonious relation between man and forces of nature and the importance of each season has been beautifully brought into light by the great poet Kalidasa in Ritu Samhaara, a poem written by him. It can be called the "Medley of Seasons" or "Garland of Seasons". The Ritusamharam has been divided into six main chapters, each chapter describing vividly, the seasons of India.

Raghuvamsa

Raghuvamsa play is a literary magnum opus written by the famous poet Kalidasa. The play is synonymous with the creator and is often called Raghuvamsa Kalidasa. The play basically traces the roots of the great lineage of Lord Rama and his descendants and the great conqueror Raghu. Raghuvamsam basically talks about the valor and strength of the great warrior Raghu.

Puranas

The corpus of the Hindu Puranas likewise falls into the classical period of Sanskrit literature, dating to between the 5th and 10th centuries, and marks the emergence of the Vaishna and Shaiva denominations of classical Hinduism. The Puranas are classified into a Maha- ("great") and a Upa- ("lower, additional") corpus. Traditionally they are said to narrate five subjects, called *pancalaksana* ("five distinguishing marks"):

> Sargasca pratisargasca vamso manvantarani ca I
>
> Vamsanucaritam caiva Puranam pancalaksanam II
>
> They are:

1. Sarga—The creation of the universe.
2. Pratisarga—Secondary creations, mostly re-creations after dissolution.
3. Vamœa—Genealogy of royals and sages.
4. Manvantara—Various eras.
5. Vamuanucaritam—Dynastic histories.

A Purana usually gives prominence to a certain deity (Shiva, Vishnu or Krishna, Durga) and depicts the other gods as subservient.

Later Sanskrit Literature

Some important works from the 11th century include the *Katha-sarit-sagara* and the *Gita Govinda* of Jayadeva. Nagananda, attributed to King Harsha, is an outstanding drama that outlines the story of King Jimutavahana, who sacrifices himself to save the tribe of serpents. It is also unique in that it invokes Lord Buddha in what is a predominantly Hindu drama.

The *Katha-sarita-sagara* (An Ocean of Stories) by Somadeva was an 11th century poetic adaptation in Sanskrit of *Brihat-katha,* written in the 5th century BC in the *Paishachi* dialect. One of the famous series of stories in this work is the *Vikrama and Vetala* series, known to every child in India. On the other side of the spectrum, of the 'Bhana' style of drama, Ubhayabhisarika is a one-person drama of an endearing lecher who knows every courtesan and her family by name.

The *Gita Govinda* (The song of Govinda) by the Oriya composer Jayadeva is the story of Krishna's love for Radha, and is written in spectacularly lyrical and musical Sanskrit.

Basohli painting (circa 1730 AD) depicting a scene from Jayadeva's *Gita Govinda.*

A central text for several Hindu sects in eastern India, the *Gita Govinda* is recited regularly at major Hindu pilgrimage sites such as Jagannath temple at Puri, Orissa. The *Ashtapadis* of the *Gita Govinda* also form a staple theme in Bharatanatyam and Odissi classical dance recitals.

Beyond the 11th century, the use of Sanskrit for general literature declined, most importantly because of the emergence of literature in vernacular Indian languages (notably Hindi, Marathi, Telugu, and Kannada). Sanskrit continued to be used, largely for Hindu religious and philosophical literature. Sanskrit literature fueled literature in vernacular languages, and the Sanskrit language itself continued to have a profound influence over the development of Indian literature in general.

5

Buddhist Literature

Buddhist texts come in numerous variety, however not all of them command the same kind of respect from the Buddhist community. There are texts which are respected to an extent of being worshipped. At the same time, there are other texts that have comparitively less or even miniscule significance for Buddhists.

Buddhist texts can be categorized in a number of ways. The Western terms "scripture" and "canonical" are applied to Buddhism in inconsistent ways by Western scholars: for example, one authority refers to "scriptures and other canonical texts", while another says that scriptures can be categorized into canonical, commentarial and pseudo-canonical.

A rather more definite division is that between Buddhavacana (the Word of the Buddha) and other texts. The former, including the Sutras (Sanskrit) or Suttas (Pali), are held to be the literal words of the historical Buddha or close approximations thereof. The latter are the various commentaries on canonical texts and other treatises on the Dharma, as well as collections of quotations, histories, grammars, and other texts.

Sometimes texts that are considered commentaries by some are regarded by others as Buddhavacana. Within Buddhavacana, there is a chronological difference between the early Buddhist texts (e.g. the Pali Canon and the Agamas), and the Mahayana sutras. Whereas some scholars believe that some portions of the Pali Canon and Agamas could contain the actual substance of the historical teachings (and possibly even the words) of the Buddha, this is not the case for the Mahayana sutras, for which only adherence to the spirit of the Buddha would be claimed by non-fundamentalist Mahayanists.

Some of these distinctions are arbitrary, and some texts fall between categories or can be associated with more than one. Many later Chinese scriptures were explicitly not of Indian origin, but have been widely accepted as valid sutras on their own merits by Chinese and East Asian Buddhists of the Mahayana tradition.

Recently an important archaeological discovery was made, consisting of the earliest known Buddhist manuscripts, recovered from the ancient civilization of Gandhara in north central Pakistan (near Taxila just south west of the capital Islamabad). These fragments, written on birch bark, are dated to the 1st century and have been compared to the Dead Sea scrolls in importance. Donated to the British Library in 1994, they are now being studied in a joint project at the University of Washington

Classification

The most important categorisation that is accepted of Buddhist literature is between canonical and non canonical texts.

Canonical Text

Canonical texts are those that are linked to Gautama Buddha in one way or another. Differences, however exist among different Buddhist schools as to which texts are canonical. Also, there are a number of revised versions of Buddhist canons as well. Consensus as to which one of them is canonical is also not there.

Canonical texts comprise three different kind of texts – the sutras (discourses), vinaya (discipline) and abhidharma (analytical texts).

Together they are called the The 'Three Baskets' or Tipitaka (in Pali language) and Tripitaka (in Sanskrit).

Non Canonical Texts

Non Canonical texts or semi canonical texts have held a significant place for themselves since a long time now. These include commentaries in Pali, Tibetan, Chinese and other East Asian languages on the canonical texts. Apart from this, non canonical texts also include treatise on the dharma, collection of quotations, histories and grammars.

Buddhavacana

These are, in some way or other, texts associated with one of the Buddhas. Different schools, however, are not always in agreement about which texts are Buddhavacana, and the various collections of Buddhist literature contain widely varying numbers and types of texts. According to most early schools of Buddhism, the texts come in three types:

– sutras (i.e. discourses)
– vinaya (relating to the rules of monastic discipline)
– abhidharma (analytical texts)

Together these three make up what is known in Sanskrit as the Tripitaka and in Pali as the Tipitaka. Both the sutras and the vinaya of every Buddhist school contain a huge variety of documents including discourses on the Dharma, commentaries on other teachings, cosmological and cosmogonical texts, stories of the Buddha's previous lives, and various lists.

Traditionally, the Theravada and other Nikaya schools believe, more or less literally, that most of these texts contain the actual words of the Buddha. The Theravada canon, also known as the Pali Canon after the language it was written in, contains some four million words. Theravada is practiced mainly in southern Asian countries such as Sri Lanka, Thailand, and Myanmar.

Later texts, such as the Mahayana Sutras, are also traditionally considered by Mahayanists to be the word of the Buddha, but transmitted either in secret, via lineages of supernatural beings (such as the nagas), or revealed directly from other Buddhas or bodhisattvas. Some 600 Mahayana Sutras have survived in Sanskrit, or in Chinese and/or Tibetan translation.

The earliest Mahayana texts were composed in a 'Middle Indo-ryan' language which was Sanskritised during the Gupta era when Sanskrit became the official language of the Indian court. Most of the Mahayana sutra texts are composed in what is called Buddhist Hybrid Sanskrit, a Middle Indo-ryan Prakrit with ornaments and flourishes designed to imitate Sanskrit.

The Tibetan Kangyur, which belongs to the various schools of Tibetan Vajrayana Buddhism, in addition to containing sutras and vinaya, also contains tantras.

The division of texts into the traditional three yanas may obscure the process of development that went on, and there is some overlap in the traditional classifications. For instance, there are so-called *proto-Mahayana* texts, such as the Ajitasena Sutra, which are missing key features that are associated with Mahayana texts. Some Pali texts also contain ideas that later became synonymous with the Mahayana. The Garbhvakrnti Sktra is included in both the Vinaya Pitaka of the Mulasarvastivada, one of the early schools, and the Ratnakuta, a standard collection of Mahayana sutras. Some Mahayana texts are also thought to display a distinctly tantric character, particularly some of the shorter Perfection of Wisdom Sutras. An early tantra, the Mahavairocana Abhisambodhi Tantra, is also known as the Mahavairocana Sutra. At least some editions of the Kangyur include the Heart Sutra in the tantra division. Such overlap is not confined to "neighbouring" yanas: at least nine "Sravakayana" ("Hinayana") texts can be found in the tantra divisions of some editions of the Kangyur. One of them, the Atanatiya Sutra, is also included in the Mikkyo (esoteric) division of the standard modern collected edition of Sino-Japanese Buddhist literature. (A variant of it is also found in the Digha Nikaya of the Pali Canon.)

Some Buddhist texts evolved to become a virtual canon in themselves, and are referred to as *vaipulya* or extensive sutras. Scholars think, for instance, that the Golden Light Sutra constellated around the celebrated third chapter. The Avatamsaka Sutra is another example of a single Sutra made up of many other sutras, many of which, particularly the Gandavyuha Sutra still circulate as separate texts. The Avatamsaka Sutra and the White Lotus Sutra are associated with the idea of the Ekayana or One Vehicle. The texts claim to unify all the teachings that have come before into a greater whole.

Shingon Buddhism developed a system which assigned authorship of the early sutras to Gautama Buddha in his physical manifestation, of the *Ekayana* sutras to the Buddhas as Sambhoghakaya, and the Vajrayana texts to the Buddha as Dharmakaya.

Other Texts

Other texts have been important from very early in Buddhism. Extensive commentaries exist in Pali for the Pali Canon and in Tibetan, Chinese and other East Asian languages.

Important examples of non-canonical texts are the Visuddhimagga, or *Path of Purification*, by Buddhaghosa, which is a compendium of Theravada teachings that include quotes from the Pali Canon. The Milinda Pañha or *Questions of Milinda*, sometimes included in the Pali Canon and perhaps regarded by some as Buddhavacana, is a popular condensation of the Dharma in the form of a dialogue between the Buddhist sage Ngasena and the Indo-Greek King Menander.

The treatise *Awakening of Faith in the Mahayana* strongly influenced east Asian Mahayana doctrine and inspired numerous commentaries authored by early Chinese and Korean Buddhist teachers. Shantideva's *Bodhicaryavatara* has been influential in both Mahayana and Vajrayana, and his Shikshasamucaya contains references to texts which are no longer extant in any other form.

The Platform Sutra attributed to Huineng is on the borders of Buddhavacana; it is one of a very few texts not thought to be spoken by the Buddha that has the label "sutra."

Tibetan Buddhism has a unique and special class of texts called terma. These are texts (or ritual objects, etc.) which are held to have been either composed or hidden by tantric masters and/or elementally secreted or encoded in the elements and retrieved, accessed or rediscovered by other tantric masters when appropriate. Termas are discovered by a tertön, whose special function is to discover these texts. Some termas are hidden in caves or similar places, but a few are said to be 'mind termas' which are 'discovered' in the mind of the tertön. The Nyingma school (and Bön tradition) has a large terma literature. Many of the terma texts are said to have been written by Padmasambhava, who is particularly important to the Nyingmas. Probably the best known terma text is the so-called "Tibetan book of the dead", the Bardo thodol.

Other types of texts which have been important are the histories of Buddhism in Sri Lanka, the Dipavamsa and Mahavamsa.

Texts of the Early schools

Although many versions of the texts of the early Buddhist schools exist, the most complete canon to survive is the Pali Canon of the Theravadin school, which preserved the texts in the Pali language. Also large parts of the Sarvastivada and Dharmaguptaka texts are extant. The Pali literature has been divided by one scholar into roughly three periods. The early, or classical, period begins with the Pali Canon itself and ends with the Milindha-pañha about the turn of the Christian era. After a period of being in comparative disuse or decline, Pali underwent a renaissance in the 4th or 5th century with the help of Buddhaghosa, and this period lasted until the 12th Century. The third period coincides with major political changes in Burma and lasted for some time in Sri Lanka, and much longer in Burma.

The other (parts of) extant versions of the Tipitakas of early schools include the agamas, which includes texts of the Sarvastivada and the Dharmaguptaka. Parts of the what is likely to be the canon of the Dharmaguptaka can be found amongst the Gandharan Buddhist Texts. Several early Vinaya Pitakas (from various schools) are also kept in the Chinese (Mahayana) Canon.

Vinaya

The vinaya literature is primarily concerned with aspects of the monastic discipline. However, vinaya as a term is also contrasted with Dharma, where the pair (Dhamma-Vinaya) mean something like 'doctrine and discipline'. The vinaya literature in fact contains a considerable range of texts. There are, of course, those which discuss the monastic rules, how they came about, how they developed, and how they were applied. But the vinaya also contains some doctrinal expositions, ritual and liturgical texts, biographical stories, and some elements of the "Jatakas", or birth stories.

Paradoxically, the text most closely associated with the vinaya, and the most frequently used portion of it, the *Pratimoksha,* is in itself not a canonical text in Theravada, even though almost all of it can be found in the canon.

Six complete vinayas survive:

- Theravada, written in Pali
- Mula-Sarvstivda, written in Sanskrit, but surviving complete only in Tibetan translation
- Mahsnghika, Sarvstivda, Mah+shsika, and Dharmagupta, originally in Indian languages, but only surviving in Chinese translation.

In addition, portions survive of a number of vinayas in various languages.

The *Mahvastu* compiled by the Lokottaravadin sub-school of the Mahsnghika was perhaps originally the preamble to their vinaya that became detached; hence, rather than dealing with the rules themselves, it takes the form of an extended biography of the Buddha, which it describes in terms of his progression through ten bhumis, or stages. This doctrine was later taken up by the Mahayana in a modified form as Vasubandhu's Ten Stages Sutra.

Sutra

The Sutras are mostly discourses attributed to the Buddha or one of his close disciples. They are all, even those not actually spoken by him, considered to be 'Buddhavacana' or the word of the Buddha, just as in the case of all canonical literature. The Buddha's discourses were perhaps originally organised according to the style in which they were delivered; there were originally nine, but later twelve, of these. The Sanskrit forms are:

- Sktra: prose discourses, especially short declarative discourses.

- Geya: mixed prose and verse discourse. Identified with the Sagthvagga of the SaAyutta Nikya
- Vykarana: explanation, analysis. Discourses in question and answer format.
- Gth: verse
- Udna: inspired speech
- Ityukta: beginning with 'thus has the Bhagavan said'
- Jtaka: story of previous life
- Abhutadharma: concerning wonders and miraculous events
- Vaipulya either 'extended discourses' or 'those giving joy'
- Nidna: in which the teachings are set within their circumstances of origin
- Avadna: tales of exploits
- Upadesha: defined and considered instructions

The first nine are listed in all surviving agamas, with the other three added in some later sources. In Theravada, at least, they are regarded as a classification of the whole of the scriptures, not just suttas. The scheme is also found in Mahayana texts. However, some time later a new scheme of organisation was imposed on the canon, and it is this scheme which most people are familiar with. The scheme organises the suttas into:

Long Discourses

These range in length up to 95 pages. The Pali Digha Nikaya contains 34 texts, including the Mahparinibbna Sutta and the Brahmajla Sutta. The D+rghgama of the

Dharmagupta also survives, in Chinese translation, and contains 30 sutras.

Medium-length Discourses

These are the rest of the sutras of any length, and the Pali Majjhima Nikaya has 152 suttas. The Madhyamgama of the Sarvstivada containing 222 sutras survives in Chinese translation.

Connected Discourses

This grouping consists of many short texts connected by theme, setting, or interlocutor. The Pali Samyutta Nikaya contains more than 2,800 suttas. The Samyuktgama of the Sarvstivada containing only 1,300 sutras survives in Chinese translation.

Numbered Discourses

Sutras which have the same number of doctrinal items, comprising over 2,300 suttas in the Pali Anguttara Nikaya. The Chinese canon contains an Ekottargama which is thought by some scholars to belong to the Mahsanghika school.

Abhidharma

Abhidharma means 'further Dharma' and is concerned with the analysis of phenomena. It grew initially out of various lists of teachings such as the 37 Bodhipaksika-dharmas or the 37 Factors leading to Awakening. The Abhidharma literature is chiefly concerned with the analysis of phenomena and the relationships between them.

The Theravda Abhidhamma survives in the Pali Canon. Outside of the Theravada monasteries the Pali Abhidharma texts are not well-known.

A Sarvastivada Abhidharma, composed in Sanskrit, survives in Chinese and Tibetan traditions. Though the Theravdin Abhidhamma is well preserved and best known, it should be noted that a number of the early Eighteen Schools each had their own distinct Abhidharma collection with not very much common textual material, though sharing methodology.

Not all schools accepted the Abhidharma as canonical. The Sautrntika, for instance, held that the canon stopped with the vinaya and sutras. The rejection by some schools that dharmas (i.e. phenomena) are ultimately real, which the Theravada Abhidhamma, for instance, insists, is thought to be an important factor in the origin of the Mahayana.

Pali Canon

The Pali Canon is the standard collection of scriptures in the Theravada Buddhist tradition, as preserved in the Pali language. It is the only completely surviving early Buddhist canon, and one of the first to be written down. It was composed in North India, and preserved orally until it was committed to writing during the Fourth Buddhist Council in Sri Lanka in the 1st century BCE, approximately three hundred years after the death of Shakyamuni. The Pali Canon was first printed in the nineteenth century, and is now also available in electronic form and on the Internet.

The Pali Canon falls into three general categories, called *pitaka* (pitaka, basket) in Pali. Because of this, the canon is traditionally known as the Tipitaka (Tipitaka; *three baskets*). The three pitakas are as follows:

1. Vinaya Pitaka, dealing with rules for monks and nuns

2. Sutta Pitaka, discourses, mostly ascribed to the Buddha, but some to disciples
3. Abhidhamma Pitaka, variously described as philosophy, psychology, metaphysics etc.

The Vinaya Pitaka and the Sutta Pitaka are remarkably similar to the works of other early Buddhist schools. The Abhidhamma Pitaka however is a strictly Theravada collection, and has little in common with the Abhidhamma works recognized by other Buddhist schools

The Canon is traditionally described by the Theravada as the Word of the Buddha (Buddhavacana), though this is obviously not intended in a literal sense, since it includes teachings by disciples.

The traditional Theravadin (Mahaviharin) interpretation of the Pali Canon is given in a series of commentaries covering nearly the whole Canon, compiled by Buddhaghosa (fl. 4th–5th century CE) and later monks, mainly on the basis of earlier materials now lost. Subcommentaries have been written afterwards, commenting further on the Canon and its commentaries. The traditional Theravadin interpretation is summarized in Buddhaghosa's Visuddhimagga.

An official view is given by a spokesman for the Buddha Sasana Council of Burma: the Canon contains everything needed to show the path to nirvana; the commentaries and subcommentaries sometimes include much speculative matter, but are faithful to its teachings and often give very illuminating illustrations. In Sri Lanka and Thailand, "official" Buddhism has in large part adopted the interpretations of Western scholars.

Although the Canon has existed in written form for two millennia, its earlier oral nature has not been forgotten in actual Buddhist practice within the tradition: memorization and recitation remain common. Among frequently recited texts are the Paritta. Even lay people usually know at least a few short texts by heart and recite them regularly; this is considered a form of meditation, at least if one understands the meaning. Monks are of course expected to know quite a bit more. A Burmese monk named Vicittasara even learnt the entire Canon by heart for the Sixth Council (again according to the usual Theravada numbering). Recitation is in Pali as the ritual language.

The relation of the scriptures to Buddhism as it actually exists among ordinary monks and lay people is, as with other major religious traditions, problematical: the evidence suggests that only parts of the Canon ever enjoyed wide currency, and that non-canonical works were sometimes very much more widely used; the details varied from place to place. Dr Rupert Gethin says that the whole of Buddhist history may be regarded as a working out of the implications of the early scriptures.

Origins

According to a late part of the Pali Canon, the Buddha taught the three pitakas. It is traditionally believed by Theravadins that most of the Pali Canon originated from the Buddha and his immediate disciples. According to the scriptures, a council was held shortly after the Buddha's passing to collect and preserve his teachings. It was recited orally from the 5th century BCE to the first century BCE, when it was written down. The tradition holds that only a few later additions were made.

Much of the material in the Canon is not specifically "Theravadin", but is instead the collection of teachings that this school preserved from the early, non-sectarian body of teachings. According to Peter Harvey, it contains material which is at odds with later Theravadin orthodoxy. He states that "the Theravadins, then, may have *added* texts to the Canon for some time, but they do not appear to have tampered with what they already had from an earlier period." A variety of factors suggest that the early Sri Lankan Buddhists regarded canonical literature as such and transmitted it conservatively.

Attributions

The views of scholars concerning the attribution of the Pali Canon can be grouped into three categories:

1. Attribution to the Buddha himself.
2. Attribution to the period of pre-sectarian Buddhism.
3. Agnosticism.

Scholars have both supported and opposed the various existing views.

Attribution to the Buddha

Various scholars have voiced that some of the contents of the Pali Canon (and its main teachings) can be attributed to Gautama Buddha. Richard Gombrich thinks that the main preachings of the Buddha (as in the Vinaya and Sutta Pitaka) probably go back to the Buddha individually. Some scholars argue that the teachings are coherent and cogent, and must be the work of a single genius: the Buddha himself, not a committee of followers after his death.

J.W. de Jong has stated that parts of the Pali Canon could very well have been proclaimed by the Buddha, and subsequently transmitted and developed by his disciples and, finally, codified in fixed formulas. A. Wynne has said that the Pali Canon includes texts which go back to the very beginning of Buddhism, which perhaps include the substance of the Buddha's teaching, and in some cases, maybe even his words.

A.K. Warder has stated that there is no evidence to suggest that the shared teaching of the early schools was formulated by anyone else than the Buddha and his immediate followers.

Some scholars say that little or nothing goes back to the Buddha. Prof. Ronald Davidson has little confidence that much, if any, of surviving Buddhist scripture is actually the word of the historical Buddha. Some of these scholars argue that some passages contradict the main teachings, and that the Buddha must have been consistent. Some believe only one of the variant teachings can have been the teaching of the Buddha, and that if the Buddha had taught the main teachings, contradictory teachings would never have got in. Some believe that because of this, the Buddha must have taught the divergent teachings, and that the main teachings were elaborated by his followers after his death.

Attribution to the Period of Pre-sectarian Buddhism

Most scholars do agree that there was a rough body of sacred literature that a relatively early community maintained and transmitted. Much of the Pali Canon is found also in the scriptures of other early schools of

Buddhism, parts of whose versions are preserved, mainly in Chinese. Many scholars have argued that this shared material can be attributed to the period of Pre-sectarian Buddhism. This is the period before the early schools separated in about the fourth or third century BCE.

Views Concerning Agnosticism

Some scholars see the Pali Canon as expanding and changing from an unknown nucleus. Arguments given for an agnostic attitude include that the evidence for the Buddha's teachings dates from (long) after his death.

Some scholars have said that the application of text-critical methods derived from Biblical criticism is invalidated by the fact that the Bible was a written text while the Pali Canon was oral.

Some scholars have stated that it would be hypocritical to assert that nothing can be said about the doctrine of earliest Buddhism.

Dr Gregory Schopen, argues that it is not until the fifth to sixth centuries CE that we can know anything definite about the contents of the Canon. This position did not attract much support, and was criticized by A. Wynne.

Earliest books of Pali Canon

Different positions have been taken on what are the earliest books of the Canon. The majority of Western scholars consider the earliest identifiable stratum to be mainly prose works, the Vinaya (excluding the Parivara) and the first four nikayas of the Sutta Pitaka, and perhaps also some short verse works such as the

Suttanipata. However, some scholars, particularly in Japan, maintain that the Suttanipata is the earliest of all Buddhist scriptures, followed by the Itivuttaka and Udana. However, some of the developments in teachings may only reflect changes in teaching that the Buddha himself adopted, during the 45 years that the Buddha was teaching.

Most of the above scholars would probably agree that their early books include some later additions. On the other hand, some scholars have claimed that central aspects of late works are or may be much earlier.

According to the Sinhalese chronicles, the Pali Canon was written down in the reign of King Vattagamini (Vattagamini) (1st century BCE) in Sri Lanka, at the Fourth Buddhist council. Most scholars hold that little if anything was added to the Canon after this, though Schopen questions this.

Texts and Translations

The climate of Theravada countries is not conducive to the survival of manuscripts. Apart from brief quotations in inscriptions and a two-page fragment from the eighth or ninth century found in Nepal, the oldest manuscripts known are from late in the fifteenth century, and there is not very much from before the eighteenth.

The first complete printed edition of the Canon was published in Burma in 1900, in 38 volumes. The following editions of the Pali text of the Canon are readily available in the West:

i) Pali Text Society edition, 1877–1927 (a few volumes subsequently replaced by new editions),

57 volumes including indexes, individual volumes also (for sale) separately.

a) The Pali scriptures and some Pali commentaries were digitized as an MS-DOS/ extended ASCII compatible database through cooperation between the Dhammakaya Foundation and the Pali Text Society in 1996 as *PALITEXT version 1.0: CD-ROM Database of the Entire Buddhist Pali Canon* ISBN 978-9748235875. The Dhammakaya Foundation are currently negotiating with the Pali Text Society to make available an updated database which adds the English translations and Windows/Unicode compatibility.

ii) Thai edition, 1925–28, 45 volumes; more accurate than the PTS edition, but with fewer variant readings;

a) BUDSIR on Internet, free with login; and electronic transcript by BUDSIR: Buddhist scriptures information retrieval, CD-ROM and online, both requiring payment.

iii) Sixth Council edition, Rangoon, 1954–56, 40 volumes; more accurate than the Thai edition, but with fewer variant readings;[l]

a) electronic transcript by Vipassana Research Institute available online in searchable database free of charge, or on CD-ROM (p&p only) from the Institute

b) Another transcript of this edition, produced under the patronage of the Supreme Patriarch of Thailand, World Tipitaka Edition, 2005, 40 volumes, published by the Dhamma Society Fund, claims to include the full extent of changes made at the Sixth Council, and therefore reflect the results of the council more accurately than some existing Sixth Council editions.

iv) Sinhalese (Buddha Jayanti) edition, 1957–?1993, 58 volumes including parallel Sinhalese translations, searchable, free of charge (not yet fully proofread.) Available at Journal of Buddhist Ethics.

   a) Transcript in BudhgayaNews Pali Canon. In this version it is easy to search for individual words across all 16,000+ pages at once and view the contexts in which they appear.

No one edition has all the best readings, and scholars must compare different editions.

Translation: *Pali Canon in English Translation,* 1895- in progress, 43 volumes so far, Pali Text Society, Bristol; for details of these and other translations of individual books see the separate articles. In 1994, the then President of the Pali Text Society stated that most of these translations were unsatisfactory. Another former President said in 2003 that most of the translations were done very badly. The style of many translations from the Canon has been criticized as "Buddhist Hybrid English", a term invented by Paul Griffiths for translations from Sanskrit. He describes it as "deplorable", "comprehensible only to the initiate, written by and for Buddhologists".

Contents of the Canon

The Canon consists of three pitakas.

a) Vinaya Pitaka (vinayapitaka)

b) Sutta Pitaka or Suttanta Pitaka

c) Abhidhamma Pitaka

Details are given below. For more complete information, see standard references on Pali literature.

Vinaya Pitaka

The first category, the Vinaya Pitaka, is mostly concerned with the rules of the *sangha,* both monks and nuns. The rules are preceded by stories telling how the Buddha came to lay them down, and followed by explanations and analysis. According to the stories, the rules were devised on an ad hoc basis as the Buddha encountered various behavioral problems or disputes among his followers. This pitaka can be divided into three parts.

i) *Suttavibhanga* (-vibhanga) Commentary on the Patimokkha, a basic code of rules for monks and nuns that is not as such included in the Canon. The monks' rules are dealt with first, followed by those of the nuns' rules not already covered.

ii) *Khandhaka* Other rules grouped by topic in 22 chapters.

iii) *Parivara* (parivara) Analysis of the rules from various points of view.

Sutta Pitaka

The second category is the *Sutta Pitaka* (literally "basket of threads", or of "the well spoken"; Sanskrit: *Sutra Pitaka,* following the former meaning) which consists primarily of accounts of the Buddha's teachings. The Sutta Pitaka has five subdivisions or nikayas.

i) *Digha Nikaya* (dighanikaya) 34 long discourses. Joy Manné argues that this book was particularly intended to make converts, with its high proportion of debates and devotional material.

ii) *Majjhima Nikaya* 152 medium-length discourses. Manné argues that this book was particularly intended to give a solid grounding in the teaching to converts, with a high proportion of sermons and consultations.

iii) *Samyutta Nikaya* (samyutta-) Thousands of short discourses in fifty-odd groups by subject, person etc. Bhikkhu Bodhi, in his translation, says this nikaya has the most detailed explanations of doctrine.

iv) *Anguttara Nikaya* (anguttara-) Thousands of short discourses arranged numerically from ones to elevens. It contains more elementary teaching for ordinary people than the preceding three.

v) *Khuddaka Nikaya* A miscellaneous collection of works in prose or verse.

Abhidhamma Piṭaka

The third category, the *Abhidhamma Pitaka* (literally "beyond the dhamma", "higher dhamma" or "special dhamma", Sanskrit: *Abhidharma Pitaka*), is a collection of texts which give a systematic philosophical description of the nature of mind, matter and time. There are seven books in the Abhidhamma Pitaka.

a) *Dhammasangani* (-sangani or -sangani) Enumeration, definition and classification of dhammas

b) *Vibhanga* (vibhanga) Analysis of 18 topics by various methods, including those of the Dhammasangani

c) *Dhatukatha* (dhatukatha) Deals with interrelations between ideas from the previous two **books**

d) *Puggalapannatti* (-pannatti) Explanations of types of person, arranged numerically in lists from ones to tens

e) *Kathavatthu* (katha-) Over 200 debates on points of doctrine

f) *Yamaka* Applies to 10 topics a procedure involving converse questions

g) *Patthana* (patthana) Analysis of 24 types of condition.

The traditional position is that the Abhidhamma is the absolute teaching, while the suttas are adapted to the hearer. Most scholars describe the abhidhamma as an attempt to systematize the teachings of the suttas: Harvey, Gethin. Cousins say that where the suttas think in terms of sequences or processes the abhidhamma thinks in terms of specific events or occasions.

The other two main canons in use at the present day are the Tibetan Kangyur and the Chinese Buddhist Canon. The former is in about a hundred volumes and includes versions of the Vinaya Pitaka and the Dhammapada (the latter by the title *Udanavarga*) and of parts of some other books. The standard modern edition of the latter is the Taisho published in Japan, which is in a hundred much larger volumes.

It includes both canonical and non-canonical (including Chinese and Japanese) literature and its arrangement does not clearly distinguish the two. It includes versions of the Vinaya Pitaka, the first four nikayas, the Dhammapada, the Itivuttaka and the Milindapanha and of parts of some other books. These Chinese and Tibetan versions are not usually translations of the Pali and differ from it to varying extents, but are recognizably the "same" works. On the other hand, the Chinese abhidharma books are different works from the Pali Abhidhamma Pitaka, though they follow a common methodology.

6

Assamese Literature

Assamese literature is the entire corpus of poetry, novels, short stories, documents and other writings in the Assamese language. It also includes popular ballads in the older forms of the language during its evolution to the contemporary form. The literary heritage of the Assamese language can be traced back to the 6th century in the Charyapada, where the earliest elements of the language can be discerned.

Assamese literature has a glorious and deep-rooted past Popular folk compositions of wisdom and light hearted mirth like the Bihu songs, ban-gets, the cradle songs, and the pastoral ballads, characterised by spontaneity and simplicity, are early specimens of unwritten Assamese poetry. The aphorisms of Dak Mahapurush, wise maxims om economic activities as well as social behaviour, constitute the earliest didactic compositions in Assamese, so far recorded in books. Assam has an unbroken heritage of written literature starting from at least the 13th century. The earliest known patronage of such efforts had come from the Kamata royal court since two of the earliest Assamese poets Harivara Vipra and Hema Saraswati wrote benedictory verses in praise of the Kamata King Durlabh Narayan.

In the 14th century emerged Madhava Kandali, an extremely powerful and sensitive poet on whom was bestowed the patronage of the Barahi King Mahamanikya Kandali rendered the Valmiki Ramayana into most graceful and elegant Assamese verse. It is interesting to note that of all the versions of Valmiki's great epic into other Indian languages, Madhava Kandali's was the earliest.

But the most glorious period of Assamese literature was the 15th and 16th centuries, when rose to the fore two uncommon luminaries- Sankaradeva and Madhavadeva, both of whom are being considered Mahapurushas by the people.

Both being great Sanskrit scholars, Sankaradeva and Madhavadeva took Assamese language and literature to unprecedented heights of artistic excellence. What is more, the high spiritual and artistic ideals combined with a whole some sense of direction held aloft first by Sankaradeva and then by Madhavadeva, inspired a whole lot of creative writers, both during their lifetimes and after. As a result, Assamese Vaishnavite literature is exceptionally rich in volume, range and flavour. Literature of Shakta affiliation as well as works on various secular subjects also equally developed through the centuries.

Apart from poetry of which Assamese literature possesses many real gems like the Kirtana-ghosha of Sankaradeva and the Namghosha of Madhavadeva, the two field in which it excels are drama and prose. The plays written by the two Mahapurushas are recognised as the earliest specimens of purely vernacular dramatic literature in the sub-continent.

As for prose, Assamese literature has a would-standing for at least one particular reason. It was as early as the sixteenth century that Vaikunthanath Bhattacharyya, more popularly known as Bhattadeva, rendered the Bhagavata and Gita into such mature prose that evoked spontaneous and unstinted admiration from the most enlightened quarters.

" Indeed the prose Bhattadeva composed in the sixteenth century is unique in its kind. ...... It is a priceless treasure that Assamese prose literature developed in the distant sixteenth century which no other literature of the world reached except the writings of Hooker and Latimer in England, " says Acharya Prafulla Chandra Roy.And then Rabindra Nath Tagore is on record, saying : " You may very well be proud of the author of this book who could handle prose in such a remarkably lucid style more than a century before we had any prose book in Bengal."

Historical literature is yet another wealth of Assam. This tradition of writing buranji, as history is called in Assamese, is the contribution of the Ahom dynasty. These are chronicles of royal courts and noble families first written in the Tai language and then in Assamese. Assamese buranji literature is unique in the whole of India not only because they contain invaluable historical material, but also because they represent an unmatched literary style.

Sir G. A. Grierson, the eminent scholar, commenting on this unique character of the buranji, said : "The Assamese are justly proud of their national literature. In no department have they been more successful than in a branch of study in which, India , as a rule is curiously deficient. The historical works of buranjis are numerous and voluminous. A knowledge of buranjis was an indispensable qualification for an Assamese gentleman."

Early Assamese Literature

The Charyapadas are often cited as the earliest example of Assamese literature. The Charyapadas are Buddhist songs composed in 8th-12th century. These writings bear similarities to Oriya and Bengali languages as well. The phonological and morphological traits of these songs bear very strong resemblance to Assamese some of which are extant.

After the Charyapadas, the period may again be split into Pre-Vaishnavite and Vaishnative sub-periods. The earliest known Assamese writer is Hema da Charita". In the time of the King#Saraswati, who wrote a small poem "Prahra Indranarayana (1350-1365) of Kamatapur the two poets Harihara Vipra and Kaviratna Saraswati composed *Asvamedha Parva* and *Jayadratha Vadha* respectively. Assam is known as the state of Vaishnava dharma. Because two great apostles, Mahapurusha Srimanta Shankardeva and Mahapurush Madhabdeva had undertaken pivital roles in Assamese literature. The *Kirtan Ghosa, Dasham, Ankia Nat, Gunamala, Namghosa* are the most popular and widely held books in Assam. Srimanta Sankardev And Madhabdev has changed the literature of Assam by writing these books. The *Borgit* written by both Sankardev And Madhabdev is known as the soul song of Assam. The Ankia Nat and Jumura are the first Indian cultural drama and these are acts that came before Shakespeare wrote Hamlet. Another poet named Rudra Kandali translated *Drona Parva* into Assamese. But the most well-known poet of the Pre-Vaishnavite sub period is Madhav Kandali, who rendered Valmiki's Ramayana into Assamese verse (Kotha Ramayana, 14th century) under the patronage of Mahamanikya, a Kachari king of Jayantapura.

Middle Age Assamese Literature

This is a period of the prose chronicles (*Buranji*) of the Ahom court. The Ahoms had brought with them an instinct for historical writings. In the Ahom court, historical chronicles were at first composed in their original Tibetian-Chinese language, but when the Ahom rulers adopted Assamese as the court language, historical chronicles began to be written in Assamese. From the beginning of the seventeenth century onwards, court chronicles were written in large numbers. These chronicles or buranjis, as they were called by the Ahoms, broke away from the style of the religious writers. The language is essentially modern except for slight alterations in grammar and spelling.

Modern Assamese Literature

The history of modern Assamese literature begins with the merger of Assam with British India in 1826. The initial years were difficult, especially with the British making Bengali and not Assamese the language of the schools and courts from 1835 to 1871. This situation however was reversed and Assamese was restored to its rightful position, with the American Baptist Mission taking a lead role. The Mission also brought out the first Assamese newspaper, Orunodoi in 1846. The Mission's efforts to promote Assamese literature was followed by the nationalistic zeal and single-minded devotion of literary stalwarts like Ananda Ram Dhekial Phukan, Lakshminath Bezbaroa, Padmanath Gohain Barual, Hem Chandra Goswami. Chandra Kanta Agarwala, and others.

The British imposed Bengali in 1836 in Assam after the state was occupied in 1826. Due to a sustained campaign, Assamese was reinstated in 1873 as the state language. Since the initial printing and literary activity occurred in eastern Assam, the Eastern dialect was introduced in schools, courts and offices and soon came to be formally recognized as the Standard Assamese. In recent times, with the growth of Guwahati as the political and commercial center of Assam, the Standard Assamese has moved away from its roots in the Eastern dialect.

Influence of Missionaries

The modern Assamese period began with the publication of the Bible in Assamese prose by the American Baptist missionaries in 1819. The currently prevalent standard Asamiya has its roots in the Sibsagar dialect of Eastern Assam. As mentioned in Bani Kanta Kakati's "Assamese, its Formation and Development" (1941, Published by Sree Khagendra Narayan Dutta Baruah, LBS Publications, G.N. Bordoloi Road, Gauhati-1, Assam, India) – "The Missionaries made Sibsagar in Eastern Assam the centre of their activities and used the dialect of Sibsagar for their literary purposes". The American Baptist Missionaries were the first to use this dialect in translating the Bible in 1813.

The Missionaries established the first printing press in Sibsagar in 1836 and started using the local Asamiya dialect for writing purposes. In 1846 they started a monthly periodical called *Arunodoi*, and in 1848, Nàthan Brown published the first book on Assamese grammar. The Missionaries published the first Assamese-English Dictionary compiled by M. Bronson in 1867. One of the major contributions of the American Baptist missionaries to the Assamese language is the reintroduction of Assamese as the official language in Assam. In 1848 missionary Nathan Brown published a treatise on the Assamese language. This treatise gave a strong impetus towards reintroducing Assamese the official language in Assam. In his 1853 official report on the province of Assam, British official Moffat Mills wrote:

> "...the people complain, and in my opinion with much reason, of the substitution of Bengalee for the Vernacular Assamese. Bengalee is the language of the court, not of their popular books and shashtras, and there is a strong prejudice to its general use. ...Assamese is described by Mr. Brown, the best scholar in the province, as a beautiful, simple language, differing in more respects from, than agreeing with, Bengalee, and I think we made a great mistake in directing that all business should be transacted in Bengalee, and that the Assamese must acquire it. It is too late now to retrace our steps, but I would strongly recommend Anandaram Phukan's proposition to the favourable consideration of the Council of Education, viz., the substitution of the vernacular language in lieu of Bengalee, and completion of the course of the Vernacular education in Bengalee. I feel persuaded that a youth will, under this system of tuition, learn more in two than he now acquires in four years. An English youth is not taught in Latin until he is well grounded in English, and in the same manner, an Assamese should not be taught in a foreign language until he knows his own.. "

Modern Trends

The period of modern literature began with the publication the Assamese journal *Jonaki* (1889), which introduced the short story form first by Laxminath Bezbarua. Thus began the Jonaki period of Assamese literature. In 1894 Rajanikanta Bordoloi published the first Assamese novel *Mirijiyori.*

Modern Assamese literature is as the literature in any other major language in India. People like Birendra Kumar Bhattacharyya (also only winner of the coveted Jnanpith Award), Bhabendra Nath Saikia, Syed Abdul Malik, Homen Borgohain, Nava Kanta Baruah, Devkanta Barua, Nirmal Prabha Bordoloi, Nilmani Phikan, Mmoni Raisom Goswami etc. have been recognized as writers of great repute all over the country.As for the tribal languages, Bodo has developed noticeably in the last few decades. But the other tribal languages are also no less poor, taking intoconsideration the fact that each is a rich storehouse of oral folk literature,with myths, legends, tales, songs, proverbs, riddles, lullabies and rhymes.

The Asam Sahitya Sabha, the biggest literary body in Eastern India, is the organisation which plays the most important role in co-ordinating efforts of the writers and bringing the masses closer to the written word. In fact the annual sessions of the Sabha are worth seeing going by the fact that they draw crowds in lakhs, thus proving the Sabha's mass following.

The Bodo Sahitya Sabha on the other hand is a pioneer body in co-ordinating the activities of Bodo writers, Of late, the Asam Sahitya Sabha and the Bodo Sahitya Sabha have taken up joint programmes to encourage writers coming from the tribal Communities.

7

Bengali Literature

The term Bengali literature refers to literary works written in Bengali language particularly from Bangladesh and the Indian provinces of West Bengal and Tripura. The history of Bengali literature traces back hundreds of years while it is impossible to separate the literary trends of the two Bengals during the pre-independence period. Post independent Bangladesh has given birth to its own distinct set of literature.

Early History Bengali Literature

The first evidence of Kamrupi literature is known as Charyapada or Chari-Siddha-Pada in dedication on the names of four sons of Brahma, a collection of 8th-12th century CE Buddhist mystic poems from eastern India or ancient Kingdom of Kamarupa now read as Kamrup that provides early examples of Assamese, Oriya and Bengali languages. Poets of these Charyapadas, the Siddhas belonged to the various regions of ancient Kamarupa kingdom or present Assam, Bengal, Orissa and Bihar. Charyapada is also the oldest known written form of Kamrupi.

The famous Bengali linguist Harprashad Shastri discovered the palm leaf Charyapada manuscript in the Nepal Royal Court Library in 1907.

In the middle of 19th century, Bengali literature gained momentum. During this period, the Bengali *Pandits* of Fort William College did the tedious work of translating the text books in Bengali to help teach the British some Indian languages including Bengali. This work played a role in the background in the evolution of Bengali prose. In 1814, Raja Ram Mohan Roy arrived in Calcutta and engaged in literary pursuits. Translating from Sanskrit to Bengali, writing essays on religious topics and publishing magazines were some the areas he focussed on. He established a cultural group in the name of 'Atmiya Sabha' (Club of Kins) in 1815. Another significant contributor of Bengali literature in its early stage was Ishwar Chandra Bandyopadhyaya.

In 1857, the famous 'Sipahi Bidroha' (Sepoy Mutiny) took place. With the wind of it, 'Nil Bidroho' (Indigo Revolt) scattered all over then Bengal region. This Nil Bidroha lasted for more than a year (In 1859-1860). The literature world was shaken with this revolt. In the light of this revolt, a great drama was published from Dhaka in the name of 'Neel Dorpon' (The Indigo

Michael Madhusudan Dutt

In this time, Michael Madhusudan Dutt emerged as the first epic-poet of modern bangla literature. Dutt, a Christian by conversion, is best known for his Ramayana-based masterpiece, "The Slaying of Meghnadh," (in Bengali *"Meghnadh Bodh Kabbo"*, which essentially follows in the poetic tradition of Milton's

Paradise Lost. Those who have read it consider this work a world-class epic poem of the modern era. Michael Madhusudan Dutta is also credited with the introduction of sonnets to Bangla literature. He ruled the Bangla literature wold for more than a decade (1858-1863).

Bankim Chandra Chattopadhyay

Bankim Chandra Chattopadhyay starts his journey through bangla literature with his first published novel 'Durgeshnondini' (Daughter of the Fort Lord) in 1865. He is considered as one of the leading Bengali novelists and is popularly known as the author of India's first *national song*, "Bande Matarom". The song appears in his novel "Anandamath", considered to be a masterpiece in Bengali literature.

Rabindranath Tagore

Possibly the most prolific writer in Bangla is Nobel laureate Rabindranath Tagore. Tagore dominated both the Bengali and Indian philosophical and literary scene for decades. His 2,000 *Rabindrasangeets* play a pivotal part in defining Bengali culture, both in West Bengal and Bangladesh. He is the author of the national anthems of both India and Bangladesh, both composed in Bangla. Other notable Bangla works of his are *Gilunjali*, a book of poems for which he was awarded the Nobel Prize for Literature in 1913, and many short stories and a few novels. It is widely accepted that Bangla Literature accomplished its contemporary look by the writings and influence of Rabindranath.

Kazi Nazrul Islam

In a similar category is Kazi Nazrul Islam, who was

invited to post-partition Bangladesh as the National Poet and whose work transcends sectarian boundaries. Adored by Bengalis both in Bangladesh and West Bengal, his work includes 3,000 songs, known as both as *nazrul geeti* and "nazrul sangeet". He is frequently called the rebel poet mainly because of his most famous and electrifying poem "Bidrohi" or "The Rebel", and also because of his strong sympathy and support for revolutionary activities leading to India's independence from British Rule.

His songs and poems were frequently used during the Bangladesh Liberation War as well. Though he is acknowledged as the rebel poet, Nazrul very effectively contributed in all branches of literature. He wrote poems that light the fire against inequality or injustice and at the same time is known for his poignant romantic poems as well. He wrote a lot of Islami Ghazals and in the same time wrote a number of *Shyama Sangeet* (songs for the Hindu Mother Goddess, Kali). Nazrul was not only a poet, he was writer, musician, journalist and philosopher. He was sent to jail for his literary works against the then prevailing British rule.

Novelists

Sarat Chandra Chattopadhyay was one of the most popular novelists of early 20th century whose speciality was exploring life and sufferings of women in contemporary rural Bengal. His sympathy towards the common rural folks in "pallisamaj" and a trademark simplified Bengali as a writing style made him one of the most popular writer in his time. Even long after his death many Bengali and Bollywood blockbusters were based on his novels.

After him Tarashankar Bandopadhyay, Bibhutibhushan Bandopadhyay, Manik Bandopadhyay, are the three Bandopadhyays who broke out into a new era of realistic writing style. Where the two of the above Bibhutibhusan and Manik had long standing influence on the two of the most brilliant film directors from Bengal, Satyajit Ray and Ritwik Ghatak respectively. Other famous bengali novelists are Jagadish Gupta, Satinath Bhaduri, Balai Chand Mukhopadhyay (Banophool), Saradindu Bandopadhyay, Kamal Kumar Majumdar, Sunil Gangopadhyay, Sandipan Chattopadhyay, Shumotho Nath Ghosh, Gagendra Kumar Mitra, Bimal Mitra, Bimal Kar, Samaresh Basu, Mani Shankar Mukherjee (Shankar), etc.

Seeds of bengali science fiction could be observed in the writings of Jagadish Chandra Bose, which was later put into a definite genre by writers such as Jagadananda Roy, Hemlal Dutta, Begum Roquia Sakhawat Hussain, Premendra Mitra, Satyajit Ray. Where Satyajit Ray is also notable for his short stories where he revives the tradition of Thakurmar Jhuli into a mixture of fantasy, mystery, science, and fairy tale. The genre of parallel novel-writing started from the 1960s with the Hungryalist Movement. Malay Roy Choudhury, Subimal Basak and Basudeb Dasgupta are known to be the most experimental novelists belonging to this movement. Basudeb is known to his readers for his only novel Kheladhula. Malay is famous for his Dubjaley trilogy and Subimal for his broken narrative CHHATAMATHA.

More experimental novelists who came into the scene in the midst of surging change in Bengali Literature are: Udayan Ghosh, Rabindra Guha, Kamal Chakraborty, Barin Ghoshal, Subimal Mishra, Arupratan Basu, Nabarun Bhattacharya.

Short Story Writers

Bengali literature is also famous for short stories. Some of the famous short story writers are Rabindranath Tagore, Manik Bandopadhyay, Jagadish Gupta, Tarashankar Bandopadhyay, Bibhuti Bhushan Bandopadhyay, Rajshekhar Basu (Parasuram), Premendra Mitra, Kamal Kumar Majumdar, Shibram Chakrabarti, Saradindu Bandopadhyay, Subodh Ghosh, Narendranath Mitra, Jyotirindra Nandi, Bimal Kar, Narayan Gangopadhyay, Shumotho Nath Ghosh, Gagendra Kumar Mitra, Santosh Ghosh, Debesh Roy, Anish Deb, Abhijnan Roychowdhury, Satyajit Roy,Lila Majumder, Shiresendu Mukhopaddhyay, Ratan Lal Basu,Sayed Walliullaha, Sandipan Chattopadhyay, Basudeb Dasgupta, Subimal Mishra, Arupratan Basu, Kamal Chakraborty, Aboni Dhar, Nabarun Bhattacharya, Akhtaruzzaman Ilias, Mahmudul Huq, Hasan Azizul Huq, etc. Malay Roy Choudhury has introduced a completely new genre of Bengali short story writing called 'Atibastab' or 'Hyperreal' during 1990s.

New writers and experimental short stories (apart from the mainstream ones) were not in the scene over the last two decades (1980's and 90's). A revival of new experimental short stories is observed in the New Age (21st Century). Pratishedhak, a New Age magazine (which first revived the experimental short story culture in early 2000), has played a major influential role to promote further revival of the experimental short story writing culture. Some New Age short story writers are: Souptik Chakraborty, Arko Chattopadhyay, Arupratan Ghosh, Sudeshna Majumdar and Ratul Paul.

Poets

Jatindramohan Bagchi, Kazi Nazrul Islam, Jibanananda Das, along with Buddhadeva Bose, marks the beginning of the major move to transcend the Tagore legacy. Even though Jibanananda went through a terbulent and difficult financial troubles and met an unfortunate accident caliming his life early in his writing career, he remains to be the most influential poet of post-Rabindranath era. The new genre of Bengali poets departed considerably from Tagore's ideological style and adopted various themes and philosophies such as Marxism , Freudian interpretation of mind, which were avoided and often criticized by Rabindranath Tagore. These three marked the beginning of the era that will burst with activities and urge to merge with the greater world of poetry absorbing elements from them. Commonly called polli-kobi (*pastoral poet*) Jasimuddin, Shamsur Rahman, widely known for his 'playing with words' are also notable.

Literary Movements

Hungryalism

There has been only one pathbreaking literary movement in West Bengal, namely The Hungry generation or Hungryalism. The famous poets of this movement are Malay Roy Choudhury, Shakti Chattopadhyay, Benoy Majumdar, Samir Roy choudhury, Falguni Ray, Saileswar Ghose, Pradip Chowdhuri, Subo Acharya, Arunesh Ghose, Tridib Mitra and Debi Ray. The fiction writers are Sandipan Chattopadhyay,Basudeb Dasgupta, Subimal Basak, Malay Roy Choudhury and Samir Roychoudhury. The painters are Anil Karanjai and Karunanidhan Mukhopadhyay.

Prakalpana Movement

Prakalpana Movement, branded by Steve LeBlanc, the noted US critic, as 'a tiny literary revolution', 'nurtured' by Kolkata, has been fostering its new genres of Prakalpana fiction, Sarbangin poetry and Chetanavyasism for over four decades, spearheaded by Vattacharja Chandan, beginning in 1969. It is probably the only bilingual (Bengali-English) literary movement in India mothered by Bengali literature, that has spread its wings world wide through the participation of well known international avant-garde writers and mail artists such as Richard Kostelanetz, John M. Bennett, Sheila Murphy, Don Webb, John Light, Carla Bertola &c, with notable Bengali poets, writers and artists like Vattacharja Chandan, Dilip Gupta, Asish Deb, Bablu Roy Choudhury, Syamoli Mukherjee Bhattacharjee, Boudhayan Mukhopadhyay, Ramratan mukhopadhyay, Nikhil Bhaumik, Utpal, Abhijit Ghosh, Arun Kumar Chakraborty, Niva De etc.

Parallel Poetry

Kaurab Cult

Some major changes occurred in the 1970s in the Bengali Poetry, chiefly around Kaurab - a literary & cultural magazine nearly four decades old. Prime cult-figures of Kaurab are :

Swadesh Sen, Kamal Chakraborty, Barin Ghosal, Debajyoti Dutta, Shankar Lahiri, Shankar Chakraborty and Aryanil Mukhopadhyay.

Poets who lead Left-movement since 1970

Biplab Majee, Ananya Ray, Tusar Roy, Monibhushan Bhattacharya, Pranab Chattopadhya, Saroj Dutta.

New Poetry

Since the mid 80's Bengali Literature experienced a new genre of Bengali poetry called New Poetry. From the early 90's a Kolkata based poetry journal Kabita Campus has organized various workshops and poetry-camps focusing on this genre. In 2003 some poets of that journal have separately started another one named Natun Kabita containing their ideas and poems, through both online and print media. Another new age poetry magazine in the same sphere is Boikhoribhashya. Poets associated with this literary movement are: Barin Ghosal, Ranjan Maitra, Swapan Roy, Dhiman Chakraborty, Alok Biswas, Pronob Pal, Soumitra Sengupta, Arupratan Ghosh, Indranil Ghosh, Amitava Praharaj and Debanjan Das.

Rajarshi Chattopadhyay, Atanu Bandopadhyay, Pradip Chakraborty are the poets who joined this movement in mid 90's.

The first decade of this century (2000-09) is considered to be the period of a *New Age* of Bengali poetry. Prominent poets rising from the period are: Sankha Subhra Devbarman, Aritra Sanyal, Animikh Patra, Souptik Chakraborty, Saibal Sarkar, Deb Maity, Arindam Ray, Arup Ghosh, Tanmay Mandal, Arjun Bandopadhyay, Susnata Jana, Himalay Jana, Kaushik Bhowmik, Pallab Chakrabarti, Sanghamitra Haldar, Himadri Mukhopadhyay, Somnath Ghosal, Swagata Dasgupta, Nabendu Bikash Ray, Ripon Fio, Atanu Sinha, Sandip Kumar, Paramita Das.

Seminal Hindu religious works in Bangla include the many songs of Ramprasad Sen. His works (still sung today) from the 17th century cover an astonishing range of emotional responses to the goddess Kali, detailing complex philosophical statements based on Vedanta teachings and more visceral pronouncements of his love of the goddess. They are known as *Shyama Sangeet* and were the literary inspiration for Kazi Nazrul Islam's later, famed Shyama Sangeet. There are also the laudatory accounts of the lives and teachings of the Vaishnava saint Chaitanya Mahaprabhu (the *Choitanyo Choritâmrit*) and Shri Ramakrishna (the *Ramakrishna Kathamrita,* translated roughly as Gospel of Ramakrishna). There is also a large body of Islamic literature, that can be traced back at least to *Noornama* by Abdul Hakim. *Bishad Sindhu* depicting the death of Hussain in Karbala is very popular novel written by Mir Mosharraf Hossain. Later works influenced by Islam include devotional songs written by Nazrul, and popularized by Abbas Uddin, among others.

The literature discussed so far can be more or less regarded as the common heritage of both Bangladesh and West Bengal. Since the partition of Bengal in 1947, the east and west parts of Bengal have also developed their own distinctive literatures. For example, the Naxalite movement has influenced much of West Bengal's literature, whereas the Liberation War has had a similarly profound impact on Bangladeshi literature.

8

Hindi Literature

Hindi literature, is broadly divided into four prominent forms or styles, being *Bhakti* (devotional); *Shringar* (beauty); *Veer-Gatha* (extolling brave warriors); and *Adhunik* (modern). The Mahatma Gandhi Antarrashtriya Hindi Vishwavidyalaya is an Indian central university established for the promotion and development of Hindi language and literature, through teaching and research.

Hindi language, the official language of India, according to the Constitution of India and is spoken in Indian states of Haryana, Rajasthan, Uttar Pradesh, Uttarakhand, Bihar, Madhya Pradesh, Chhatisgarh, Jharkhand and Himachal Pradesh. Thus, Hindi literature contains literature in all Hindi languages, including its dialects like: Brij Bhasha, Bundeli, Awadhi, Kannauji, Marwari, Maithili, Magahi, Bhojpuri and Bihari languages and Khariboli (Modern Standard Hindi) in Devnagari script, the dialect which is one of India's official languages.

History of Hindi Literature

Adi Kaal or Veer Gatha Kaal

In the ancient period of Hindi or *Adi Kaal* (before 1400

CE), Hindi literature was developed in the states of Kannauj, Delhi, Ajmer, stretching up to central India, modern Madhya Pradesh.

Delhi was ruled by Prithviraj Chauhan (1168-1192 CE), that is when his court poet, Chand Bardai, composed a eulogy to him, titled Prithviraj Raso, which was considered one of the first works in the History of Hindi Literature.

Kannauj's last Rathore ruler was Jayachand, who gave more patronage to Sanskrit (which was no longer the common man's language). His court poet was Harsha (whose major poetic work was *Naishdhiya Charitra*). Mahoba's royal poet Jagnayak (or Jagnik) and Ajmer's Nalha were other literary figures in this period. However, after Prithviraj Chauhan's defeat, most literary works belonging to this period were destroyed during Muhammad Ghori's campaign. Very few scriptures or manuscripts from this period are available and their genuineness is also doubted.

Some Siddha and Nathpanthi poets' works belonging to this period are also found, but their genuineness is again, doubted. Siddhas belonged to Vajrayana, a later Buddhist cult. Many argue that the language of Siddha poetry is not earlier Hindi, but Magadhi Prakrit. Nathpanthis were yogis who practised Hatha yoga. Some Jain and *Rasau* (heroic poets) poetry works are also available from this period.

In the Deccan region in South India, Dakkhini or Hindavi was used. It flourished under the Delhi Sultanate and later under the Nizams of Hyderabad. It was written in the Persian script. Nevertheless, the Hindavi literature can be considered as proto-Hindi literature. Many Deccani experts like Sheikh Ashraf or Mulla Vajahi used the word *Hindavi* to describe this dialect. Others such as Roustami, Nishati etc preferred to call it Deccani. Shah Buharnuddin Janam Bijapuri used to call it Hindi. The first Deccani author was Khwaja Bandanawaz Gesudaraz Muhammad Hasan. He wrote three prose works - Mirazul Aashkini, Hidayatnama and Risala Sehwara. His grandson Abdulla Hussaini wrote *Nishatul Ishq*. The first Deccani poet was Nizami.

During the later part of this period and early Bhakti Kala, many saint-poets like Ramanand and Gorakhnath became famous. The earliest form of Hindi can also be seen in some of Vidyapati's Maithili works.

Bhakti Kaal

The medieval Hindi literature is marked by the influence of Bhakti movement and composition of long, epic poems.

Avadhi and Brij Bhasha were the dialects in which literature was developed. The main works in Avadhi are Malik Muhammad Jayasi's *Padmavat* and Tulsidas's *Ramacharitamanas*. The major works in Braj dialect are Tulsidas's *Vinaya Patrika* and Surdas's *Sur Sagar*. Sadhukaddi was also a language commonly used, especially by Kabir in his poetry and dohas.

The Bhakti period also marked great theoretical development in poetry forms chiefly from a mixture of older forms of poetry in Sanskrit School and the Persian School. These included Verse Patterns like *Doha* (two-liners), *Sortha, Chaupaya* (four-liners) etc. This was also the age when Poetry was characterized under the various Rasas. Unlike the Adi Kaal (also called the Vir Gatha Kaal) which was characterized by an overdose of Poetry in the *Vir Rasa* (Heroic Poetry), the Bhakti Yug marked a much more diverse and vibrant form of poetry which spanned the whole gamut of rasas from *Shringara rasa* (love), *Vir Rasa* (Heroism).

Bhakti poetry had two schools - the *Nirguna* school (the believers of a formless God or an abstract name) and the *Saguna* school (the believers of a God with attributes and worshippers of Vishnu's incarnations). Kabir and Guru Nanak belong to the Nirguna school, and their philosophy was greatly influenced by the Advaita Vedanta philosophy of Adi Sankaracharya. They believed in the concept of Nirgun Nirakaar Bramh or the Shapeless Formless One. The Saguna school was represented by mainly Vaishnava poets like Surdas, Tulsidas and others and was a logical extension of the Dvaita and Vishishta Advaita Philosophy propounded by the likes of Madhavacharya etc. This school was chiefly Vaishnava in orientation as in seen in the main compositions like Ramacharitamanas, Sur Saravali, Sur Sagar extoling Rama and Krishna.

This was also the age of tremendous integration between the Hindu and the Islamic elements in the Arts with the advent of many Muslim Bhakti poets like Abdul Rahim Khan-I-Khana who was a court poet to Mughal emperor Akbar and was a great devotee of Krishna. The Nirgun School of Bhakti Poetry was also tremendously secular in nature and its propounders like Kabir and Guru Nanak had a large number of followers irrespective of caste or religion.

Ritikavya Kaal

In *Ritikavya* or *Ritismagra Kavya* period, the erotic element became pre-dominant in the Hindi literature. This era is called Riti (meaning 'procedure') because this was the age when poetry forms and theory developed to the fullest, as in the theoretical aspects and procedures of poetry writing as an Art Form, following traditional forms. But this emphasis on poetry theory greatly reduced the Emotive Aspects of Poetry which was the chief aspect of the Bhakti movement and poetry content gradually started degenerating. The Saguna School of the Bhakti Yug split into two schools (Rama bhakti and Krishna bhakti) somewhere in the interregnum of the Bhakti and the Reeti Eras. The Reeti Era saw most of its work under the Krishna Bhakti banner, but the works had greatly degenerated in philosophical content from the pure forms of total Devotion to the Dualistic Supreme Being, more towards the erotic description of Shringar aspects of Krishna's life, his Leela, his pranks with the Gopis in Braj, the description of the carnal/physical aspects of the beauty of Radha (Krishna's Consort). The poetry of Bihari, and Ghananand Das fit this bill. The most well known book from this age is Bihari Satsai by Bihari which is a collection of Dohas (couplets), about *Bhakti* (devotion), *Neeti* (Moral policies) and *Shringar* (love).

Modern Hindi Literature

In 1800, the British East India Company established Fort William College at Calcutta. The College President J. B. Gilchrist hired professors to write books in Hindi and Urdu. Some of these books were *Prem sagar* (or *Prem Sagur*) by Lallu Lal, *Naasiketopaakhyan* by Sadal Mishra, *Sukhsagar* by Sadasukhlal of Delhi and *Rani Ketaki ki kahani* by Munshi Inshallah Khan.

A depiction of Surya in a 1884 book, *Indrajalakala* (The Art of Magic); Jwala Prakash Press, Meerut. By this time, Hindustani had become the general public's language. To distinguish themselves from the general masses, the learned Muslims used to write in Urdu (filled with Persian and Arabic vocabulary), while Khadiboli became prominent among educated Hindus. Khadiboli with heavily Sanskritized vocabulary or *Sahityik* Hindi (Literary Hindi) was popularized by the writings of Swami Dayananda Saraswati, Bhartendu Harishchandra and others. Bhartendu Harishchandra preferred Braj Bhasha for poetry, but for prose, he deliberately used Khadiboli. Other important writers of this period are Mahavir Prasad Dwivedi, Maithili Sharan Gupt, R N Tripathi and Gopala Sharan Sinha. The rising numbers of newspapers and magazines made Khadiboli popular among the educated people. Chandrakanta, written by Devaki Nandan Khatri, was considered the first authentic work of prose in the Adhunik kaal (modern period). A story of magical characters, kings and kingdoms, it reminds one of The Lord of the Rings series and was successfully manifested into an eponymous TV Serial.

The person who brought realism in the Hindi prose literature was Munshi Premchand, who is considered as the most revered figure in the world of Hindi fiction and progressive movement. Before Premchand, the Hindi literature revolved around fairy or magical tales, entertaining stories and religious themes. Premchand's novels have been translated into many other languages.

Dwivedi Yug

The *Dwivedi Yug* ("Age of Dwivedi") in Hindi literature lasted from 1900 to 1918. It is named after Mahavir Prasad Dwivedi, who played a major role in establishing modern Hindi language in poetry and broadening the acceptable subjects of Hindi poetry from the traditional ones of religion and romantc love. He encouraged poetry in Hindi dedicated to nationalism and social reform.

Dwivedi founded the magazine *Sarasvati* in 1900 and used it to crusade for reforms in Hindi literature. One of the most prominent poems of the period was Maithilisharan Gupta's *Bharat-bharati*, which evokes the past glory of India. Shridhar Prathak's *Bharatgit* is another renowned poem of the period.

Some scholars have labeled much of the poetry of this period as "versified propaganda". According to Lucy Rosenstein: "It is verse of public statement; its language is functional but aesthetically unappealing. Earnest, concerned with social issues and moral values, it is puritanical poetry in which aesthetic considerations are secondary. Imagination, originality, poetic sensibility and expression are wanting, the metre is restrictive, the idiom clumsy." She adds, however, that the period was important for laying the foundations for modern Hindi poetry, it did reflect sensitivity to social issues of the time, and the inelegance is a typical feature of a "young" poetry, as she considers Modern Hindi.

Without a poetic tradition in modern Hindi, poets often modeled their forms on Braj, and later on Sanskrit, Urdu, Bengali and English forms, often ill-suited to Hindi. The subjects of the poems tended to be communal rather than personal. Characters were often presented not as individuals but as social types.

Chhayavaadi Yug

In 20th century, Hindi literature saw a romantic

upsurge. This is known as *Chhayavaad* (*shadowism*) and the literary figures belonging to this school are known as *Chhayavaadi*. Jaishankar Prasad, Suryakant Tripathi 'Nirala', Mahadevi Varma and Sumitranandan Pant, are the four major *Chhayavaadi* poets.

This period of Neo-romanticism, represents the adolescence of Hindi Poetry. It is marked by beauty of expression and flow of intense emotion. The four representative poets of this era represent the best in Hindi Poetry. A unique feature of this period is the emotional (and sometimes active) attachment of poets with national freedon struggle, their effort to understand and imbibe the vast spirit of a magnificent ancient culture and their towering genius which grossly overshadowed all the literary 'talked abouts' of next seven decades.

Other important genres of *Adhunik Sahitya* (Modernism) are: Prayogvad (Experimentalism) of Ajneya and the *Tar Saptak* poets, also known as *Nayi Kavita* (New Poetry) and *Nayi Kahani* (New Story) of Nirmal Verma and others; followed by Pragativad (Progressivism) of Gajanan Madhav Muktibodh and other authors.

Nakenwad

Among the numerous schools of poetry which sprang up in the fifties of this century was *Nakenwad*, a school deriving its nomenclature from the first letters of the names of its three pioneers - Pandit Nalin Vilochan Sharma, Kesari Kumar, and Naresh Mehta all poets of note in their own right. Apart from being a poet, Nalin Vilochan was also a brilliant critic, with a wide perspective on literary history. His critical attitude is marked by a synthesis or coordination of various disciplines of human knowledge - philosophy, history, art and culture, all pressed into the service of literary appraisal and analysis.

Uttar Adhunik Kaal

Uttar Adhunik is the post-modernist period of Hindi literature, marked by a questioning of early trends that copied the West as well as the excessive ornamentation of the Chhayavaadi movement, and by a return to simple language and natural themes. Jainendra Kumar, Phanishwar Nath Renu and Agyeya (Satchidananda Hiranand Vatsyayan) are the other popular figures of this time. Jainendra Kumar explored the human psyche in novels like *Sunita* and *Tyagapatra*. Renu's *Maila Aanchal* is one of the major works of this period. Agyeya brought experimentalism (*Prayogvaad*) into the Hindi literature. His most famous novel is *Shekhar Ek Jivani* (1941).

In this period the voices of the women appeared in feminist writings and also of other long marginalized social groups, have started emerging, exemplied by the Dalit literature, which represents the most fierce and important genres of the contemporary Indian literature.

Travel Literature

Rahul Sankrityayan and Baba Nagarjun were some of the great Indian writers who dedicated themselves entirely to the Hindi Travel Literature (*Yatra Vritanta*). Rahul Sankrityayan was one of the greatest traveled scholars of India, spending forty-five years of his life on travels away from his home. He is known as the (*"Father of Hindi Travel literature"*). Baba Nagarjun was a major Hindi and Maithili poet who has also penned a number of novels, short stories, literary biographies and travelogues, and was known as ("*Janakavi- the People's Poet*").

Essay-writing

Acharya Kuber Nath Rai is one of the writers who dedicated themselves entirely to the form of essay-writing. His collections of essays *Gandha Madan, Priya neel-kanti, Ras Aakhetak, Vishad Yog, Nishad Bansuri, Parna mukut* have enormously enriched the form of essay. A scholar of Indian culture and western literature, he was proud of Indian heritage. His love for natural beauty and Indian folk literatures and preference for agricultural society over the age of machines, his romantic outlook, aesthetic sensibility, his keen eye on contemporary reality and classical style place him very high among contemporary essayists in Hindi.

9

Kannada Literature

Kannada literature is the corpus of written forms of the Kannada language, a member of the Dravidian family spoken mainly in the Indian state of Karnataka and written in the Kannada script. Attestations in inscriptions span something like one and a half millenia, with some specific literary works surviving in rich manuscript traditions, extending from the 9th century to the present. The Kannada language is usually divided into three linguistic phases: Old (850–1200 CE), Middle (1200–1700 CE) and Modern (1700–present); and its literary characteristics are categorised as Jain, Veerashaiva and Vaishnava—recognising the prominence of these three faiths in giving form to, and fostering, classical expression of the language, until the advent of the modern era. Although much of the literature prior to the 18th century was religious, some secular works were also committed to writing.

Starting with the *Kavirajamarga* (c. 850), and until the middle of the 12th century, literature in Kannada was almost exclusively composed by the Jains, who found eager patrons in the Chalukya, Ganga, Rashtrakuta and Hoysala kings. Although the *Kavirajamarga*, authored during the reign of King Amoghavarsha, is the oldest extant literary work in the language, it has been hypothesized that prose, verse and grammatical traditions must have existed earlier. However, other scholars believe the literary tradition in Kannada to have begun with *Kavirajamarga* itself, pointing to the absence of references in other early works (such as the *Sabdamanidarpanam* of Kesiraja) to any preceding literature prior to the ninth century.

The Veerashaiva movement of the 12th century created new literature which flourished alongside the Jain works. With the waning of Jain influence during the 14th-century Vijayanagara empire, a new Vaishnava literature grew rapidly in the 15th century; the devotional movement of the itinerant Haridasa saints marked the high point of this era.

After the decline of the Vijayanagara Empire in the 16th century, Kannada literature was supported by the various rulers, including the Wodeyars of Mysore and the Nayakas of Ikkeri. In the 19th century, some literary forms, such as the prose narrative, the novel, and the short story, were borrowed from English literature. Modern Kannada literature is now widely known and recognised: during the last half century, Kannada language authors have received seven Jnanpith awards and 51 Sahitya Akademi awards in India.

Content and Genre

In the early period and beginning of the medieval period, between the 9th and 13th centuries, writers were predominantly of the Jain and Veerashaiva faiths. Jains were the earliest known cultivators of Kannada literature, which they dominated until the 12th century, although a few works by Veerashaivas from that period have survived. Jain authors wrote about

Jain Tirthankars and other aspects of the Jain religion. The Veerashaiva authors wrote about the Hindu God Shiva, his 25 forms, and the expositions of Shaivism. Veerashaiva poets belonging to the Vachana tradition advanced the philosophy of Basavanna from the 12th century.

During the period between the 13th and 15th centuries, there was decline in Jain writings and an increase in the number of works from the Veerashaiva tradition; there were also contributions from Vaishnava writers. Thereafter, Veerashaiva and Vaishnava writers dominated Kannada literature. Vaishnava writers focused on the Hindu epics, the Ramayana, the Mahabharata and the Bhagavata, as well as the Vedanta and other subjects from the Hindu puranic traditions. The devotional songs of the Haridasa poets, performed to music, were first noted in the 15th century. Writings on secular subjects remained popular throughout this period.

An important change during the *Bhakti* (devotion) period starting from the 12th century was the decline of court literature and the rise in popularity of shorter genres such as the *vachana* and *kirthane,* forms that were more accessible to the common man. Writings eulogising kings, commanders and spiritual heroes waned, with a proportional increase in the use of local genres. Kannada literature moved closer to the spoken and sung folk traditions, with musicality being its hallmark, although some poets continued to use the ancient *champu* form of writing as late as the 17th century.

The *champu* Sanskritic metre (poems in verses of various metres interspersed with paragraphs of prose, also known as *champu-kavya*) was the most popular written form from the 9th century onwards, although it started to fall into disuse in the 12th century. Other Sanskritic metres used were the *saptapadi* (seven line verse), the *ashtaka* (eight line verse) and the *shataka* (hundred-line verse). There were numerous translations and adaptations of Sanskrit writings into Kannada and, to a lesser extent, from Kannada into Sanskrit. The medieval period saw the development of literary metres indigenous to the Kannada language. These included the *tripadi* (three-line verse, in use from 7th century), one of the oldest native metres; the *shatpadi* (six-line verse, first mentioned by Nagavarma I in *Chhandombudhi* of c. 984 and in use from 1165), of which six types exist; the *ragale* (lyrical narrative compositions, in use from 1160); the *sangatya* (compositions meant to be sung with a musical instrument, in use from 1232) and the *akkara* which came to be adopted in some Telugu writings. There were rare interactions with Tamil literature, as well.

Though religious literature was prominent, literary genres including romance, fiction, erotica, satire, folk songs, fables and parables, musical treatises and musical compositions were popular. The topics of Kannada literature included grammar, philosophy, prosody, rhetoric, chronicles, biography, history, drama and cuisine, as well as dictionaries and encyclopedias. According to critic Joseph T. Shipley, over fifty works on scientific subjects including medicine, mathematics and astrology have been written in the Kannada language.

Kannada literature of this period was mainly written on palm leaves. However, more than 30,000 more durable inscriptions on stone (known as *shilashasana*) and copper plates (known as *tamrashasana*) have survived to inform modern students of the historical development of Kannada literature. The Kappe Arabhatta inscription (c. 700), and the Hummacha and Soraba inscriptions (c. 800) are good examples of poetry in *tripadi* metre, and the Jura (Jabalpur) inscription of King Krishna III (964) is regarded as an epigraphical landmark of classical Kannada composition, containing poetic diction in *kanda* metre, a form consisting of a group of stanzas or chapters. Elegiac poetry on hundreds of *veeragallu* and *maastigallu* (hero stones) written by unknown poets in the *kanda* and the *vritta* (commentary) metre mourn the death of heroes who sacrificed their lives and the bravery of women who performed *sati*.

The pace of change towards more modern literary styles gained momentum in the early 19th century. Kannada writers were initially influenced by the modern literature of other languages, especially English. Modern English education and liberal democratic values inspired social changes, intertwined with the desire to retain the best of traditional ways. New genres including short stories, novels, literary criticism, and essays, were embraced as Kannada prose moved toward modernisation.

Classical Period

Rashtrakuta Court

The reign of the imperial Rashtrakutas and their powerful feudatory, the Gangas, marks the beginning of the classical period of writings in the Kannada language under royal patronage and the end of the age of Sanskrit epics. There was an emphasis on the adoption of Sanskritic models while retaining elements of local literary traditions, a style that prevailed in Kannada literature throughout the classical period. *Kavirajamarga,* written during this period, is a treatise on the Kannada speaking people, their poetry and their language. A portion of the writing qualifies as a practical grammar. It describes defective and corrective examples (the "do's and don't's") of versification, native composition styles recognised by *puratana kavis* (*lit,* "early poets") (the *bedande,* the *chattana* and the *gadyakatha* – compositions written in various interspersed metres), and in some contexts, the term *puravcharyar,* which may refer to previous grammarians or rhetoricians. Some historians attribute *Kavirajamarga* to the Rashtrakuta king Amoghavarsha I, but others believe that the book may have been inspired by the king and co-authored or authored in full by Srivijaya, a Kannada language theorist and court poet.

The earliest existing prose piece in old Kannada is *Vaddaradhane* ("Worship of Elders", 9th century) by Shivakotiacharya. It contains 19 lengthy stories, some in the form of fables and parables, such as "The Sage and the Monkey". Inspired by the earlier Sanskrit writing *Brihatkatha Kosha,* it is about Jain tenets and describes issues of rebirth, karma, the plight of humans on earth, and social issues of the time such as education, trade and commerce, magic, superstition, and the condition of women in society.

The works of Jain writers Adikavi Pampa, Sri Ponna and Ranna, collectively called the "three gems of Kannada literature", heralded the age of classical Kannada in the 10th century. Pampa, who wrote *Adipurana* in 941, is regarded as one of the greatest Kannada writers. Written in *champu* style, *Adipurana* narrates the life history of the first Jain Thirtankar, Rishabhadeva. In this spiritual saga, Rishabhadeva's soul moves through a series of births before attaining emancipation in a quest for the liberation of his soul from the cycle of life and death. Pampa's other classic, *Vikramarjuna Vijaya* (or *Pampa Bharata,* 941), is loosely based on the Hindu epic the Mahabharata.

Sri Ponna, patronised by King Krishna III, wrote *Santipurana* (950), a biography of the 16th Jain Tirthankar Shantinatha. He earned the title *Ubhaya Kavichakravathi* ("supreme poet in two languages") for his command of both Kannada and Sanskrit. Although Sri Ponna borrowed significantly from Kalidasa's earlier works, his *Santipurana* is considered an important Jain purana.

Chalukya Court

From the late 10th century, Kannada literature made considerable progress under the patronage of the new overlords of the Deccan, the Western Chalukyas and their feudatories: the Hoysalas, the southern Kalachuris, the Seuna Yadavas of Devagiri and Silharas of Karad. The skill of Kannada poets was appreciated in distant lands. King Bhoja of Malwa in central India presented Nagavarma I, a writer of prosody and romance classics, with horses as a mark of his admiration.

Ranna was the court poet of the Western Chalukya kings Tailapa II and Satyasraya. He was also patronised by Attimabbe, a devout Jain woman. Ranna's poetic writings reached their zenith with *Sahasa Bhima Vijaya* ("Victory of the bold Bhima", also called *Gada Yudda* or "Battle of Clubs", 982), which describes the conflict between Bhima and Duryodhana in his version of the Mahabharata epic, one of the earliest poetic elegies in the Kannada language. Unlike Pampa, who glorified Arjuna and Karna in his writing, Ranna eulogised his patron King Satyasraya and favourably compared him to Bhima, whom he crowned at the end of the Mahabharata war. His other well-known writing is the *Ajitha purana* (993), which recounts the life of the second Jain Tirthankar Ajitanatha. Ranna was bestowed the title *Kavi Chakravathi* ("Emperor among poets") by his patron king.

Among grammarians, Nagavarma-II, *Katakacharya* (poet laureate) of the Chalukya king Jagadhekamalla II made significant contributions with his works in grammar, poetry, prosody, and vocabulary; these are standard authorities and their importance to the study of Kannada language is well acknowledged. Among his other writings, the *Kavyavalokana* on grammar and rhetoric and the *Karnataka Bhashabhushana* (1145) on grammar are historically significant. However, the discovery of *Vardhamana Puranam* (1042), which has been ascribed by some scholars to Nagavarma II, has created uncertainty about his actual lifetime since it suggests that he may have lived a century earlier and been patronised by King Jayasimha II.

Hoysala Period

In the late 12th century, the Hoysalas, a powerful hill tribe from the Malnad region in modern southern Karnataka, exploited the political uncertainty in the Deccan to gain dominance in the region south of the Krishna River in southern India. A new chronological era was adopted, imperial titles were claimed and Kannada literature flourished with such noted scholars as Janna, Harihara, Rudrabhatta, Raghavanka, Keshiraja and others. An important achievement during this period was the establishment of native metres in literature (the *ragale,* the *tripadi,* the *sangatya* and the *shatpadi*).

Two renowned philosophers who lived during this time, Ramanujacharya and Madhvacharya, influenced the culture of the region. The conversion of the Hoysala King Vishnuvardhana in early 12th century from Jainism to Vaishnavism was to later prove a setback to Jain literature. In the decades to follow, Jain writers faced competition from the Veerashaivas, to which they responded with rebuttals, and from the 15th century, from the writers of the Vaishnava cadre. These events changed the literary landscape of the Kannada-speaking region forever.

One of the earliest Veerashaiva writers who was not part of the *Vachana* literary tradition, poet Harihara (or Harisvara) came from a family of *karnikas* (accountants), and worked under the patronage of King Narasimha I. He wrote *Girijakalyana* in ten sections following the Kalidasa tradition, employing the old Jain *champu* style, with the story leading to the marriage of Shiva and Parvati. In a deviation from the norm, Harihara avoided glorifying saintly mortals. He is credited with more than 100 poems in *ragale* metre, called the *Nambiyanana ragale* (or *Shivaganada ragale,* 1160) praising the saint Nambiyana and Virupaksha (a form of Hindu god Shiva). For his poetic talent, he has earned the honorific *utsava kavi* ("poet of exuberance").

Harihara's nephew, Raghavanka, was the first to introduce the *shatpadi* metre into Kannada literature in his epic *Harishchandra Kavya* (1200), considered a classic despite occasionally violating strict rules of

Kannada grammar. Drawing on his skill as a dramatist, Raghavanka's story of King Harishchandra vividly describes the clash of personalities between sage Vishvamitra and sage Vashisht and between Harishchandra and Vishvamitra. It is believed that this interpretation of the story of Harishchandra is unique to Indian literature. The writing is an original and does not follow any established epic traditions. In addition to Hoysala patronage, Raghavanka was honoured by Kakatiya king Prataparudra I.

Rudrabhatta, a Smartha Brahmin (believer of monistic philosophy), was the earliest well-known Brahminical writer, under the patronage of Chandramouli, a minister of King Veera Ballala II. Based on the earlier work of *Vishnu Purana,* he wrote *Jagannatha Vijaya* (1180) in the *champu* style, relating the life of Lord Krishna leading up to his fight with the demon Banasura.

In 1209, the Jain scholar and army commander Janna wrote *Yashodhara Charite,* a unique set of stories dealing with perversion. In one of the stories, a king intended to perform a ritual sacrifice of two young boys to Mariamma, a local deity. After hearing the boys' tale, the king is moved to release them and renounce the practice of human sacrifice. In honour of this work, Janna received the title *Kavichakravarthi* ("Emperor among poets") from King Veera Ballala II. His other classic, *Anathanatha Purana* (1230), deals with the life of the 14th Tirthankar Ananthanatha.

Vijayanagara Period

Vaishnava Literature

The 14th century saw major upheavals in geo-politics

of southern India with Muslim empires invading from the north. The Vijayanagara Empire stood as a bulwark against these invasions and created an atmosphere conducive to the development of the fine arts. In a golden age of Kannada literature, competition between Vaishnava and Veerashaiva writers was fierce and literary disputations between the two sects were common, especially in the court of King Deva Raya II. Acute rivalry led to "organised processions" in honour of the classics written by poets of the respective sects.

To this period belonged Kumara Vyasa (the pen name of Naranappa), a doyen of medieval epic poets and one the most influential Vaishnava poets of the time. He was particularly known for his sophisticated use of metaphors and had even earned the title *Rupaka Samrajya Chakravarti* ("Emperor of the land of Metaphors"). In 1430, he wrote the *Gadugina Bharata,* popularly known as *Karnata Bharata Kathamanjari* or *Kumaravyasa Bharata* in the Vyasa tradition. The work is a translation of the first ten chapters of the epic *Mahabharata* and emphasises the divinity and grace of the Lord Krishna, portraying all characters with the exception of Krishna to suffer from human foibles. An interesting aspect of the work is the sense of humour exhibited by the poet and his hero, Krishna. This work marked a transition of Kannada literature to a more modern genre and heralded a new age combining poetic perfection with religious inspiration. The remaining *parvas* (chapters) of *Mahabharata* were translated by Timmanna Kavi (1510) in the court of King Krishnadevaraya. The poet named his work *Krishnaraya Bharata* after his patron king.

Kumara Valmiki (1500) wrote the first complete brahminical adaptation of the epic Ramayana, called

Torave Ramayana. According to the author, the epic he wrote merely narrated God Shiva's conversation with his consort Parvati. This writing has remained popular for centuries and inspired folk theatre such as the *Yakshagana,* which has made use of its verses as a script for enacting episodes from the great epic. In Valmiki's version of the epic, King Ravana is depicted as one of the suitors at Sita's *Swayamvara* (*lit.* a ceremony of "choice of a husband"). His failure to win the bride's hand results in jealousy towards Rama, the eventual bridegroom. As the story progresses, Hanuman, for all his services to Rama, is exalted to the status of "the next creator". Towards the end of the story, during the war with Rama, Ravana realises that his adversary is none other than the God Vishnu and hastens to die at his hands to achieve salvation.

Chamarasa, a Veerashaiva poet, was a rival of Kumara Vyasa in the court of Devaraya II. His eulogy of the saint Allama Prabhu, titled *Prabhulinga Lile* (1430), was later translated into Telugu and Tamil at the behest of his patron king. In the story, the saint was considered an incarnation of Hindu God Ganapathi while Parvati took the form of a princess of Banavasi.

Interaction between Kannada and Telugu literatures, a trend which had begun in the Hoysala period, increased. Translations of classics from Kannada to Telugu and vice versa became popular. Well-known bilingual poets of this period were Bhima Kavi, Piduparti Somanatha and Nilakanthacharya. In fact, so well versed in Kannada were some Telugu poets, including Dhurjati, that they freely used many Kannada terms in their Telugu writings. It was because of this "familiarity" with Kannada, that the notable writer Srinatha even called his Telugu, "Kannada". This process of interaction between the two languages continued into the 19th century in the form of translations by bilingual writers.

Mystic Literature

Veerashaiva

In the late 12th century, the Kalachuris successfully rebelled against their overlords, the Western Chalukyas, and annexed the capital Kalyani. During this turbulent period, a new religious faith called Veerashaivism (or Lingayatism) developed as a revolt against the existing social order of Hindu society. Some of the followers of this faith wrote literature called *Vachana Sahitya* ("Vachana literature") or *Sharana Sahitya* ("literature of the devotees") comprising of a unique and native form of poetry in free verse called *Vachana*. Basavanna (or Basava, 1160), the prime minister of southern Kalachuri King Bijjala II, is generally regarded as the inspiration for this movement. Devotees gathered to discuss their mystic experiences at a centre for religious discussion called Anubhava Mantapa ("hall of experience") in Kalyani. Here, they expressed their devotion to God Shiva in simple *vachana* poems. These poems were spontaneous utterances of rhythmic, epigrammatical, satirical prose emphasising the worthlessness of riches, rituals and book learning, displaying a dramatic quality reminiscent of the dialogues of Plato.

Basavanna, Allama Prabhu, Devara Dasimayya, Channabasava, Siddharama (1150), and Kondaguli Kesiraja are the best known among numerous poets (called *Vachanakaras*) who wrote in this genre. Akka Mahadevi was prominent among the several women poets; in addition to her poetry, she is credited with two short writings, *Mantrogopya* and *Yogangatrividhi*. Siddharama is credited with writings in *tripadi* metre and 1,379 extant poems (though he has claimed authorship of 68,000 poems).

The Veerashaiva movement experienced a setback with the assassination of King Bijjala and eviction of the *sharanas* (devotees) from Kalyani; further growth of *Vachana* poetry was curtailed until the 15th century when another wave of writings began under the patronage of the rulers of Vijayanagara. Chieftain Nijaguna Shivayogi originated a new philosophy called *Kaivalya*, founded on the advaitha (monistic) philosophy of Adi Shankara, synthesised with an offshoot of the Veerashaiva faith.

A prolific writer, Shivayogi composed devotional songs collectively known as the *Kaivalya sahitya* (or *Tattva Padagalu*, literally "songs of the pathway to emancipation"). His songs were reflective, philosophical and concerned with Yoga. Shivayogi also wrote a highly respected scientific encyclopaedia called the *Vivekachintamani*; it was translated into Marathi language in 1604 and Sanskrit language in 1652 and again in the 18th century. The encyclopaedia includes entries on 1,500 topics and covers a wide range of subjects including poetics, dance and drama, musicology and erotics.

Other well-known poet saints of the Veerashaiva tradition include Muppina Sadakshari, a contemporary of Shivayogi, whose collection of songs are called the *Subodhasara*, Chidananda Avadhuta of the 17th century and Sarpabhushana Shivayogi of the 18th century. So vast is this body of literature that much of it still needs to be studied.

Vaishnava

The Vaishnava Bhakti (devotional) movement involving well-known Haridasas (devotee saints) of that time made an indelible imprint on Kannada literature starting in the 15th century, inspiring a body of work called *Haridasa Sahitya* ("Haridasa literature"). Influenced by the Veerashaivism of the 12th century, this movement touched the lives of millions with its strong current of devotion.

The Haridasas conveyed the message of Vedantic philosopher Madhvacharya to the common man through simple Kannada language in the form of *devaranamas* and *kirthanas* (devotional songs in praise of god). The philosophy of Madhvacharya was spread by eminent disciples including Naraharitirtha, Jayatirtha, Vyasatirtha, Sripadaraya, Vadirajatirtha, Purandara Dasa, and Kanaka Dasa. Chaitanya Mahaprabhu, a prominent saint from distant Bengal, visited the region in 1510, further stimulating the devotional movement.

Purandara Dasa (1484–1564), a wandering bard, is believed to have composed 475,000 songs in the Kannada and Sanskrit languages, though only about 1,000 songs are known today. Composed in various *ragas,* and often ending with a salutation to the Hindu deity Vittala, his compositions presented the essence of the *Upanishads* and the *Puranas* in simple yet expressive language. He also devised a system by which the common man could learn Carnatic music, and codified the musical composition forms *svaravalis, alankaras* ("figure of speech") and *geethams*. Owing to such contributions, Purandara Dasa earned the honorific *Karnataka Sangeeta Pitamaha* ("Father of Carnatic Music").

Kanaka Dasa (whose birth name was Thimmappa Nayaka, 1509–1609) of Kaginele (in modern Haveri district) was an ascetic and spiritual seeker who authored important writings such as *Mohanatarangini* ("River of Delight"), the story of the Hindu god Krishna in *sangatya* metre; *Nrisimhastava,* a work dealing with glory of god Narasimha; *Nalacharita,* the story of Nala, noted for its narration; and *Hari Bhaktisara,* a spontaneous writing on devotion in *shatpadi* metre. The latter writing, which deals with *niti* (morals), *bhakti* (devotion) and *vairagya* (renunciation) has become popular as a standard book of learning for children. Kanaka Dasa authored a unique allegorical poem titled *Ramadhanya Charitre* ("Story of Rama's Chosen Grain"), which exalts ragi over rice. Apart from these classics, about 240 songs written by the Kanaka Dasa are available today.

The Haridasa movement returned to prominence from the 17th through 19th centuries, producing as many as 300 poets in this genre; well-known among them are Vijaya Dasa (1682–1755), Gopala Dasa (1721–1769), Jagannatha Dasa (1728–1809), Mahipathi Dasa (1750), Helavanakatte Giriamma and others. Over time, the movement's devotional songs inspired a form of religious and didactic performing art of the Vaishnava people called the Harikatha ("Stories of Hari"). Similar developments were seen among the followers of the Veerashaiva faith who popularised the *Shivakatha*

Mysore and Keladi Period

With the decline of the Vijayanagara Empire, the Kingdom of Mysore (1565–1947) and the kingdom of the Keladi Nayakas (1565–1763) rose to power in the southern and western regions of modern Karnataka respectively. Production of literary texts covering various themes flourished in these two courts. The Mysore court was adorned by eminent writers who authored encyclopaedias, epics, and religious commentaries, and composers and musicians. The Keladi court is better known for writings on Veerashaiva doctrine. The Mysore kings themselves were accomplished in the fine arts and made important contributions. A unique and native form of poetic literature with dramatic representation called *Yakshagana* gained popularity in the 18th century.

Geetha Gopala, a well-known treatise on music, is ascribed to King Chikka Devaraja Wodeyar (1673–1704), the earliest composer of the dynasty, who went by the honorific *Sahitya Vidyanikasha Prastharam* ("Expert in literature"). Inspired by Jayadeva's *Geetha Govinda* in Sanskrit, it was written in *saptapadi* metre. This is the first writing to propagate the Vaishnava faith in the Kannada language.

Also writing in this period was Sarvajna (*lit.* "The all knowing")—a mendicant and drifter Veerashaiva poet who left a deep imprint on Kannada speaking region and its people. His didactic *Vachanas*, penned in the *tripadi* metre, constitute some of Kannada's most celebrated works. With the exception of some early poems, his works focus on his spiritual quest as a drifter. The pithy *Vachanas* contain his observations on the art of living, the purpose of life and the ways of the world. He was not patronised by royalty, nor did he write for fame; his main aim was to instruct people about morality.

The writing of Brahmin author Lakshmisa (or Lakshmisha), a well-known story-teller and a dramatist, is dated to the mid-16th or late 17th century. The *Jaimini Bharata,* his version of the epic Mahabharata written in *shatpadi* metre, is one of the most popular poems of the late medieval period. A collection of stories, the poem includes the tale of the *Sita Parityaga* ("Repudiation of Sita"). The author successfully converted a religious story into a very human tale; it remains popular even in modern times.

The period also saw advances in dramatic works. Though there is evidence that theatre was known from the 12th century or earlier, modern Kannada theatre is traced to the rise of *Yakshagana* (a type of field play), which appeared in the 16th century. The golden age of *Yakshagana* compositions was tied to the rule of King Kanteerava Narasaraja Wodeyar II (1704–1714). A polyglot, he authored 14 *Yakshaganas* in various languages, although all are written in the Kannada script. He is credited with the earliest *Yakshaganas* that included *sangeeta* (music), *nataka* (drama) and *natya* (dance).

Mummadi Krishnaraja Wodeyar (1794–1868), the ruler of the princely state of Mysore, was another prolific writer of the era. More than 40 writings are attributed to him, including a poetic romance called *Saugandika Parinaya* written in two versions, *sangatya* and a drama. His reign signalled the shift from classical genres to modern literature which was to be complemented by the influence of colonial period of India.

Modern Period

The development of modern Kannada literature can be traced to the early 19th century when Maharaja Krishnaraja Wodeyar III and his court poets moved away from the ancient *champu* form of prose toward prose renderings of Sanskrit epics and plays. Kempu Narayana's *Mudramanjusha* ("Seal Casket", 1823) is the first modern novel written in Kannada.

Modern Kannada literature was cross-fertilized by the colonial period in India as well, with translations of Kannada works and dictionaries into European languages as well as other Indian languages, and vice versa, and the establishment of European style newspapers and periodicals in Kannada. In addition, in the 19th century, interaction with European technology, including new printing techniques accelerated the development of modern literature.

The first Kannada newspaper called *Mangalore Samachara* was published by Hermann Mögling in 1843; and the first Kannada periodical, *Mysuru Vrittanta Bodhini* was published by Bhashyam Bhashyacharya in Mysore around the same time. Hermann Mögling translated Kannada classics into a series called *Bibliotheca Carnataca* during 1848–1853, while British officers Benjamin L. Rice and J. H. Fleet edited and published critical editions of literary classics, contemporary folk ballads and inscriptions. Following the rich tradition of dictionaries in Kannada since the 11th century, the first dictionaries expressing meanings of Kannada words in European languages were published in the 19th century, the most prominent of them being Ferdinand Kittel's Kannada-English dictionary in 1894.

There was a push towards original works in prose narratives and a standardisation of prose during the late 19th century. Translations of works from English, Sanskrit and other Indian languages like Marathi and Bengali continued and accelerated. Lakshman Gadagkar's *Suryakantha* (1892) and Gulvadi Venkata

Rao's (1899) *Indira Bai* signalled the move away from the highly stylised mores and aesthetics of prior Kannada works to modern prose, establishing the modern novel genre and fundamentally influencing the essay, literary criticism and drama genres.

Navodaya

At the dawn of the 20th century, B. M. Srikantaiah ('B. M. Sri'), regarded as the "Father of modern Kannada literature", called for a new era of writing original works in modern Kannada while moving away from archaic Kannada forms. This paradigmatic shift spawned an age of prolificacy in Kannada literature and came to be dubbed the *Navodaya* (*lit.* 'A new rise') period—a period of awakening.

B. M. Sri led the way with his *English Geethagalu* ("English Songs")—a collection of poems translated from English set the tone for more translations using a standardisation of a modern written idiom. Original and seminal works which drew greatly from native and folk traditions also emerged alongside the translations. Stalwarts like S. G. Narasimhachar, Panje Mangesha Rao and Hattiangadi Narayana Rao also contributed with celebrated efforts. Literary subjects now veered from discussing kings and gods to more humanistic and secular pursuits. Kannada writers experimented with several forms of western literature, the novel and the short story in particular. The novel found an early champion in Shivaram Karanth while another prominent writer, Masti Venkatesh Iyengar ('Masti'), laid the foundation for generations of story tellers to follow with his *Kelavu Sanna Kathegalu* ("A few Short Stories", 1920) and *Sanna Kathegalu* ("Short Stories", 1924).

The consolidation of modern drama was pioneered by T. P. Kailasam, with his *Tollu Gatti* ("The Hollow and the Solid", 1918). Kailasam followed this with *Tali Kattoke Cooline* ("Wages for tying the Mangalsutra"), a critique on the dowry system in marriage. His plays mainly focused on problems affecting middle class Brahmin families: the dowry system, religious persecution, woes in the extended family system and exploitation of women. Novels of the early 20th century promoted a nationalist consciousness in keeping with the political developments of the time. While Venkatachar and Galaganath translated Bankim Chandra and Harinarayana Apte respectively, Gulvadi Venkata Rao, Kerur Vasudevachar and M. S. Puttanna initiated the movement toward realistic novels with their works. Aluru Venkatarao's *Karnataka Gatha Vaibhava* had a profound influence on the movement for Karnataka's unification.

The Golden Age

While the first quarter of the 20th century was a period of experiment and innovation, the succeeding quarter was one of creative achievement. This period saw the rise of acclaimed lyricists whose works combined native folk songs and the mystic poetry of the medieval *vachanas* and *kirthanas* with influences from modern English romantics. D. R. Bendre, with his collection of 27 poems including such masterpieces as *Gari* ("Wing", 1932), *Nadaleela* (1938) and *Sakhigeetha* (1940), was perhaps the most outstanding Kannada lyricist of the period. His poems covered a wide range of themes including patriotism, love of nature, conjugal love, transcendental experiences and sympathy for the poor. Govinda Pai narrated the story of Christ's crucifixion in his work *Golgotha* (1931). The success of this work encouraged Pai to follow with three panegyrics in 1947; *Vaishakhi, Prabhasa* and *Dehali,* narrated the last days of the Buddha, God Krishna and Gandhi respectively. His *Hebberalu* ("Thumb", 1946) dramatises the story of Drona and Ekalavya, characters from the epic Mahabharata.

K.V. Puttappa ('Kuvempu'), who would subsequently become Kannada's first Jnanpith awardee, demonstrated great talent in writing blank verse with his *magnum opus Sri Ramayana Darshanam* (1949). This work marks the beginning of modern Kannada epic poetry. The work, through the use of metaphors and similes, focuses on the concept that all living creatures will eventually evolve into perfect beings. Other important works of the period are Masti's *Navaratri* and P. T. Narasimhachar's *Hanathe.* D. V. Gundappa's *Mankuthimmana Kagga* ("Dull Thimma's Rigmarole", 1943) harkened back to the wisdom poems of the late medieval poet Sarvajna. A celebrated writer of conjugal love poems, K. S. Narasimhaswamy won critical acclaim for *Mysore Mallige* ("Mysore Jasmine", 1942), a description of the bliss of everyday marital life.

Growth in poetic drama was inspired by B.M. Sri's *Gadayuddha Natakam* (1925), an adaptation of Ranna's medieval epic. While Kuvempu and B.M. Sri were inspired by old Kannada, Masti and later P. T. Narasimhachar ('Pu. Ti. Na') explored modern sensibilities in their *Yashodhara* (1938) and *Ahalye* (1940). The 1930s saw the emergence of Sriranga, who joined forces with Samsa and Kailasam to pen some of the most successful plays in Kannada. Samsa completed his trilogy about Ranadhira Kantirava, a Mysore king of yore, with his *Vijayanarasimha* (1936) and *Mantrashakti* (1938). Kailasam's mastery over wit and stage rhetoric come to the fore in his *Home Rule* (1930) and *Vaidyana Vyadi* ("A Doctors Ailment", 1940) while he explores his serious side in *Bhahishkara* (1929); with *Soole* ("Prostitute", 1945), he unleashed his contempt for outdated quasi-religious mores. Societal ills were also examined in Bendre's *Nageya Hoge* ("Fumes of Laughter", 1936), and in Karanth's *Garbhagudi* ("Sanctum", 1932), which decried the exploitation of society in the name of religion.

The novel came of age during this period, with Karanth (*Chomana Dudi,* 1933), Masti (*Subbanna,* 1928) and Kuvempu ("Subbamma Heggadathi of Kanur", 1936) leading the charge. Significantly, writers chose to carry on from where Puttanna, Gulvadi and Kerur had left off at the turn of the century rather than continue with popular translations in the style of Venkatachar and Galaganath. Aesthetic concerns replaced the didactic and a sense of form developed. Devudu Narasimha Shastri distinguished himself with his *Antaranga* (1931) and *Mayura* (1928); the former was a much acclaimed work which delved into the psychology of the protagonist, while the latter was a historical novel tracing the emergence of the Kadamba dynasty. Another high point of this period is Karanth's *Marali Mannige* (1942), the saga of three generations of a family, reflecting the social, cultural and economic developments of over a hundred years.

Literary criticism, which had its beginnings in the first quarter-century, also made significant progress. B.M. Sri's *Kannada Sahitya Charitre* (1947), Gundappa's *Sahitya Shakti* (1950), Masti's *Adikavi Valmiki* (1935),

Bendre's *Sahitya Hagu Vimarshe* ("Literature and Criticism", 1932) and Krishna Shastry's *Samskrita Nataka* (1937) are particularly notable. The essay, another form adopted from western literature, was richly served by A N Murthy Rao (*Hagaluganasugalu,* 1937), Gorur Ramaswamy Iyengar's ('Gorur') humorous *Halliya Chitragalu* (1930) and Karanth's *Hucchu manassina Hatt*

Rise of Progressives

As the *Navodaya* period waxed, the *Pragatishila* (progressives) movement led by novelist A. N. Krishna Rao ('Anakru') gained momentum in the early 1940s. This left-leaning school contended that literature must be an instrument of social revolution and considered the *Navodaya* to be the product of aesthetes, too puritanical to be of any social relevance. This movement drew both established and young writers into its fold and, while it produced no poetry or drama of special merit, its contributions to short story and novel forms were appreciable. *Pragatishila* was credited with broadening readers' horizons; works produced during this period dealt extensively with subjects of everyday life, rural themes and the common man.

The language was less inhibited and made generous use of colloquialism and slang. Anakru himself was a prolific writer of novels but the best works of this school are attributed to T. R. Subba Rao ('Ta Ra Su'), Basavaraju Kattimani and Niranjana. T. R. Subba Rao initially wrote short stories, although he later turned his talents to novels, which were popular. His early novels, *Purushavatara* and *Munjavininda Munjavu,* told the stories of the underprivileged, the downtrodden and the outcast. Best known among his novels—some of whose plots are centred on his native Chitradurga—are *Masanada Hoovu* ("Flower from a cemetery"), a story about the plight of prostitutes, and historical novel *Hamsa Gite* ("Swan Song"), a story about a dedicated musician of the late 18th century during annexation of Chitradurga by Tipu sultan.

Marked as its influence had been, the *Pragatishila* wave was already in decline by the close of the 1950s. Legendary writers of the previous era continued to produce notable works in the *Navodaya* style. In poetry, Bendre's *Naku Tanti* ("Four Strings", 1964) and Kuvempu's *Aniketana* (1964) stand out. V.K. Gokak brought out the innate insufficiencies of the more advanced western cultures in *Indilla Nale* (1965). *Navodaya*-style novels continued to be successful with such noteworthy works as Karanth's *Mookajjiya Kanasugalu* ("Mookajji's visions", 1968), where Karanth explored the origins of man's faith in the mother goddess and the stages of evolution of civilisation. Kuvempu's *Malegallali Madumagalu* ("The Bride of the Hills", 1967) is about loving relationships that exist in every level of society.

Masti's two classic novels of this era were *Channabasavanayaka* (1950), which describe the defeat of Bidanur's chief Channabasava Nayaka (on Karnataka's coast) by Haider Ali in the late 18th century, and *Chickavirarajendra* (1950), which describes the fall of the tiny kingdom of Coorg (ruled by Chikka Virarajendra) to the British East India Company. The common theme in both works is the despotism and tyranny of the incumbent native rulers resulting in the intervention of a foreign power appearing on the scene to restore order, but with its own imperialistic intentions.

S. L. Bhyrappa, a charismatic young writer, first came to attention in the 1960s with his first novel *Dharmasri*, although it was his *Vamsavriksha* ("Family Tree", 1966) that put him in the spotlight as one of Kannada's most popular novelists. It is a story of a respected scholar, Srinivasa Srotri, his family and their long-held values. The protagonist's young and widowed daughter-in-law wishes to re-marry, putting his family tradition at risk. Bhyrappa's best novel of the period was *Grihabhanga* ("Breaking of a Home", 1970), a story of a woman surviving under tragic circumstances. The characters in the story are rustic and often use vulgar language. His other important novel is *Parva*, a major work in Kannada fiction acclaimed as an admirable attempt at recreating life on the sub-continent during the time of the epic Mahabharata.

Navya Kavitegalu

In the 1950s, even as the *Pragatishila* merged back into the *Navodaya* mainstream, a new modernist school of writing called *Navya* emerged. Though formally inaugurated by V. K. Gokak with his *Navya Kavitegalu* ("Modern Poems", 1950), it was Gopalakrishna Adiga who best exemplified the ethos of the movement. Poetry and, later, the short story became the most effective vehicles of the movement. With the passing of the Gandhian era and its influences, a new era in which to express modern sensibilities had arrived. The *Navya* writers questioned the time-honoured standards of plot of the *Navodaya*; life was seen not as a pursuit of already existing values, but as an introspective search for them, occasionally narrated in stream of consciousness technique. Events and details were increasingly treated metaphorically and the short story grew closer to poetry. Gopalakrishna Adiga is considered the father of this form of expression with his *Nadedu Banda Dari* ("The Path Traversed", 1952) where he sought inspiration from T. S. Eliot and W. H. Auden. His other well-known poems include *Gondalapura* ("Pandemonium", 1954) and *Bhoota* (1959).

G. S. Shivarudrappa made his mark in the Navya period with *Mumbai Jataka* ("A Horoscope of Bombay", 1966), which takes a closer look at urbanised society in Mumbai. A protégé of Kuvempu, Shivarudrappa's fame came the peak of popularity of romantic poems with his *Samagma* ("Songs of Equanimity", 1951), poems distinguished by an idealistic bent. He continued to write poems in the same vein, although in his later poems there is a gradual shift to social issues with a streak of admiration for god's creation. His critical essay, *Anuranana* (1980), is about the Vachana poets of the 12th century, their tradition, style and influence on later poets.

K.S. Narasimhaswamy remained prominent through this era, writing such landmark poems as *Silalate* ("The Sculptured Creeper", 1958) and *Gadiyaradangadiya Munde* ("Before the Clock Shop"). Chandrashekhara Kambar, Chandrashekar Patil, P. Lankesh, and K. S. Nissar Ahmed are among the best-known later generation Navya poets.

Outstanding playwrights from this period are Girish Karnad, P. Lankesh, Chandrashekhara Kambara and Chandrashekar Patil. Karnad's *Tughlaq* (1964) portrays violence caused by idealism gone astray. Considered an important creation in Kannada theatre, the play depicts the 14th-century Sultan of Delhi, Mohammad Tughlaq in contrasting styles, a tyrannical and whimsical ruler and at the same time, an idealist who sought the best for his subjects. Most plays written by Karnad have either history or mythology as their theme, with a focus on their relevance to modern society.

The most acclaimed novel of the era was *Samaskara* by U.R.Anantha Murthy (1965). The novel details the search for new values and identity by the protagonist, a Brahmin, who had sexual intercourse with the untouchable mistress of his heretic adversary. Another notable work is the *Swarupa* (1966) by Poornachandra Tejaswi. Anantha Murthy's *Prasne* (1963) contains his best collection of short stories including *Ghatashraddha,* which describes the tragedy that befell a young pregnant widow, from the point of view of a boy. His collection *Mouni* (1973) includes the stories *Navilugulu* ("Peacocks") and *Clip Joint.*

The Navya movement was not without its critics. The doubt, dilemmas and indecision in every turn of the plot resulted in increasingly sophisticated and complex narrations, which some readers found uninteresting. It was derided as an intellectual exercise of the middle class intelligentsia; in its extreme sophistication, it was thought to have lost its touch with realities of life. This led to a gradual waning of the Navya school as it was supplanted by emerging waves of *Navyottara, Bandaya* (protest) and *Dalit* schools.

Post-modern Trends

From the early 1970s, a segment of writers including many "Navya" writers started to write novels and stories that were anti-"Navya". This genre was called *Navyottara* and sought to fulfil a more socially responsible role. The best-known authors in this form of writing were Poornachandra Tejaswi and Devanur Mahadeva. Tejaswi moved from writing poetry to writing novels, going on to win "most creative novel of the year" for his *Karvalo* in 1980 and *Chidambara Rahasya* in 1985 from the Sahitya Akademi.

Modernisation and westernisation continue to inform sensibilities and spawn new literary techniques and genres. The most striking developments in recent times have been the rise of the prose form to a position of predominance—a position earlier held by poetry—and the prodigious growth in dramatic literature. More recently *Bandaya* (Rebellion) and Dalit literature, in some ways a throwback to the *Pragatishila* days, have come to the fore. Mahadeva's *Marikondavaru* ("Those who sold themselves") and *Mudala Seemeli Kole Gile Ityadi* ("Murder in the Eastern Region") are examples of this trend.

10

Malayalam Literature

Malayalam is the language spoken by around 35 million people, mainly the inhabitants of the state of Kerala and the union territory of Lakshadweep Islands in India. Malayalam is a Dravidian language and thus has close association with the other Dravidian languages, especially Tamil. Historically, Kerala had been receptive to foreign influence and this has had effect on the Malayalam literature also, which has evolved over time.

The story of Malayalam literature can be associated simultaneously with the origin of Malayalam itself. The first recorded evidence of its literature is dated back to 13th century. Malayalam is often referred to as a poetic language. The language is affluent in every genre of literature. Although each successive generation has added its own contribution to Malayalam literature, the ancient texts are still influential. Due to the lack of printed medium, the literature of ancient period reached their audience through performances like dramas, art forms like Kathakali, Ottenthullal, Koodiattam etc. and through recitation like indigenous ballads and folk songs. It also found its way to the younger generations in the form of bedtime stories. Apart from indigenous literary works, translations from other languages have further enriched the Malayalam literature.

Early Literaure

Even up to 500 years since the start of the Malayalam calendar, the Malayalam literature remained in preliminary stage. During this time, Malayalam literature consisted mainly of various genres of songs. The most prominet among them were songs praising the Goddesses of the land, ballads of brave warriors, songs related to the work of a particular caste and those which were used for entertainment. Bhardakali pattu, thottam pattu, mavaratham pattu, sasthanga pattu, nizhalkoothu pattu, sarpa pattu, sastham pattu, thiyyattu pattu, pulluvar pattu, mannar pattu, panar pattu, krishi pattu, thamburan pattu, pada pattu, villadichan pattu, onappttu, kummi and lullaby were some of the major subgenres. All these names were not used historically, but are used in modern times to describe the song genres of at that time.

Malayalam is a language of the Dravidian family. It is very close to Tamil, one of the major languages of the same family. This was due to the extensive cultural synthesis that took place between the speakers of the two languages. Tamil, in Kerala, was for long, the language of administration. This has resulted in Tamil being used in literature too. In addition, Malayalam was influenced by Sanskrit also. Malayalam absorbed a lot from Sanskrit, not only in the lexical level, but also in the phonemic, morphemic and grammatical levels of language. Looking back, we see that early Malayalam literature consists of three streams namely, (1) Folk Literature (2) Early Tamil Literature (3) Manipravalam Literature

Folk Literature

A major part of folklore includes the oral tradition, where songs, stories, riddles, proverbs, sayings etc. are transmitted through generations. Oral folklore is the throbbing pulse of the people. It constitutes the themes of wisdom conceived in the minds of the ordinary people during work or play. This rich wealth of folk imaginations has a very great role, when one goes through the history of any language.

The folk songs in Malayalam were related to agriculture, worship, war and other day - to- day activities. Often they depicted the sorrow and hardship of a group. Different occupational groups had their own songs.

Folk literature has great importance, since they are true reflections of day-to-day life. Moreover, their transmission from one generation to the next, makes them dynamic effective, and never forgotten.

Early Tamil Literature

Among the ancient Tamil classics *Pathittuppath* (Ten of ten) is a very important work. Originally it consisted of ten cycles each, having ten poems praising a Chera ruler. However the first and last have been lost. The rulers described in this work belong to the fourth and fifth centuries A.D.

The social life as reflected in Pathittuppath is very advanced and prosperous. Everything was based on sound ecological principles. Kuravas inhabited the hills. They were basically hunters and fruit cultivaters. The pasture lands were inhabited by Itayas who reared the cattle. Flat land was the land of the Uzhavas who were farmers and coastal region was the land of

Valayas who were fishermen : At this time there was no caste differentiation. Trade relations with Yavanas were prosperous. It has to be noted that Greeks, Romans, Persians, Turks and Arabs were referred to as Yavanas.

The great Tamil Classic *Chilappatikaaram* (Epic of the anklets) written by a Chera prince is a product of the early seventh century. This epic gives vivid details of the three dynasties of the Dravidian land, namely, the Cholas, Pandyas and the Cheras. Kulasekara, the founder of the Second Chera empire, wrote the work '*Mukundamala*' in Sanskrit and '*Perumaạl Thirumozhi*' in Tamil. This was during the 9th century A.D. During the eighth century, the Brahmins entered Kerala from Kolhapur and its surroundings.

Their influx and blend of cultures caused the caste system to emerge, thus forming distinct groups like Namboodiris, Kshtriyas, Sudras and untouchables. The Sanskrit language now started to gain ground and became the language of literature. The 9th century witnessed the domination of Sanskrit language over the native Dravidian.

Beginning of the Malayalam Period

During the first half of the thirteenth century, there appeared a narrative poem known as *Vaisika Tantram*. The diction was far away from the spoken variety. This work on poetics was an elaborate appraisal of the poetry which was highly influenced by Sanskrit .

At this time due to the great influence of Sanskrit, Sanskrit cases and verbal inflections were added to Malayalam, thus forming a new poetic language called *Manipravaalam*. Mani is 'ruby' and Pravalam is 'coral'.

Ruby and coral are of the same color, and when a garland is made out of them they appear indistinguishable. Similarly the blend of the Malayalam 'Mani' and the Sanskrit 'coral' resulted in a perfect blend of the two languages, Malayalam and Sanskrit.

Manipravaalam Literature

One of the most famous works of this time was *'Lilatilakam'*. Lilathilakam is a work on the grammar and rhetorics of Malayalam. Lilathilakam states that the colloquial language of Kerala was known as Tamil. A literary language higher than the colloquial, existed. Lilathilakam explicitly defines the Manipravaalam style of poetry. Sanskrit elements that were assimilated by Malayalam, were governed by Malayalam grammatical rules.

Although Lilathilakam, was a very popular work of the time, the name of the author is unknown. Historical evidences suggest that it was a product of the last quarter of the 14th century A.D.

Champu Poems

Most of the Manipravaalam works extolled the beauty of the woman. This trait can be observed in the champu poems of which the first appeared in the 14th century. *Unniyachi Charitam* the first Champu poem is the first kaavya or narrative composition in the language. Following this model, similar works like *Unnichirutevi Charitam,* and *Unniyaati Charitam* appeared. Unnichirutevi Charitam, cannot be called a champu, because its narration is wholly in prose. Generally, the prose in Malayalam Champus is poetical. It has got a definite meter. All these works as reffered to earlier have a predominating sensuous import.

In the beginning of the 14th century, there appeared a work called *Anantapura Varnanam* (Description of Trivandrum). It takes us right into the markets of Trivandrum, describing vividly the sights normally seen there.

The message poems following Kalidasa's Cloud Messenger, that appeared in Kerala are *Unnuneeli Sandesam,* and *Kooka sandesam.* They depict the agonies of a lover separated from his beloved. Another important work which is a great contribution to literature is *Chandrotsavam* (Festival of the Moon) that appeared around 1500A.D. This work is exceptionally brilliant in composition and texture.

Most of the earlier Champus dealt with eroticism. The later Champus switched over to puranic themes. Of these, the *Raamayana Champu,* the Champu written in Malayalam, deserves mention. It consists of two thousand stanzas dealing with the story of Rama and Sita. The work has in it the main theme, interspersed with humorous descriptions. The *Bhaarata Champu,* is another puranic composition. Another exquiste Champu, of the sixteenth century depicts the story of Nala and Damayanti in a moving manner. *Kaama-Dahanam* is yet another work which deals with a puranic theme.

Ramacharitam

A variety of poetry, called *Paattu* (song) belonging to a totally different genre grew simultaneously. In this group which can be called song-mould, the most prominent work was *Raamacharitam* belonging to the late twelfth or early thirteenth century. The author of this work is named as Cheeraman (Sri Rama), who has been identified by some historians as the ruler of

Venad. The work is a blend of Tamil and Malayalam. Raamacharitham has been created on the model of Valmiki's Raamaayanam.

Niranam Poets

The poets who helped to stabilize the classical import of Ramacharitam were the three Niranam poets whose period was between 1350 and 1450. They were members belonging to a family called Niranam. Their names were Madhava Panikar, Sankara Panikar and Rama Panikar. Their diction was also in the mould of Raamacharitam. Madhava Panikkar's most important contribution was his transilation of '*The Gita*'. Sankara Panikkar's work *Bharata Mala* and Rama Panikkar's *Ramaayana Bharata* and the *Bhagavata* also were based on Puranic themes.

Cherusseri

In the 15th century, one of the important works in Malayalam, which served as a landmark in the development of its literature, emerged. It was *Krishna Gatha,* written by Cherusseri Namboodiri. It is said that the author was inspired by a lullaby sung by a mother to put her child to sleep. He followed the same metrical pattern for his composition. It is in Krishna Gatha, that we see a diction, which is similar to that of the present day. The theme deals with the story of Lord Krishna. The sweet and tender aspects of maternal love are wonderfully portrayed in this work.

Ezhuthachan

It is said that it was in the sixteenth century that Malayalam Literature attained its own individuality as a full-fledged independent language. Thunchat

Ramanujan Ezhuthachan the author of the famous *Adhyaathma Raamaayanam* is considered to be the father of Modern Malayalam Literature. Ezhuthachan was from Trikkandiyur in Malabar. He was a teacher who had attained spiritual heights. The Malayalam, that he used was one that had a classical style. The grammar, was not a mixture of Sanskrit and Malayalam. It was a grammar that was purely a fully developed Malayalam. The metre that he employed was *Kilippaattu* metre. In his works, the narrator is a bird who presents to the reader the whole epic. Hence it is called Kilippaattu which means 'bird song'. The Adhyaatma Raamayana, appealed to the common man, and had such strong influence over him, that still it is sung in houses, especially in the month of scarcity, the month of Karkitaka. In addition to Ramayana, he has written *Mahabhaarata* too in *Kilippaattu* style.

Ezhuthachan through his extraordinary narrative capacity and excellent diction, brought about a revolution in poetry. He through his works served as a medium to transmit the literary and spiritual interests in the common man.

Other Poetry Forms

In addition to the poetical forms that served as purely a literary medium, there were many art forms, which were conveyed through the genre of poetry. This takes us to the evolution of the prominent dance forms of Kerala like the Kathakali and the Thullal. In addition there were entertainment forms like Sanghakkali, *Chakkiar Koothu* and *Paathakam,* which too had wonderful poetry interspersed in them.

It was in the ninth century that *Koodiyaattam* a dramatic form, emerged. The actors belonged to the

Chakkiar community. They enacted the plays of well known Sanskrit poets like Bhasa, and Harsha, with great variation in the original style. The Chakiarkoothu another form of entertainment, had something in common with Koodiyattam. Koothu was the recital of puranic legends by the Chakkiar. It was in Sanskrit. Pathakam, a similar form, had Malayalam as its language. In both Pathakam and Chakiar Koothu, the narrator had freedom to ridicule even the king. The presentation generally was loaded with satirical humour, which made the rendering attractive to the audience.

It was Manavedan, a Zamorin of Calicut, who wrote *Krishna Giiti* in Sanskrit, modeled on the Gitaa Govinda. He later developed this into *Krishnanattam,* a dance drama. The Raja of Kottarakkara in south Kerala, once requested Manavedan to send his Krishnanattam troupe to his land for a performance. But Manavedan turned down the request. Provoked by this, the Raja created *Ramanaattam* (The story of Rama). Ramanaattam was the model from which the internationally acclaimed art form, *Kathakali* had its beginnings.

Kathakali

Kathakali can be described as a ballet or an operatic form of art. The literary forms employed here, are the Manipravalam poetry and the song mould. Kathakali literature is full of classical and ornate descriptions. The actors are elaborately made up, with red, green, yellow or black visages.

The Kathakali performances had the patronage of the wealthy kings and the Namboodiris who spent their leisure time in watching and enjoying the performances. Kottarakkara's Raamanaattam thus, brought forth a new era in the field of literature as well as performing arts. In the end of the Seventeenth century, the Raja of Kottayam in Malabar, wrote poems to be enacted in a Kathakali performance. The themes of his works were from the epic Mahabharata. A landmark in the history of Kathakali literature was Unnaayi Varier's *Nalacharitam* written during the mid eighteenth century. The diction of Varier was such, that the poetic excellence transcended the limitations of a dance-drama, to a wider milieu. Varier's romantic and tender love story of Nala and Damayanti is replete with expressions of various emotions. The characters, both major and minor are blazingly alive. The blend of music and poetry is effected wonderfully.

The ruler of Travancore, Karthika Tirunal, during the latter half of the eighteenth century, wrote six Kathakali plays. His nephew Aswati Tirunal wrote four plays. Towards the middle of the nineteenth century, Irayimman Thampi wrote three plays, which were known for their exquisitive musical quality. Rajaraja Varma of Kilimanoor, is known for his work *Raavana Vijayam* which has Ravana as its hero.

At present many international themes have appeared as Kathakali plays. Buddacharitam written by N.V. Krishna Varier is one among them. Biblical tales, Persian legends, stories of Tagore and Shakespeare have been improvised into kathakali tales, making the art form more universal.

Thullal

Kunchan Nambiar, the exponent of the Thullal form of art, was born around 1705 in Central Kerala. Legend says that Nambiar who used to accompany the

Chakiar in Koothu performances, was scorned by the latter when he dogged off during a performance. Nambiar left the performance and created the Thullal play, overnight.

Nambiar's Thullal was not modeled on then highly influenced Kathakali. But it was definitely away from it in every manner, because it catered to the lower rungs of society. The Thullals of Nambiar were of three types, namely, the fast type called *oottan Thullal,* the medium type called *Seethankan Thullal* and the slow type called the *Parayan Thullal.*

The Thullal has a narrative form in verse, very much like the Kathakali. But while Kathakali has many actors on the stage, Thullal has only one actor. Unlike in Kathakali, the actor in Thullal sings the songs also. The face-painting and costumes are picturesque and attractive. Narration and dancing go side by side.

Regarding the form of poetry employed, it was overwhelmingly caricatural. Humour formed the essence of Nambiar's works. Nambiar, it occurs to us, is gleeful when he portrays scenes of weddings, feasts and battles going into the details of human frailty, stupidity and greed.

Nambiar's works were essentially social criticisms, where we see in him the picture of a sarcastic observer. His themes were essentially puranics with the characters symbolizing the contemporary stock.

Thullals continued to be produced after Nambiar's time too, but nothing excelled Nambiar's works of cynical humour. In the 19th century, Poonthottam (Junior) and Venmani (Junior) tried to re-establish the lost humour of this unique stream of poetry. At present, Thullal, as a dance - drama has achieved a lot of popularity and ordinary tales are converted into Thullal forms for stage performances. But their merit as literary works is very inferior.

Hymnal Poetry

When one thinks of hymnal poetry in Kerala, apart from Ezhuthachan, one of the names that arise foremost in the mind is that of Poonthaanam. He was a contemporary of Ezhuthachan. His *Sreekrishna Karnaamritam* tells the story of Lord Krishna. Poonthaanam was an ardent devotee of Lord Krishna. Being childless himself, he loved the Lord as his own child, which is revealed in the following verse:

> "When Unnikrishna, plays in the heartwhere is the need for another boy as son?"

Along with the hymnal poetry, there evolved ethical and didactic verses, which pointed out to the theory of a universal God. Poonthanam in his last section of *Karnaamritham* gives a clear picture of man, who does not realize the transitory nature of life.

There were a number of versions of epics and puranas during the course of the development of Malayalam literature. In the sixteenth century, there appeared a Ramayana which had twenty four sections, each having a different metre. The author is greatly indebted to Punam's Champu. Vira Kerala Varma was another person who attempted to render a work based on Ramaayana. He wrote his poem in a clear style, since he felt that Niranam's work was obsolete in diction. He wanted his poetry to be intelligible to the layman. In the eighteenth century, there appeared another Ramayana in the song - mould called paana. The author of this work is unknown. Rama Varma a ruler of Cochin rendered a section of Valmiki's original in Malayalam. Later Subhadra, a princess of Cochin added another section to it.

There are other works which have taken certain parts of epics as their themes. The important works belonging to this category are *Putrakaameeshti* (18th century), *Baalivatham*(18th century), *Seetu Bandanam* (15th century), and *Raamaasvameedham* (16th century).

A monumental work related to the epic *Mahaabhaarata* appeared in the 19th century. It was written by Kunjikuttan Thampuran of Kudamalloor. The work was a complete and instant translation of the great epic. It has a very simple style and diction. Kathulli Achutha Menon, encouraged by Kunjikuttan Thampuran wrote a translation of *Aswamedha,* the only canto that has survived in the Mahabharata written by Jaimini.

Ezhuthachan's *Bhagavatham* in the Kilippattu style needs special mention. Another important work belonging to this category is Kunchan Nambiar's *Sreekrishana Charitham*. Puranas like *Devi Maahaatmyam, Brahmanda Purana,* and *Skanda Purana* also have their renderings in Malayalam. There arose poems also describing holy places. Examples of these are *Vilvaadri Maahaatmyam* (17th century) and *Vrishapura Maahaatmyam* (18th century).

Beginning of Prose

The evolution of prose was comparatively later than that of poetry. Its evolution also is of the same pattern as that of poetry. As the spoken language form blended with the classical form, and gave rise to a new hybrid form of poetry, the prose too developed after such hybridization.

The imperial and royal decrees on stone, copper plate, etc. from the 9th century to the 13th century reveal the infiltration of the spoken language into Tamil. This is revealed in *Kautiyam* the translation of Kautilya's treatise on political tactics. This translation appeared by the end of the 12th century.

The early prose renderings were instruction manuals associated with Koodiyaattam. The most important among them is *Doota Vaakyam* (14th century). The structure is Sanskritic although there are a few Tamil words here and there. In addition to this, there are other instruction manuals which are known as *Krama Deepika* or *Aattaprakaaram*. The prose employed in these manuals is very close to the spoken language. The sentences are simple and close to that employed in the present day.

The *Brahmaanda Puraanam* belonging to the 14th century was meant for the common man. Hence it did not contain too much of Sanskrit. During the same time there appeared prose works dealing with the story of King Ambarisha, the story of Nala and a Devi Mahatmyam. In the early 15th century there was a prose *Raamayana,* which was a heavily Sanskritized work. In contrast there was a *Bhaagavatha* during the same time which had very simple style. The *Uttara Raamayana* of the 16th century is another prose rendering of the story of Rama.

Although prose is closer to the spoken form of language, its early developments was not as dynamic or vibrant as that of poetry. Still it has its streaks of growth and acceleration.

The eighteenth century witnessed the work of the Christian missionaries in Kerala. Along with this there developed a form of prose which catered to the common man. During the end of the 19th century, Pachu Moothath wrote his autobiography. Romance prose had its beginnings with the works of Ayilyam Tirunal (1831-1880), the ruler of Travancore. A.R. Rajaraja Varma (1863-1918) was a great scholar who wrote his famous treatise Kerala Paanineeyam, a work on grammar. Kerala Paanineeyam is still considered to be the most authoritive work on Malayalam grammer. His other important contributions are Bhashaa Bhuushanam and the Saahitya Saahyam.

By the middle of the 19th century, there was the rise of periodicals like *jnaana niksepam* (1840) and *Paschima Taaraka* (1864), which were propagators of the doctrine of Chirtianity. In 1881, there appeared the first secular periodical, called *Kerala mitram*. The famous Malayala Manorama, still very popular, had its origin in 1890. Kandattil Varghese Mappila was its editor. In 1896, the journal *Bhashaa Poshini* had its birth. K. Ramakrishna Pilla's newspaper 'Svadesaabhimaani' was very important among newspapers because of its exposition of radical views.

Contribution of Muslims

The Muslims of the past used to study only the Quran. They knew how to write only Arabic just for the purpose of reciting the Quran. But creativity needed self expression. It was this self expression that created the special 'language form' known as Arabi Malayalam. It followed the grammar and syntax of Malayalam. But its vocabulary included words from Arabic, Urdu and Tamil. It was written in Arabic script, with some new symbols to denote unfamiliar Malayalam consonants.

Arabi-Malayalam works are mainly in verse form. There are narrative poems, war poems and romantic stories in this group. There is a rich collection of wedding songs which are beautiful when sung.

Contributions of Christians

The work of the Christian missionaries to aid conversion, was instrumental to bring about a surge of prose works. Of the foreign missionaries who came to Kerala, the name of Arnos Padri deserves special mention. He reached Kerala in 1699 and was here till his death in 1732. He was the first European to have written a Sanskrit grammar. Another great contribution of Arnos is his poems and hymns. The story of Virgin Mary and the life and death of Christ are his important works. The other missionaries who left indelible marks in the history of kerala are Paulino and Hermann Gundert (1814-1893). Paulino wrote two poetical works. Gundert has two very important works to his credit. These are a Malayalam Grammar (1851) and a Malayalam English Dictionary (1872). The dictionary is still popular, and reveals the sincere and laborious field work that he undertook to collect the words. As a result, the dictionary has a unique place among the lexicographical works in Malayalam.

Kattakkayam's (1859-1936), work was the first full fledged literary attempt made by native Christians. His early poems were published in a journal called *Satyananda Kahalam.* He has written plays .on the temptation of Christ on the story of Oliver and Charlemagne and St. Thomas, the Apostle. His greatest work was the epic *Yesu Vijayam* (Triumph of Jesus). Succeeding Kattakkayam's epic, came K.V. Simon's *Veda Vihaaram*. Kandattil Verghese Mappila, the editor of Manorama has written poems and hymns also. Regarding, contributions to prose the name of Joseph Kariyatti is worth mentioning. His main work is a critique of the ecclesiastic controversy of his time. The book is entitled *Veda Tarkam*. Kariyatti's friend Thoma wrote a book called *Vartamana- Pustakam* which is a record of their travel to Europe.

George Mathan (1820-70) a Jacobite priest was another person who contributed a lot in the form of articles and books. He has also written a grammar.

Poetry in the 19th century

The origin of the Malayalam Manorama in 1890, and the importance it gave to original contributions, gave impetus to the native poets to get their poems published. Pantalom Kerala Varma started as magazine called *Kavana Kaumudi*. In this journal, everything was in verse. This included announcements, reports, editorials, book reviews and advertisements. In such a poetic temper, there awakened a number of poetical works. There arose a new current of poetry, which can be termed as the Venmani movement. Those included in this group were the Senior Venmani (1816-90), his sons Kunjikuttan Thampuran (1865-1913) and Junior Venmani (1843-92), the Senior Natuvath Namboodiri (1840-1912), the junior Natuvath Namboodiri (1867-1943), Oravankara (1856-1916), Kochunni Thampuran (1857-1925) and Kundoor (1860-1935). The group used to have informal get togethers. This was a group which preferred single stanza poems called *Muktaka* poems.

Among the poems of this group, *Poora Prabandham* by Venmani Junior narrates the famous Pooram festival of Trichur: This group of poets had a carefree life devoid of worries, which is reflected in their compositions. Their works had a wonderful clarity about them. Poetry was a passion for them, that even mutual correspondence was effected in verse. The Venmani current, however reminds us of the Manipravalam times, where the main theme for poetry was the beauty of the female body. Still there remains the holy hymnal and didactic elements which are sometimes evident in their poems.

During this time, there lived Kerala Varma (1845-1914) who wrote his *Mayura Sandesam* (Peacock message) modeled on Kaalidasa's *Mega Sandesam* (Cloud messenger). This was written when Kerala Varma was in house arrest. His longing for his wife is expressed through the work. In 1902 there appeared the long poem Ramachandra Vilaasam by Azhakath. A.R. Rajaraja Varma's *Malayala Vilaasam* that was in 1895 had a lyrical quality about it. But modern lyricism had its beginnings in V.C. Balakrishna Panikkar's works. Within a short span of the only 26 years of his life he contributed a lot which clearly reveal his poetic genius. He wrote a book on poetics when he was only fifteen and was the editor of a literary journal when he was sixteen.

Romantic Poetry

The lyrical poetry gave way to Romantic poetry in course of time. Romanticism flourished with the appearance of the great trio Asan, Ulloor and Vallathol.

Kumaran Asan

Kumaran Asan belonged to the Ezhava community

which was socially backward. He represented his community's struggle for social equality.

Kumaran Asan was the disciple of the great spiritual master and great seer Sri Narayana Guru (1856-1929). Guru was the person who inspired the Ezhava community towards social revolution. He himself has authored a number of books in Tamil, Sanskrit and Malayalam. Asan's poems are primarily pessimistic. He has always had a serious approach to poetry. In his poem *Viina puuvu* (fallen flower), he draws parallels between the fallen flower and the human life. When the flower falls on the ground, he mourns for it asking himself to turn away his eyes from the pathetic sight. The flower will go back to dust very soon. This, he states, is the lot of the human being.

His two Narrative poems *Nalini* (1911) and *Leela* (1914) although apparently love stories depicting human relationships have got deeper messages to convey. The ultimate victory of love over life is the point that is stressed in these poems. Asan's work *Chintaavishtayaaya sitaa* (Thoughtful sita) (1919) is one of the best works in Malayalam. His *Duravasta* deals with the love affair of a Namboodiri girl and a Pulaya youth. Another work *Chandaala bhikshuki* (outcaste) depicts the growth of personal love into the wider realm of love of humanity itself. *Karuna* (compassion), his last work gives an account of a courtesan who falls in love with Buddha's young disciple Upagupta. Here too love is not personalized nor physical.

Ulloor

Ulloor Parameswara Iyer (1877-1949) was a poet who attempted to revive the classical heritage of Malayalam poetry. He was a Brahmin and therefore unlike Asan he did not suffer social ostracism of any kind. He was a government servant who finally became the Chief Secretary to the Travancore Government.

Ulloor was an erudite scholar which is reflected in his work *Kerala Saahitya Charitham* (History of the Literature of Kerala), which consists of five volumes. His long poem-mahaakaavya-named *Umaakeralam* (1914) has as its theme, a particular phase in Kerala's history. The poem deals with the politics related to the monarchical power of Travancore in the 17th century. Among his shorter narrative poems, *Pingala* and *Karnabhuushanam* are important.

Vallathol

Vallathol Narayana Menon (1878-1958) was a very expressive poet who was well known for his extremely musical compositions. Vallathol could create musical verses from a very young age. He was an ardent patriot who created poems that have revealed his deep love for his motherland.

Some of Vallathol's poems narrate certain incidents, taken from Puranas, and ancient texts like Kathaasaritsaagaram. His *Chitrayogum* deals with the theme of a love story from the Kathaasaritsaagaram. Another small narrative poem *Bhandanasthanaaya Aniruddhan* (1914) is taken from the Puranas. *Saahityamanjari* (7vols.) is a collection of his poems.

Vallathol was always attracted by the simplicity and innocence of young children. In *Kilikonchal* (Parrot prattling), we see the Sita of the Ramayana as the main Character. She is a five year old girl who happens to see two parrots that come to her garden the birds recite the Raamayana poem When they say that Rama marries Sita, her mother is happy. But she cries and says, that she wants to be married to no one else other than her mother. This gives a clue that at the end of the Ramayana story Sita finds refuge in her mother's arms and not Rama's.

Another poem where Vallathol describes Akrura's visit to Vrindavan, gives picturesque accounts of the pure and rustic atmosphere around. His *Magdalana Mariyam* describes the story of Mary Magdalene.

Romanticism found wonderful expression in other poets like Edappalli (1909-36) and Changampuzha (1914-48). Edapalli belonged to a poor family. He was not fortunate enough to get employment. He was unlucky in love, and he committed suicide, when he was only twenty seven.

Changampuzha

Edappally's close friend Changampuzha was a person who was very emotional. This excessive emotionalism made him enter into a number of emotional involvements. He was addicted to alcohol. However, his life style resulted in wasted health and an attack of T.B. which claimed his life in 1948 when he was thirty four.

Changampuzha's most famous work *Ramanan* is a lament on the death of Edappalli. Ramanan was written when Changampuzha was only twenty. The poem is of the pastoral elegy type. It is characterized by beautiful, straight forward verses, that appeal to the sensitive heart. His expression of passions is intense, as can be observed in the work *Mohini,* which is the story of a lover who cannot even imagine that the beauty of his beloved would fade ultimately. So he **stabs her** to death, in the prime of her youth and beauty.

Novel and Short Stories

Kundalatha published in 1887, is considered to be the first Malayalam novel. Even before that Malayalam translations of English works were becoming popular. The second Malayalam novel was *Indulekha* (1889) which has taken an English novel as its model. Indulekha was a strong critique of the existing social situation of the time. It was an attack against the Namboodiri community which was steeped in conservatism. The author has attacked the feudal lordship, and the Namboodiri-Nair marriage pact called Sambandham which was prevalent during those times.

The second novel of Chandu Menon was *Sarada,* which was published in 1892. Due to his death in 1899, Chandu Menon was not able to complete the second part of Sarada.

In 1891, C.V. Raman Pillai published his novel *Marthanda Varma.* It was followed by his other works, namely, *Dharma Raja* (1913), and *Rama Raja Bahadur* (2vols.) (1917-1920). C.V. in his novels portrays a time when Kerala was ruled by the princes and the nairs. Marthanda Varma has in it both history and romance. C.V.'s language was highly dramatic and intense that still it is considered to be a unique contribution in the annals of Kerala's literary history. C.V., thus was the person who paved the way for the historical novel.

Paarappuram by Kurukkal was the first political novel and *Bhaskara Menon* (1904) by Appan Thampuran was the first detective novel. Appan Thampuran's novel *Bhuta Rayar* (1923) is a portrayal of Kerala in the second century. The narration is very attractive. *Kerala Simham* (1941) by K.M.Panikkar has an epic quality about it.

The first Malayalam novel that dealt with the socially backward classes was *Saraswathy Vijayam* by Kunjambu in 1892. Novels on Christian life were written by Kochuthomman (1892), and Kocheeppan Tharakan. Latter Ponjikkara Rafi wrote *Papikal* in 1949. Kochu Thresia (1964) by Joseph Mattom, also belong to this group.

The late forties was the time of "Progressive literature" in Kerala. Vaikkom Muhammad Basheer with his unique style and rare humour wrote works portraying the Muslim community. Basheer's *Baalyakaala sakhi* (Playmate of childhood) is a brilliant exposure of the fate of two young lovers. The passages in this novel are exquisite. Yet, another work of Basheer which has won international acclaim is *'Ntuppaappaakkoraanendaarunnu'* (Me Grandad 'ad an elephant) (1951). The novel deals with the disparity that existed between the orthodox Muslims, and the progressive Muslims.

During this time feudalism was the cause of social distancing, and many other social ills in different communities. M.T. Vasudevan Nair's (1933) *Naalukettu* picturizes the feudalship and its associated struggles. His yet another novel *Asuravittu* (Dragon seed) also has as its theme, the conflicts and problems of a Nair Family. Malayattoor Ramakrishnan was popular through his *Verukal* (roots) and *Yantrom* (machine).

Thakazhi Sivasankara Pillai's *Rantitangazhi* (Two measures of paddy) focuses on the lower community. His description and picturisation have a real life force which is appreciable. His another work *Chemmeen* (shrimps), is a story of the fishermen community of Purakkad in Kuttanad. The theme is an intense love story, but tuffeted around the theme we see a whole world of human emotions of love and hatred. Moreover, the work reveals the tradition bound society of the fisherfolk which stick on stubbornly to their values and beliefs. Yet another work of Thakazhi is *Thottiyute Makan* (Scavenger's son) which deals with the life of the scavengers of Alleppey.

Kesava Dev, another noted writer of the time, wrote *otayilninnu* (from the gutter) in 1942. He has written other works too, but otayil ninnu is the most important one.

Karur Neelakanda pillai was known for his short stories like *Bhrityan* (Male-servant), *Makan* (son), *Potichoru* (rice-packet) and *Velakkaari* (maid servant). He has not written novels.

S. K.Pottakkat is an author of renown, whose work *Oru Desattinte Katha* (story of a land) fetched him the *gyaanapiith* award. He has written short stories and travelogues. His other works include *Stri* (woman), *Muutupatam* (veil), *Oru teruvinte Katha* (story of a street).

Uroob (P.C. Kuttikrishnan) was a writer whose simple prose and rustic themes attracted readers. He has novels, short stories and plays which have been acclaimed. His works include novels like *Ummaachu, Sundarikalum Sundaranmaarum* (beautiful women and handsome men) and *Mintaappennu* (non-talking girl). His famous stories are *Raachiyamma* and *Velutta Kutti* (fair child). His important play is *Ti konttu Kaliykkarutu* (don't play with fire).

M. T. Vasudevan Nair, whose two works have been mentioned earlier is a narrator with exceptional skill. His important short stories include *Eruttinte aatmaavu* (soul of darkness), *Kuttyetatti and Vaanaprastham*. He has won the *gyaanapiith* award.

Thikkotian is an author who is known for his plays and humorous poems. His autobiography *Arangu Kaanaatta natan* (The actor who didn't see the stage) makes interesting reading. *Cherukaatu* is another writer who also has written short stories, humorous poems and plays. He has written his autobiography called *Jivitappaata* (Life- path).

Muttathu Varkey is the author who popularized the romance movement in the history of Malayalam novel. His works paralleled the Mills and Boon romances, popular in English. Varkey's setting was some village in central Kerala, where the plot unfolds to its romantic heights. His main novels are *Paataatta painkili* (The bird that does not sing), and *Mayilaatum Kunnu* (The hill on which the peacock dances).

N.P.Muhammed is an author whose many novels unfold the cultural intricacies of the Muslim community of Malabar. His important novels are *Ennappaatam* and *Deivattinte Kannu* (God's eyes). He has written a novel along with M.T.Vasudevan Nair. Its name is *Arabiponnu* (Arabian gold).

Kovilan and Nandanar are known for their short stories which portray the trials and travails in the life of a soldier. Nandanar has also a work called *Unnikuttante lokam* (The world of Unnikuttan), which beautifully narrates a story in the perspective of a small boy. Another author Parappurattu has also focused his themes on military life. His important novels are *Ninamaninja kaalpaatukal* (foot prints of blood) and *Aranaazhikaneram.*

Rajalekshmi was a woman novelist who faced an untimely death. Her works include *Oru Vazhiyum Kure nizhalukalum* (One way and many shadows) and *Njaanenna bhaavam* (ego).

T. Padmanabhan, one of the most important story writers of modern times has written a number of short stories, which have a special beauty. His main stories are *Prakaasam parattunna oru penkutti* (A girl who spreads light) and Gauri.

During this time, there were a number of authors like Vettoor Raman Nair, K.M. Kovoor and Nagavally R.S.Kurup, whose works were popular and acclaimed.

Lalithambika Antharjanam was born in the Namboodiri community which was shifted in orthodoxy. Prior to this, during the end of the 19th century and the beginning of the 20th century, some women and men in Namboodiri community were breaking the rigid shackles of conventionalism in the community, that caused shocking social practices to exist. In the attempt at social revolution authors like V.T.Bhattathiripad (V.T), M.R. Bhattathiripad (M R B) and M.P.Bhattathiripad (MP) wrote works which focused on the existing malpratices prevalent in the community. V.T.'s play *Attukkalayil ninnu arangatteykku* (from kitchen to stage) was a famous work belonging to this category. His autobiographical work *Kannirum Kinaavum* (Tears and dreams) also needs special mention. M.R.B. has written a skit called *Marakkutaykkullile mahaanarakam* (The big hell within the umbralla veil) and many other short stories. His simple travelogues also are very attractive M.P.'s main work known as *Ritumati* (Girl who has attained puberly) also exposes the picture of a convention - ridden community. Moothirigode Bhavathrathan Namboodiripad has through his works expressed the intense anguish of the community, to be set free. His main novel is *Apphante makal* (father's younger brother's daughter). It was in this social background that Lalithambika Antherjanam set her works. Her most important work *Agnisaakshi* (fire witness) reflects the conflicts between the convention - ridden, and the progressive elements in the community. Her other works are *Kotumkattil petta oru ila* (a leaf caught in a typhoon) and *maanikyan.* Antharjanam's son N.Mohanan is also known for his adeptness in story telling.

K. Saraswati Amma is another woman writer, \ portrayed the woman in the man's world. Her works were intensely liberation - oriented and portrays the innate strength of the woman. Her important works are the short stories *Cholamarangal* (shady trees) and *Orukkattinte otuvil* (At the end of the preparation).

K. Surendren is an author who delves deep into the complexities of the human mind. His famous works are Taalam (rhythm),and *Kaattukurangu* (forest - monkey). G.Vivekanadan is another author who portrays the society in his works. *Kallu* (Toddy) is his important work. E.Vasu is an author who gives a description of the drudgery of the government servants, in his novel *Chuvappu Naata* (Red tape). K.T. Muhammed has written a number of novels of which the most important is *Itu bhumiyaanu* (This is earth).

Madhavikutty (Also known as Kamala Das and at present as Kamala Surayya) has a unique place in the history of Malayalam literature. Her diction, presented with an extraordinary simplicity makes her works attractive and readable. She has a special way of exposing the bitter truths of life in a stunningly simple manner. She is a versatile writer, fluent in both Malayalam and English. Her important works are the autobiographical work *Ente Katha* (My story), and the short stories *Puzha vintum ozhuki* (the rever flowed again), *Ammu, Driksaakshi* (eye witness) and *Pakkshiyute manam* (smell of the bird).

O.V. Vijayan brought forth a revolution in Malayalam fiction, by his true exposition portrayed in the novel *Khasaakinte Itihaaśam* (the legend of the Khasak). All his works are deeply philosophical and many a time mystical. His other main works are *Gurusaagaram* (the ocean of Guru), *Dharmapuraanam* (the saga of Dharmapuri) and *Thalamurakal* (generations). He has written short stories too of which *Oru yudhattinte aarambham* (beginning of a war), *Appukkili* and *Irinjaalakuda* are important.

C. Radhakrishnan is a scientist, turned into an author. His important works are *Mumpe parakkunna pakshikal* (birds that are flying ahead), *Puzha mutal puzha vare* (from river to river) and *Pullippulikalum Vellinakshtrangalum* (spotted tigers and silver stars).

Vilasini (M.K.Menon) has to his credit the largest novel in Malayalam. This novel, *Avakaasikal* (interitors) has as its plot, the wide canvas of an extended family settled in Malaysia. His other important novels are *unjaal* (swing) and *Inaangaatta kannikal* (incompatible links).

M. Mukundan is an author who has written works set in the milieu Mahe, the French occupied province in Kerala. Two such works are *Mayyazhipuzhayute tiirangalil* (In the banks of the Mayyazhi river) and *Deivattinte Vikritikal* (God's pranks). Another important novel written by Mukundan is *Keshavante Vilaapangal* (Keahavan's laments). His short stories include 1981, and *Haridvaril Mani Muzhangumbol* (When the bell tolls in Haridwar).

M.P. Narayana Pillai through his novel *Parinaamam* (change) brilliantly exposes the set-values in a society. He has written short stories too. V.K.N. is an eminent Malayalam author whose sense of humour is second to none. He has paved the way to a unique humour literature in Malayalam. With the efficient strategy of language manipulation, he reveals a world so different from the ordinary one.

The present generation has got a number of gifted people like Sarah Joseph. Her works are essentially liberalistic, and have always been powerful enough to convey the pathetic of any suppressed group.

11

Manipuri Literature

Manipuri literature is the literature written in the Manipuri Language, including literature composed in Manipuri Language by writers from Manipur, Assam, Tripura, Myanmar and Bangladesh.It is also known as Meetei Literature. The history of Manipuri literature trace back to thousands of years with flourish of its civilization. Nevertheless, Puya Meithaba (burning of Ancient Manipuri Scriptures) can not be overlooked in the history of Manipuri Literature. The terror event of history, the Puya Meithaba in 1729 A.D., during the reign of Meidingu Pamheiba (1709 –1748 A.D.), totally devastated the ancient Manipuri scriptures and cultural history and begin with a new era of Manipuri literature. Most of the early literary works found in Manipuri Literature were in Poetry and Prose. Some of the books were written with combination of both the Prose and Poetry. Meetei Scholars have broadly divided the History of Manipuri Literature into the following periods.

Ancient Period

The Meeteis had a long tradition of writing. It is not able to completely clear when the archaic Meetei

Puyas(Old Scriptures) and Meetei Mayek (Manipuri Scripts) were first came into existence. However, the written Constitution of the country (i.e. Meitrabak or Manipur), Loiyamba Shinyen(1110 A.D.), during the regime of Meidingu Loiyamba (1074–1122A.D.) vividly connote the practice of writing in this era. It has further confirmed that from the time of Meidingu Thangwai Ningthouba(1467–1508 A.D.),later as Kyamba, the Royal Chronicle -Chitharon Kumpaba, was kept meticulously and continued till the end of kingship (Meidingu Bodhchandra,1941-1955 A.D.).

As he was the worthy son of the mighty father Meidingu Ningthoukhomba(1432-1467 A.D.) and warrior mother Linthoingambi, the kingdom was full fledged sovereign country and lots of evidence for the considerable literary works during his reign. But the use of writing was referred back to Mariya Phambalcha (in B.C.) era by many Meetei scholars.

The skill of writing was the prerogative of the professional scribes and scholars of the traditional Meetei culture, the Maichous. The later proliferation of religious, proto-scientific and astrological text would suggest that as time progressed writing was expanded beyond these professional scribal classes. However, most the ancient Meetei Puyas (Scriptures) were anonymous and undated. The period from prehistory till the reign of Meidingu Charairongba(1697-1709 A.D.),that is before the Puya Meithaba(1729 A.D.), is considered to be the Ancient Period of the Manipuri Literature.

Early Manipuri Literature consists of ritual hymn, cosmogony, history, folks in Prose and Poetry. Most of the ancient Manipuri literature were written in archaic Meeteilon, which had attained the same fortune like

Sanskrit and Latin language. Few of the remarkable works of Ancient Meeteilon(i.e.Manipuri Language) poetries were – Numit Kappa, Ougri, Khencho, Sana Lamoak(6th or 7th A.D), Ahonglon(11th A.D.), Khoiju Lamoak(12th A.D.), Hijin Hirao, Ningthauron(17th A.D.)

Numit Kappa: The excerpt below in archaic Meeteilon is from the Numit Kappa:

"Haya he Liklaio

Yipungthou nongthourel o lahalnong

Laicha tarang ipakthakta

... ... "

One of the oldest literary work, Numit Kappa, was written in archaic Meeteilon with Meetei Mayek (i.e.Manipuri Script) in poetry verse.Though this Puya was anonymous and undated,the researchers believed that it can be dated to the first A.D. Since ancient time, its verse had been used by Meetei Amaiba (Priest) in Chup Shaba (a funeral ceremony).

According to Tutenglon Puya, the two sons of Khuyoi Tompok(154 A.D.), – Yoimongba and Taothingmang, personally participated in the dredging of the rivers in Meitrabak(i.e. Manipur). The two royal brothers entrapped the giant bird (Kakyen Meengamba) and killed it. Numit Kappa hymn was sung when the giant bird wounded Yoimongba. T.C.Hodson was the first English who attempted to translate this archaic Meeteilon literary work into English in his book – The Meitheis.

Ougri: The excerpt below rendering in Meeteilon is from the beginning part of the Ougri Sheireng (i.e.Ougri Poem).

"Hoirou haya haya ... ...
He hupe he
Ougri O kollo
Lamlenmada madaimada
Kangleiyonda pungmayonda
Yoimayaibu Taodanbabu
Taoroinaibu Anganbabu
... ..."

Ougri, which was also known as Leiroi Ngongloi Eshei, was also an anonymous and undated Poetry written in archaic Meeteilon. But it is believed to be written in pre-Christian era. It was a part of Leishemlon Puya, the old scripture about Meetei cosmogony. Meeteis had been used it as the ceremonial hymn since the time immemorial.

According to Meetei epic the KHAMBA-THOIBI in Moirang mythology, Ougri was sung by Thonglen as father of KHAMBA, when KHUMAN KHAMBA caught the Pamba Keiren (i.e.wild Tiger) in Khoirentak. Meetei Festival, Lai Haraouba is the observation of believes in Meetei Cosmogony and it interprets the philosophy by performing the Ougri Hangel Chongba. Amaiba (Priest) and Amaibi (Priestess), the spiritual guide of Meeteis, lead the Ougri Chongba and they perform very sincerely to avoid any fault in Ougri Chongba. Many of Meetei Puyas (Manipuri Scriptures) viz- Naothingkhong Phambal Kaba, Laishra Pham, Panthoibi Khongul, Cheithon Kumbaba mentioned the performance of this form of dance in different occasions in the time immemorial.

Few of the most remarkable work of Ancient Manipuri literature in Prose were–Panthoibi Khongul (prehistory), Nongshaba Laihui (prehistory), Sakok Lairamlen (prehistory), Poireiton Khunthokpa (3rd

A.D.), Kangla Haoba (5th A.D.), Loyamba Shinyen (11th A.D.), Naothingkhong Phambal Kaba (16th A.D.), Khagemba Yumlep (16th A.D.), Cheitharon Kumbaba.

The following Maichous (Scholars)- Konok Thengra, Apoimacha, Salam Sana,Yumnam Tomba, Khaidem Temba, Langgol Lukhoi were the Royal Maichou (Scholar) during the reign of Meidingu Khagemba(1597-1652A.D.). Among of the great work of these Maichous, the praiseworthy Scriptures were - Shingkhan Laikhan and Kaibaron Puya.

Konok Thengra was a great astrologer and his great contribution was the prominent Kaibaron Puya, which depicted the future of Royal life and country's fortune, and it had witness with real phenomenon in the history of Meitrabak(i.e. Manipur). The glory of Manipuri literature with it's own indigenous culture and religion was continued till the regime of Meidingu Charairongba(1697-1709 A.D.).

Medieval Period

The momentous change in Manipuri Literature and culture was during the reign of Meidingu Charairongba and his successors. With the dawn of eighteenth century, Meitrabak(Manipur) achieved the full development of her culture, economy and state system. In this revolutionary change in the Meitrabak's life, three kings - father, son, and a great grandson: Charairongba (1697-1709 A.D.), Pamheiba or Garibniwaz (1709 –1748 A.D.) and Chingthangkhomba or Bhaygyachandra (1749-1798 A.D.) played very significant roles, the stamp of which was imprinted on the history of Meitrabak. After the death of Paikhomba, his newphew Charairongba, the son of his younger brother Tonsenngamba ascended the throne in

1697 A.D. His reign was a transition period from traditional Meetei social situation to a Hinduised Meetei Society. He constructed several temples for Meitei deities like Panthoibi, Sanamahi and Hindu deities after his espousal with Vaishnavism. The relation with Burma was deteriorated and more strengthened with India after conversion into Vaishnavism. As a result, the period from the embraced of Vaishnavism by Meetei King till the advent of British in Meitrabak (Manipur) is considered to be the Medieval Period of Manipuri Literature.

Influence of Vaishnavism

As great as a conqueror, Meidingu Pamheiba(1709 – 1748 A.D.) was also a great religious and social reformer, under his royal patronage Cheitanya's school of Vaishnavism was propagated in Meitrabak. Cheitharol Kumbaba records that in October, 1717 A.D. Graibnawaz was initiated into Vaishnavism by Guru Gopal Das. Afterward, he switched over to Ramanandi School of Vaishnavism after the arrival of Shanta Das.

Puya Meithaba – Buring of the Meetei Puyas(Old Scriptures). At the instigation of Santidas Gosain, more than 123 Meetei Puyas (Holy Meetei Sciptures) had been consigned at Kangla Uttra to flames at around 9-10 a.m., on the 23rd day of wakching(December) in 1729 A.D. It was definitely unethical action on the part of king and his preceptor. When there was no fruitful result to the strong objection of this disastrous conduct of the king, the great Maichou (scholar) of Meetei religion, Laurembam Khongnangthaba concealed himself. The Name of the Puyas were recorded as – Taoroinai Yangbi, Pakhangba Yangbi, Pakhangba Naoyaom, Sanamahi Naoyom, Sanamahi Laihui, Taoroinai Picha, Pakhangba Thiren, Pakhangba Laihui,

Sanahami Laikhan Nongkhan, Leithak Leikharon, Leichinlon Yumbi, Nonglon Yumbi, Nonglon Laicham, Nonglon Kruthong, Nongdon Langbum, etc.

Since then, it had started the Sanskritised interpolation with the post-proselytisation writing for the last couple of centuries in the more than two millennia-old history of Meitrabak (Manipur).

Angom Gopi was the renowned poet and scholar in the royal court during the reign of Meidingu Pamheiba, and he was not only proficient in Meeteilon but also in Sanskrit and Bengali language. He translated the Kritibas's Ramayan and Gangadas's Mahabharat into Meeteilon. The other books which he wrote were - Parikhit, Langka Kanda, Aranya Kanda, Kishkindiya Kanda, Sundar Kanda, Uttar Kanda.

There were historical account like Shomshok Ngamba (the conquest of Samjok) written by two authors, Laishram Aroi and Yumnam Atibar. Laishram Aroi personally participated in the expeditions in Kabaw valley and Burma under the command of king Pamheiba.

Nungangbam Gobindaram was another scholar and writer of Pamheiba's court and his two praiseworthy disciples were – Mayengba Brindaban and Wahengba Madhabram. His great literary works were – Pakhangba Nongaron, the translation of Astakal from Sanskrit to Meeteilon and Takhel Ngamba, the conquest of Tripura.

In the later part of 18th century, Wangkhei Pundit Gopiram Singh was the scholar in the royal court of Medingu Chingthangkhomba (1763-1798 A.D.). In case of any adversity, King used to consult with him. In 1789, (as per Meetei calendar,28th Wakching,Thursday

) Gobindaram had started the writing of "Meihaubaron Puya".

Wahengba Madhabram was the prominent scholar during the reign of Medingu Chingthangkhomba and Labainaya Chandra. The praiseworthy books written by him were – Langlon, Mahabharat Birat Parva, Chingthongkhomba Ganga Chatpa and Sana Manik.

In 20th century, Langlon was first published in 1924 by Education Minister of Manipur, Waheingbam Yumjao Singh, with archaic and modern Meeteilon. It is also known as the "Sloka of Meetei Chaneika".

Another landmark in the history of Manipuri literature was the evidence of novel in 1779 A.D., while religious books were only the mainstream in this era. Sana Manik can be considered as one of the earliest Manipuri novel, which was written during the regime of Meidingu Chingthangkhomba.

The eldest son of Meidingu Chingthangkhomba, Nabananda Yubaraj, was one the renowned writer from the royal family, and he had translated Virat Parva of Ram Krishnadas into Meeteilon as "Virat Shathuplon".

Chingthangkhomba Ganga Chatpa was written by Haricharon Khangyenba, Barmani Lauremba, Khagendra Yimnaba, Khongchen Aheiba with the recommendation from Meidingu Labanya Chandra.

Ashamedha Parva of Gangadas sen in Bengali was translated into Meeteilon by a group of Meetei scholars with the title "Langoi Shagol Thaba". Longjam Parshuram was played a major role for this work with the great contributions from Chirom Avimaynu, Wairokpam Gangaram,Oinam Nabashyam,Thokchom Ganashyam, Maibam Aviram, Hiamcha Madan and Khanglenbam Aviram.

Modern Period

Meitrabak lost her freedom after the Anglo-Manipuri war on 27th April 1891 and British entered to Kangla on the same day. The British Government selected Meidingngu Churachand(1891-1941 A.D.), a minor son of Chaobiyaima as the king of Meitrabak. After the advent of British, a new phase, the beginning of the modern Manipuri literature began with British influence.

In 1872, the acting political agent Nuttal began an English medium school. Later Political agent Lt-Col. Sir James Johnstone established the first Middle English School. William Pettigrew's,the Christian missionary, contribution to western education in the country was also a remarkable one. In the valley of Meitrabak, the common language of instruction was Bengali and this led to use of Bengali Script for writing of Meeteilon. As a result of this, the substantial amount of earlier literature in Meetei Mayek became inaccessible to the western educated elites and next generation Meetei peoples.

Renaissance of Literature

The pioneer in the effort to publish the Meeteilon (Manipuri language) with Bengali script was Haodijam Chaintanya, who was born of Meetei parents in Shillong, in 1867. His interest in Meetei culture led him to make translation of folk literature and ancient manuscripts like- Takhel Ngamba and Khahi Ngamba into Bengali script, and published by Chronicle Press from Sylhet in 1900 and 1902 respectively. He deserved the credit of being the first to have attempted to make some of the old manuscripts publicly available.

The decade of 1920-1930 was not only the beginnings of modern Manipuri literature, but also the renaissance of Meetei culture, language and religion. The culmination of this cultural movement was the formation of "Manipuri Sabha" in 1933, later it named as "Nikhil Hindu Manipuri Mahasabha" (NHMM). Maharaj Churachand was the president of the newly form organization and Irabot was chosen as the president of the reception committee. From the fourth session, the name of the organization changed as "Nikhil Manipuri Mahasabha"(NMM) by dropping the word "Hindu".

In the 1930s Phuratlatpam Atombapu Sharma was appointed to the Brahma Sabha and made as court Pandit. His family was migrated from North India into Meitrabak (Manipur) during the 15th Century. As per the resolution of the First session of NHMM, the court Pandi, Atombapu Sharma, was asked to established the Historical Society for Manipur.He was a prolific writer, almost entirely self-published. Many of his publication are very brief and ephemeral, and as a whole his work was very repetitive. His translation of Sanskri into Meeteilon are no doubt a valuable resource, but this work is vitiated by the fact that it provides a basis for his misinterpretation of Meetei culture. He approached Meetei Culture and religion with a number of ideological assumptions. For him the original Meetei civilization was vedic. On this basis virtually everything in the traditional Meetei culture – its deities, its rituals, its dance – are explained by drawing crude parallel with the Vedas. The foundation of all this was his belief that Manipur is referred to in the Mahabharata. In effect it was a re-writing of Meetei history to make it part of the grand Vedic tradition.

Laininghan Naoria Phulo (1888-1941) was the pioneer of Meeteis cultural renaissance and the revival movement. In opposition to the Brahmanical Hinduism,there arose a movement which sought to rediscover and reassert the religion of the past, and to purify it from all Hindu influence. This was an attempt to return to the past, to the pre-Hindu religion of the Meeteis in what was conceived to be its pure form. He founded the APOKPA LAINING in Cachar, Assam, in 1930, for revival of Meetei Laining(religion) and development of Meeteilon. In 1936 he confronted with the king and the court Pandit, Atombapu Sharma.

He is honored as a Meetei Maichou and Prophet by the Meeteis, and his literary works for the spiritual discoveries considered him also as a poet. His great contribution in Manipuri literature in poetry were –

1. Yumlai Lairon(1930)
2. Sakok Thiren (1931)
3. Apokpa Mapugee Tungnapham (1931)
4. Tengbanba Amashung Lainingthou Laibao (1933)
5. Athoiba Sheireng(1935), etc.

The important works in prose were –

1. Meetei Yelhou Mayek(1931),
2. Meetei Haobam Wari(1934),
3. Aigee Wareng(1940),

Hijam Irabot produced the first magazine, Meetei Chanu, in 1922, but it was in short lived. Yakeirol, which appeared in 1930 under the editorship of Ningthoujam Leiren. Three years later, another magazine Lalit Manjuri Patrika, came out. In the next decade, the first two daily newspaper appeared – Deinik Manipur Patrika and Manipur Matam.

There was a tradition in Meitrabak (Manipur) of dramatic presentation of ancient legends in the form of "Sumang Leela". The Dramatic Union was founded in 1905 for religious theme for Bengali language, and later Manipur Dramatic Union was established in 1932. By this decade too modern Manipuri literature was becoming a recognizable force with the appearance of works by Khwairakpam Chaoba, Dr. Lamabam Kamal and Hijam Anganghal. This flowering of the literary activities resulted into the foundation of the Manipuri Sahitya Parishad, Imphal, Manipur, which was devoted to the development of Manipuri literature and culture.

The names of most important Meetei writers in 20th century are:

a) Hijam Anganghal Singh (1892-1943),

b) Khwairakpam Chaoba Singh (1895-1950),

c) Lamabam Kamal Singh (1899-1935),

Hijam Anganghal Singh (1892-1943) - besides being a poet, he is a well-known essayist and dramatist, renowned for his magnum opus KHAMBA THOIBI (1940), which is a poem of 39,000 lines considered to be a 'national' epic of the Meeteis. Khwairakpam Chaoba Singh(1895-1950) is one of the best-known writers of modern Manipuri literature. His historical novel Lavangalata (1939) is considered as an outstanding work in Manipuri. His other prose works are:

1. Wakhalgi Icel,
2. Wakhal,
3. Phidam,
4. Kannaba Wa and
5. Chhatramacha.

Lamabam Kamal Singh(1899-1935): His Madhavi (1930) is recognised as the first modern Manipuri novel. His collection of poems called Lai Pareng (1931) has been acclaimed to be 'the most significant poetical works of this century'.

Arambam Dorendrajit Singh (1907-1944) is another pioneer poet and dramatist whose works include three dramas, viz. Miorang Thoibi, Bhagyachandra and Kaurav Parajay and two epic poems, viz. Kansa Badha and Subhadra Haran.

Laishram Samarendra Singh (b.1928) is one of the forerunners of modern Manipuri poetry. He is renowned for his poetic collections Wa Amata Hiage Telanga, Mamang Leikia Thambal Satle and Khun Amagi Vari.

H. Guno Singh (b.1927) is an acclaimed short-story writer in Manipuri. His important works include- Khudol, Langjim Mangkhrabi Kishi,Laman, Aroiba Paodam and Aikhoigi Tada. He also translated Sukumar Sen's History of Bengali Literature into Manipuri.

Pacha Meetei (1940-1990) set a new trend in Manipuri novel by introducing contemporary social problems in place of the romantic and passionate atmosphere prevalent in the Manipuri novel in the first half of the 20th century. He is acclaimed for his novel Na Tathiba Ahal Ama.

12

Marathi Literature

Marathi literature is the body of literature of Marathi, a Sanskrit-derived language spoken mainly in the Indian state of Maharashtra and written in the Devanagari script.

Early Marathi Literature

Though the earliest known Marathi inscription found at the foot of the statue at Shravanabelgola in Karnataka is dated c. 983 CE, the Marathi literature actually started with the religious writings by the saint-poets belonging to Mahanubhava and Warkari sects. Mahanubhava saints used prose as their main medium, while Warkari saints preferred poetry as the medium. The early saint-poets were Mukundaraj who wrote *Vivekasindhu*, Dnyaneshwar (1275-1296) (who wrote *Bhawarthadeepika*, which is popularly known as Dnyaneshwari, a 9000-couplets long commentary on the Bhagavad Gita) and Namdev. They were followed by the Warkari saint-poet Eknath (1528-1599). Mukteswar translated the great epic Mahabharata into Marathi. Social reformers like saint-poet Tukaram transformed Marathi into an enriched literary language. Ramdas's (1608-1681) *Dasbodh* and *Manache Shlok* are well-known products of this tradition.

In the 18th century, some well-known works like *Yatharthadeepika* (by Vaman Pandit), *Naladamayanti Swayamvara* (by Raghunath Pandit), *Pandava Pratap, Harivijay, Ramvijay* (by Shridhar Pandit) and *Mahabharata* (by Moropant) were produced. However, the most versatile and voluminous writer among the poets was Moropanta (1729-1794) whose Mahabharata was the first epic poem in Marathi. The historical section of the old Marathi literature was unique as it contained both prose and poetry. The prose section contained the Bakhars that were written after the foundation of the Maratha kingdom by Shivaji. The poetry section contained the Povadas and the Katavas composed by the Shahirs. The period from 1794 to 1818 is regarded as the closing period of the Old Marathi literature and the beginning of the Modern Marathi literature.

Modern Period

In Modern period of internet, www.marathikavita.co.in (MK) helps poets to present their talent. The period of the late nineteenth century in Maharashtra is the period of colonial modernity. Like the corresponding periods in the other Indian languages, this was the period dominated by the English educated intellectuals. It was the age of prose and reason. It was the period of reformist diadicticism and a great intellectual ferment.

The first English Book was translated in Marathi in 1817. The first Marathi newspaper started in 1835. Many books on social reforms were written by Baba Padamji (*Yamuna Paryatana,* 1857), Mahatma Jyotiba Phule, Lokhitwadi, Justice Mahadev Govind Ranade, Hari Narayan Apte (1864-1919) etc. Lokmanya Tilak's newspaper Kesari, set up in 1880, provided a platform for sharing literary views. Marathi at this time was efficiently aided by Marathi Drama. Here, there also was a different genre called 'Sangit Natya' or Musicals. The first play was V.A. Bhave's Sita Swayamvar in 1843 Later Kirioskar (1843-85) and G.B. Deval (1854-1916) brought a romantic aroma and social content. But Krishnaji Prabhakar Khadilkar (1872~1948) with his banned play Kichaka-Vadh (1910) set the trend of political playwriting. Later on this "stage" was ably served by stalwarts like Ram Ganesh Gadkari and Prahlad Keshav Atre.

The Drama Flourished in 60s and 70s with few of the best Indian actors available to take on a variety of protagonists. Mohan Agashe, Sriram Lagoo, Kashinath Ghanekar, Prabhakar Panshikar playing many immortal characters penned by greats like Vasant Kanetkar, Kusumagraj, vijay Tendulkar to name a few. This Drama movement was ably supported by Marathi films which did not enjoy a continuous success. Starting with V.Shantaram and before him the pioneer DadaSaheb Phalke, Marathi cinema went on to influence contemporary Hindi cinema.

Director Raja Paranjape, Music director Sudhir Phadke, lyricist G.Madgulkar and actor Raja Gosavi came together to give quiet a few hits in later period. Marathi Language as spoken by people here was throughout influenced by drama and cinema along with contemporary literature. Modern Marathi poetry began with Mahatma Jyotiba Phule's compositions. The later poets like Keshavsuta, Balakavi, Govindagraj, and the poets of Ravi Kiran Mandal like Madhav Julian wrote poetry which was influenced by the Romantic and Victorian English poetry. It was largely sentimental and lyrical.Prahlad Keshav Atre, the renowned satirist and a politician wrote a parody of this sort of poetry in his collection Jhenduchi Phule. Sane Guruji (1899-1950) contributed to the children's literature in Marathi. His major works are *Shyamchi Aai* (Shyam's Mother), *Astik* (Believer), *Gode Shevat* (The Sweet Ending) etc. He translated and simplified many Western Classics and published them in a book of stories titled *Gode Goshti* (Sweet Stories).

Vishnu Sakharam Khandekar (1889-1976)'s *Yayati* won him the Jnanpith Award for 1975. He also wrote many other novels, short stories, essays etc. His major works are *Don Dhruv* (Two Poles), *Ulka* (Meteorite), *Krounchavadh, Jalalela Mohar, Amrutvel.*

The major paradigm shift in sensibility began in the forties with the avant-garde modernist poetry of B.S. Mardhekar. In the mid fifties, the 'little magazine movement' gained momentum. It published writings which were non-conformist, radical and experimental. Dalit literary movement also gained strength due to the little magazine movement. This radical movement was influenced by the philosophy of Dr. Babasaheb Ambedkar and challenged the literary establishment which was largely middle class, urban, and upper caste people.

The little magazine movement threw up many excellent writers. Bhalchandra Nemade is a well known novelist, critic and poet. Dr.Sharad Rane is a well known bal-sahityakar. The poetry of Arun Kolatkar, Dilip Chitre, Namdeo Dhasal, Vasant Abaji Dahake, Manohar Oak and many other modernist poets is complex, rich and provokative. Bhau Padhye,Vilas Sarang, Shyam Manohar, Suhas Shirvalkar and Visharm Bedekar are well known fiction writers.

The another major paradigm shift in Marathi sensibility began in the nineties with the another avant-garde modernist poetry of poets associated with Abhidhanantar and Shabadavedh. In the post nineties, this 'new little magazine movement' gained momentum and poets like Manya Joshi, Hemant Divate, Sachin Ketkar, Mangesh Narayanrao Kale, Saleel Wagh, Mohan Borse, Nitin Kulkarni, Nitin Arun Kulkarni, Varjesh Solanki, Sandeep Deshpande, Vasant Gurjar touched the new areas of post-modern life. The poetry collections broughtout by Abhidhanantar Prakashan and the regular issues of the magazine Abhidhanantar is taking Marathi poetry to the global standards.

Marathi is also the one of the few Indian languages (and possibly the only one) where there is a stream of science fiction literature. A few well known Marathi science fiction authors are Dr. Jayant Narlikar, Dr Bal Phondke, Subodh Javadekar, and Laxman Londhe.

Many writers like Dnyaneshwar Mulay have added new dimensions and enriched Marathi with their literary talent. His autobiographical book 'Maati Pankh Aani Aakaash' was considered to be among the best ten autobiographies of last 100 years in Marathi by a survey conducted by Antarnaad, a respected martahi literary magazine. His other immensely likeable books are 'Russia Navya Dishanche Amantran' a book that captures post 1992 Russia. It is popular because it is the only work of its kind. His recent poetry collection 'Swatahteel Awakash' won the state literary award of governmment of Maharashtra. He is highly popular among young readers and writes regular columns in Marathi dailies like Lokmat and Loksatta and Sadhana, weekly published from Pune.

13

Oriya Literature

Oriya is an official language of the state of Orissa, India, a region known at different stages of history as Kalinga, Udra, Utkala, or Koshala. The language is also spoken by minority populations of the neighboring states of Jharkhand, West Bengal, Chhattisgarh and Andhra Pradesh. The earliest written texts in the language are about thousand years old. Orissa was a vast empire in the ancient and medieval times, which extended from the Ganges in the north to the Godavari in the south. During the British rule, however, Orissa lost its political identity and formed parts of the Bengal and Madras Presidencies. The present state of Orissa was formed in 1936.

Oriya is classified as a member of the Indo-Aryan language super family; it is a descendent of Odri Prakrit and Ardha Magadhi. This form of Prakrit was in turn derived from Sanskrit via the transitional Bibhasas. Modern Oriya vocabulary is estimated to be composed of 70% Sanskrit, 2% Hindustani/Persian/Arabic with the remaining 28% of mainly "Adivasi" origin.

The history of Oriya has been mapped by historians along three main stages, Old Oriya (spanning between the 10th century AD and 1300 AD),

Early Middle Oriya (between 1300 AD and 1500 AD), Middle Oriya (between 1500 AD and 1700 AD), Late Middle Oriya (between 1700 AD and 1850 AD) and Modern Oriya (spanning from 1850 AD till the present day), but using further subdivisons of the timeline, as below, presents the history more accurately.

Age of Charya Literature

The beginnings of Oriya poetry coincide with the development of Charya Sahitya, the literature started by Mahayana Buddhist poets. This literature was written in a specific metaphor named "Sandhya Bhasha" and the poets like Luipa, Kanhupa are from the territory of Orissa.The language of Charya was considered as Prakrita. In one of his poem, Kanhupa wrote:

> "Your hut stands outside the city
> Oh, untouchable maid
> The bald Brahmin passes sneaking close by
> Oh, my maid, I would make you my companion
> Kanha is a kapali, a yogi
> He is naked and has no disgust
> There is a lotus with sixty-four petals
> Upon that the maid will climb with this poor self and dance."

Here the image 'untouchable maid' is used for 'shakti', it resides outside the city, i.e., outside the ordinary consciousness. Though she is untouchable, the bald Brahmin, meaning the so-called wise man, has a secret hankering for her. But only a kapali or an extreme Tantric can be a fit companion for her, because he is also an outcaste; he is naked, for he does not have any social identity or artificiality. After the union with the shakti both of them would climb on the 64-petalled lotus Sahasrara Chakra, and dance there.

Evidently, the poet had drawn images and symbols from existing social milieu, social psychology, so that this deep realization could be easily grasped by the readers. This kind of poetry, full with the mystery of Tantra, spread over the Northeastern region of India from the tenth to the fourteenth century, and its style of expression was revived by the Oriya poets of sixteenth to nineteenth centuries.

Age of Sarala Das

The first great poet of Orissa is the famous Sarala-Das who wrote the Mahabharata, not an exact translation from the Sanskrit original, rather an imitation of the same. For all practical purposes it can also be seen as an original piece of work. It has provided subsequent poets with the necessary foundation for a national literature. It gives a fairly accurate idea about the culture of the Oriyas at the time. Sarala Das, belonging to 15th century Orissa of Kapilendra Dev, was acclaimed as "Adikabi" or the first poet. He is also a Shudra Muni, or a seer from backward class. He had no formal education and did not know Sanskrit. It is believed that he got his poetic gift from goddess Sarala (Sarasswati), and wrote Mahabharata as it was dictated by her. Among many of his poems and epics, he is best remembered for his Mahabharata. Chandi Purana and the Vilanka Ramayana are also two of his famous creations. Arjuna Das, a contemporary to Sarala Dasa, wrote Rama-Bibha, a significant long poem in Oriya.

Age of Panchasakha

Towards the 16th century, five poets emerged, though there are hundreds year gap in between them.But they are known as Panchasakhas as they believed to same school of thought, Utkaliya Vaishnavism.The poets are: Balaram Das, Jagannath Das, Achyutananda Das, Ananta Das and Jasobanta Das. Balaram Das's Jagamohan Ramayan provided the other pillar on which subsequent literature was to thrive. His Laksmi Purana is considered to be the first manifesto of Women's Liberaion and Feminism in India Literature. However, the most influential work was yet to come. It came in the form of Jagannath Das's Bhagabata, which made a great influence among Oriya people as a day to day philosophical guide lines and it had its effect in Oriya Culture. The Panchasakhas are very much Vaishnavas by thought. In 1509 Chaitanya came to Orissa with his Vaishnava message of love. Before him Jaydev had prepared the ground by heralding the cult of Vaishnavism through his Geetagovinda. Chaitanya's path of devotion was known as Raganuga Bhakti Marga, but the Panchasakhas differed from Chaitanyas and believed in Gyana Mishra Bhakti Marga, which has similarities with the Buddhist philosophy of Charya Literature stated above.

Age of Upendra Bhanja

At the end of age of Panchasakha, a few prominent works include the Usabhilasa of Sisu Sankara Das, the Rahasya-manjari of Deva-durlabha Dasa and the Rukmini-bibha of Kartikka Das were written. A new form of novels in verse evolved during the beginning of the 17th century when Ramachandra Pattanayaka wrote Haravali. These poets are the beginners of this age. But the prominent poets are Dinakrushna Das, Kabi Samrat Upendra Bhanja and Abhimanyu Samanta Simhar. Verbal jugglery, obscenity and eroticism as the characteristics of Shringara Kavyas, became the trend of this period to which Upendra Bhanja took a leading role. His creations were Baidehisha Bilasa, Koti Brahmanda Sundari, Lavanyabati were proved land mark in Oriya Literature. Upendra Bhanja was conferred with the title 'Kabi Samrat' of Oriya literature for the aesthetic poetic sense and verbal jugglery proficiency. Dinakrushna Das's Rasokallola and Abhimanyu samanta Simhara's Bidagdha Chintamani are prominent kavyas of this time. There was a significant influence of these poets in making modern Oriya Literature. During the end of Riti Yuga or age of Upendra Bhanja, four major poets emerged and they created the History. They are Kabi surya Baladeb Rath, Brajanath Badajena, Gopal Krushna Pattanaik and Bhima Bhoi. Kabisurya Baladev rath wrote his poems in champu and chautisha, the new form and style of poetry. But the significant role was played by Brajanath Badjena by starting a tradition of prose fiction, though he was not considered as the premier writer of prose. His Chatur Binoda (Amusement of Intelligent) seems to be the first one to deal with different kinds of rasas, but predominantly the bibhatsa rasa, often verging on nonsense.

Age of Radhanath

The first Oriya printing typeset was cast in 1836 by the Christian missionaries which made a great revolutions in Oriya literature. Instead of palm leaf inscription. The books were being printed and the periodicals and journals were published. The first Oriya Magazine of 'Bodha Dayini' was published from Balasore in 1861. The main object of this magazine was to promote Oriya literature and to draw attention to the lapses in government policy. The first Oriya paper, 'The Utkal Deepika,' made its appearance in 1866 under the editorship of late Gouri Sankar Ray with the help of late Bichitrananda. The Utkal Deepika carried on a vigorous campaign for bringing all the Oriya-speaking areas under one administration, development of Oriya language and literature and protection of Oriya interests. In 1869 late Bhagavati Charan Das started 'Utkal Subhakari' to propagate Brahmo faith. In the last three and half decades of the 19th century a number of newspapers were published in Oriya. Prominent among them were 'Utkal Deepika','Utkal Patra', Utkal Hiteisini from Cuttack, Utkal Darpan and Sambada Vahika' from Balasore, Sambalpur Hiteisini (30 May, 1889) from Deogarh. The publication of these papers during the last part of the 19th century indicated the desire and the determination of the people of Orissa to uphold the right of freedom of expression and the freedom of the press with a view to ultimately fighting for the freedom of the country from the British rule.But another great help these periodical performed was that they encouraged the modern literature and acted as a media to provide a wide readers range for the writers, The educated intellectuals came in contact with the English Literature and got influenced. Radhanath Ray (1849-1908) is the prime figure, who tried to write his poems with the influence of Western Literature. He wrote Chandrabhaga,Nandikeshwari,Usha, Mahajatra,darbar and Chilika wee the long poems or Kavyas.

Fakir Mohan Senapati (1843-1918), the prime figure of modern Oriya Fiction Prose is the product of that generation. He was considered the Vyasakabi or founder poet of Oriya language. Fakirmohan was born and brought up in the coastal town of Balasore. He grew up to be an administrator in ex-feudatory states. Enraged by the attempts of the Bengalis to marginalize even replace the Oriya language by Bengali, he took to creative writing rather late. Though he had translated from Sanskrit, wrote poetry, and attempted many forms of literature, he is now known primarily as the father of modern Oriya prose fiction. If either Fakirmohan or his progeny had preserved his short story, "Lachmania" which he had written in the late 1860s, and which was published in the journal Bodhadayini, edited by himself in Balasore, Fakirmohan would certainly been credited with having pioneered the genre in India. But as ill-luck would have it, except for a bare mention in his autobiography, the story cannot be traced, and thus his "Rebati" (1898) is widely recognized as the first Oriya short story. "Rebati" is the story of a young innocent girl whose desire for education is placed in the context of a conservative society in a backward Orissa village, which is hit by the killer epidemic cholera. His other stories are "Patent Medicine", "Dak Munshi", and "Adharma Bitta".Other than short stories, Fakir Mohan Senapati is also known for his novel Chha Maana Atha Guntha. It is the first Indian novel to deal with the exploitations of landless peasants by the feudal lord. It was written much before the October revolution of Russia or much before the emerging of Marxist ideas in India. Gangadhar Meher (1862-1924), Madhusudan Rao, Chintamani Mahanty, Nanda Kishore Bal and Gaurisankar Ray are some of eminent writers and poets of this time.

Age of Satyabadi

During Age of Radhanath the literary world was divided between the ancient, headed by a magazine *The Indradhanu* and the modernists, headed by another magazine *The Bijuli*. But Gopabandhu was a great balancer. He realized that a nation as well as its literature live by their tradition. He believed that a national superstructure of the present can endure only if it is based upon the solid foundations of the past heritage. He also wrote a satirical poem in *The Indradhanu*. This led to an ugly incident and also punishment meted out by the angry Inspector of schools for such satirical poem. He refused to apologize for such writing in lieu of punishment.

Later he joined Ravenshaw College, Cuttack to pursue graduation. He lost his father before joining college. During this period he started *Kartavya Bodhini Samiti* (Duty Awakening Society) to encourage his friends to take on social, economic & political problems to make them responsible citizens. He was leading a team to serve the flood victims, when he heard the serious illness of his son. But he preferred to save the *"sons of the soil"* rather than his son. This imbibed *Swadeshi* spirit in him. His new mission was to reform the society and to develop education. Through these activities he had the vision of social service. When he was only twenty-eight, he lost his wife. By that time he had lost all his three sons and he had two daughters whom he left with his elder brother along with the share of his property in the village. This proved that he had no love for leading a family life and for that he refused to remarry even at a marriageable age. He was not an ordinary man and that is why he did not attach much importance to worldly life. He is regarded as the Utkalmani in every Oriya's mind and heart.

With rise of freedom movement, a literary though was emerged with the influence of Gandhiji and idealistic trend of Nationalism formed as a new trend in Oriya Literature.Much respected personality of

Orissan culture and history, Utkalmani Gopabandhu Das (1877-1928) has founded a school at avillage Satyabadi near Sakshigopal of Orissa and an idealstic literary movement influenced the writers of this age. No doubt, Gopabandhu Das was the famous figure of this movement associated by other four writers like Godabarisha Mishra, Nilakantha Dash, Harihara Acharya and Krupasinshu. They are also known as Panchasakhas in comparison with the Age of Panchasakhas of the tradition. The writers of this age are mostly critiques, essayist and poets. Godabarisha Mohapatra, Kuntala-Kumari Sabat the other renowned name of this age.

Age of Marxism

With the emergence of the Soviet Union in 1935, a Communist party was formed in Orissa and a periodical named *Adhunika* was published by the party. Bhagawati Charan Panigrahi and Sachidananda Routray were founding members, and were writers and poets for the party. Bhagwati became a fiction writer and though Sachidananda Routray (who is also known as "Sachi Routra" or Sachi Babu) has written some short stories was remembered best for his poems. Sachi Babu is also considered to be the founder of Modern poetry in Orissa. He was the prime figure to introduce two European trends of English modernism - the early aestheticist phase pioneered by Pound and Eliot (1910-1930), and the second wave modernism of the 1930s poets (Auden, Spender, MacNeice, Isherwood) to Oriya Literature through his poetry.

Age of Romanticism

Influenced by the romantic thoughts of Rabindranath

tagore, during the thirties when the progressive Marxian movements was in full flow in Oriya Literature, Kalindi Charan panigrahi, the brother of Bhagabati Charan Panigrahi,the founder of Marxian Trend in Orissa, formed a group circa 1920 called "Sabuja Samiti." Along with two of his writer friend Annada Shankar Ray and Baikuntha Patnaik. Perhaps it was the very short existed period in Oriya Literature and later submerged with either Gandhian thoughts or Marxian thoughts. Later Kalindi Charan Panigrahi wrote his famous novel Matira Manish, being influenced by Gandhism. Annada Shankar Ray flew away to Bengali Literature. Mayadhar Mansingh was a renowned poet of that time though he was considered as a romantic poet, but he kept the distance away from the influence of Rabindranath successfully.

Post Colonial Age

Poetry

As the successor of Sachi babu, two poets Guruprasad Mohanty (popularly known as Guru Prasad) (1924-2004) and Bhanuji Rao highly influenced by T.S. Eliot and published their co authored poetry book "Nutan Kabita" with a preface of Professor. Jatindra Mohan Mohanty. Thus the waste land of T.S. Eliot created a great effect on the post independent Oriya poets. Later, Ramakanta Rath modified the ideas. According to him : 'After the publication of Kalapurusha (Guru Prasad's poetry collection influenced by T.S. Elliot's The Waste Land) we realized that a sense of alienation is the main ingredient of modern poetry.' Before independence of India, the Oriya poetry was mostly Sanskritic, or "literary" idiom; but after independence of India, one could notice the free use of western concepts, idioms, images and also adaption of their myths. Ramakanta Rath, Sitakanta Mohanpatra, Soubhagya Kumar Mishra, Rajendra kishore Panda and Pratibha Satpathy are the famous poets in this trend. Specially Ramakanta has a tremendous poetic aspiration in his creations. He has a unique blend of modernist esotericism, sardonic slant and a recurring vein of negation turned into art. A poet of complex man-woman relationship, that borders on oblivion, Ramakanta has the power of juxtaposing the physical and the metaphysical in a deep dark world of realizations. "I am your husband's skeleton," he may tell someone, and "you are my beautiful widow." Sitakant Mohapatra's vision of a suffering world, perpetually in the process of self-redemption, maintains a strong link with the Oriya tradition and heritage. Soubhagya Kumar Mishra is a master micro-observer, turning even trivia into art, enlivened by wit and a racy narrative. His earlier swiftness has turned into sedate subtlety. He continues to take the reader to insightful stumblings. His 'blind honeybee' finds honey-saps even in unimaginable founts. The Oriya poetic diction has become vibrant and resilient in usage and connotation in Rajendra Kishore Panda's poem, where he has many peers, with his individual strength.

Dr. Khagendranath Mallick, Brajanath Rath, Jayanta Mahapatra, Kamalakant Lenka, J P Das, Brahmotri Mohanty, Kailash Lenka, Mamata Dash, Amaresh Patnaik, Hrushikesh Mallick, Sunil Kumar Prusty, Ashok Chandra Mahapatra, Chittaranjan Misra, Sucheta Mishra, Aparna Mohanty, Sushama Mishra, Pritidhara Samal, Basudev Sunani, Gajanan Mishra, Sairindhree Sahoo, Dr. Rajani Ranjan Dash, Purna Chandra Maharana, Sunil Kumar Rath, Ajay Swain,

Krushna Ku. Mohanty, Saroj Bal, Dr Tapan Kumar Pradhan, Gayatribala Panda, Manoj Meher, Kedar Mishra, Pabitra Mohan Dash, Manuan Dash. Biraja Bal, Jajati Sahoo, Subrat Das, Goutam Das,Kanakmanjari Pattnayak, Bidyutlata Das, Akhila Nayak and Bharat Majhi, Amarendra Madhaba Dash, Dr. Basanta Kishore Sahoo are some poets of this contemporary age. A reader can find the bold approaches, the 'direct speak' dictions, the expanded open-ended observations have been charged with flashes of vision to make their poems excellent.

Fiction

In the Post-Independence Era Oriya fiction assumed a new direction.The trend which Fakir Mohan has started actually developed more after '50s of last century. Gopinath Mohanty (1914-1991), Surendra Mohanty and Manoj Das (1934-) are considered as three jewels of this time. They are the pioneer of a new trend, that of developing or projecting the "individual as protagonist" in Oriya fiction. Eminent Feminist writer and critics Sarojini Sahoo believes that it was not Gopinath, but Surendra Mohanty whose "Ruti O Chandra" has to be considered as first story of individualistic approach rather than the story "Dan" by Gopinth, which was formerly known as the first story of "individualistic attitude". The major difference between Surendra and Gopinath is that, when Gopinath is more optimistic, Surendra seems to be nihilistic. This nihilism prepares the ground for the development of "existentialist" movement of Oriya literature.

Surendra Mohanty has a mastery over language, theme and concept. Some of his famous short story collections and novels are: Krushna Chuda,

Mahanagarira Rati, ruti o Chandra, Maralara Mrutyu, Shesha Kabita, Dura Simanta, Oh Calcutta, Kabi-O-Nartaki, Sabuja Patra-O-Dhusara Golap, Nila Shaila, Andha Diganta, which bear the memorial of his success as a reputed story writer and novelist.

In his fiction Gopinath Mohanty explores all aspects of Orissan life: life, both in the plains and in the hills. He evolves a unique prose style, lyrical in style, choosing worlds and phrases from the day-to-day speech of ordinary men and women. Gopinath's first novel, Mana Gahtra Chasa, was published in 1940, which was followed by Dadi Budha (1944), Paraja (1945) and Amrutara Santan (1947). He published 24 novels, 10 collections of short stories in addition to three plays, two biographies, two volumes of critical essays, and five books on the languages of Kandh, Gadaba and Saora tribes. Moreover, he translated Tolstoy's War and Peace (Yuddh O Shanti) in three volumes (tr. 1985-86) and Togore's Jogajog (tr. 1965) into Oriya.

Started his literary career as a communist and later transformed himself to Aurobindian philosopher, Manoj Das proved himself as a successful bilingual writer as he used to write both in Oriya and English. His major works are: Shesha basantara chithi, 1966; Manoj Dasanka katha o kahani, 1971; Dhumabha diganta, 1971; Manojpancabimsati, 1977; (short stories); Tuma gam o anyanya kabita, 1992 (poetry). His notable English works include: The crocodiles lady: a collection of stories, 1975, The submerged valley and other stories, Farewell to a ghost: short stories and a novelette, 1994; Çyclones, 1987, and A tiger at twilight, 1991.

The other significant fiction writers are Chandrasekhar Rath, Shantanu Acharya, Mohapatra

Nilamani Sahoo, Rabi Patnaik and JP Das. Chandra Sekhar Rath's novel Jantrarudha (Astride the Wheel :translated by Jatindra Kumar Nayak) is one of the renowned classic of this period. Shantanu acharya's novel Nara-Kinnara also have its significant effect.

Revolution in Oriya Fiction

The trend started by the writers of '50s and the so called popular writers of 60s, were challenged by the young writers in '70s. But the process of rebellion started from 60's. In the 60s, a little magazine "Uan Neo Lu" was published from Cuttack. The title of the magazine was made up of three of the Oriya alphabets, which were not in use. The writers associated with the magazines were: Annada Prasad Ray (not Annada sankar Ray), Guru Mohanty (not Guru Prasad of Kala Purusha fame), Kailash Lenka and Akshyay Mohanty. These writers may not have become as famous as some of their contemporaries. But they started a revolution in the text and styles of Oriya fiction. They tried to break the monopoly of so called established writer. They brought sexuality into the puview of current literature and they created a new style in prose. In the late '60s the dominance of Cuttack in the field of Oriya Literature had broken when many "groups" of writers emerged from different parts of Orissa. Anamas from Puri, Abadhutas from Balugaon, Panchamukhi from Balangir, and Abujha from Berhampur and Akshara group from Sambalpur created a sensations in Oriya literary scene. Historically it does not matter the question of how many of these writers did not "make the grade," but the collective effort to break a tradition proved to be decisive in some ways.

But the actual formidable changes were confirmed by the writers of later period. Jagadish Mohanty, Kanheilal Das, Satya Mishra, Ramchandra Behera, Padmaja Pal, Yashodhara mishra and Sarojini Sahoo are few writers whose writings have created a new age in the field of fiction. Kanheilal Das and Jagadish Mohanty have started to create a new form of style and language, which was popular among the general readers as well as the intellectuals. But Kanhei lal Das was a short lived personality and his sudden demised still considered as a great loss for Oriya Fictions.

Jagadish Mohanty is considered as the introducer of existentialism and also as the trend setter in Oriya literature. Ekaki ashwarohi, Dakshina Duari Ghara, Album, Dipahara Dekhinathiba Lokotie, Nian o anyanya galpo, Mephestophelesera Pruthibi are some of his famous short story collections and Nija Nija Panipatha, Kanishka Kanishka, Uttaradhikar and Adrushya Sakal are some of his memorable novels which make him most renowned.

Dwitiya Shmashana, Abashishta Ayusha, Omkara Dhwani, Bhagnangshara Swapna, Achinha Pruthibi are some of the most famous short story collection of Ramchandra Behera.

Padmaj Pal is known for his short story collections such as Eaglera Nakha Danta, Sabuthu Sundar Pakshi, Jibanamaya and Uttara Purusha.

Sarojini Sahoo, another prominent writer, later famed for her idea of feminism also made a significant approach to Oriya fiction.Her novel Gambhiri Ghara is proved as a land mark among Oriya novel and has gained international fame for her feministic and liberal ideas. Amrutara Pratikshare, Chowkatha, Upanibesh, Pratibandi, Paksibasa, Tarlijauthiba Durga, Dukha

Apramita are some of her short story collections and Upanibesh,Pratibandi, Gambhiri Ghara, Pakshibasa, Mahajatra are her novels which have a significant effect in the Oriya Literature.

Rabi kanungo: A prominent and versatile story writer and the creator of modern feature writing in Oriya newspaper, journals and magazines uninterruptedly from 1973 and still continues. He has good national and international recognition of Oriya readers. His stories are a brand by themselves, blended with facts and fascinations, sarcasm and humour - and absolutely on down-to-earth subjects. He has received many literary awards - including 'Bishuva', 'Sarala Samman', 'Lions International Award for Oriya Creative Writing' and several others. His feature writing is unique. His works have been translated in to many Indian languages.

Popular Fiction Writings

Parallel to aesthaticism in literature, a parallel trend of populist literature also appeared after '60s which was accepted by half literate rural people, especially by the female folk. Bhagirathi Das, Kanduri Das, Bhagwana Das, Bibhuti Patnaik and Pratibha Ray are some of the best selling writer of Oriya Literature, among them Bibhuti Patnaik and Pratibha Ray have some sense of literary aesthetics. Badhu Nirupama, Gare Kajjala Dhare Luha, Topaye Sindura Dipata Shankha and Chapala Chhanda are some of popular novels of Bibhuti Patnaik.

Barsha Baishakha Basanta, Aparichita, Nishiddha Pruthibi, Upanayika and Jangyaseni are some of popular novels of Pratibha Ray. Jangyaseni proved itself different from Pratibha's other novel and has gained literary reputation. These writers able to attract the commercial producers to celluloid their stories in commercial Oriya movies.

Drama

In the field of drama, the traditional Oriya theatre is the folk opera, or Jatra, which flourishes in the rural areas of Orissa. Modern theatre is no longer commercially viable. But in the 1960, experimental theatre made a mark through the works of Manoranjan Das, who pioneered the new theatre movement with his brand of experimentalism. Bijay Mishra, Biswajit Das, Kartik Rath, Ramesh Chandra Panigrah, Ratnakar Chaini, Ranjit Patnaik, Prof. Purna Chandra Mallick continued the tradition. Though commercially modern theatre movement is a failure one still it is existing through different amateur theatre units and by different Drama Competition but unlike these modern theatre the commercialized Operas have their economical success.

14

Punjabi Literature

Punjabi literature refers to literary works written in the Punjabi language particularly by peoples from the historical Punjab region of India and Pakistan including the Punjabi diaspora. The Punjabi language is written in several different scripts, of which the Shahmukhi, the Gurmukhî scripts are the most commonly used.

Early Punjabi Literature

Whereas the oldest Punjabi literature can be found in the fragments of writings of the 11th Nath yogis Gorakshanath and Charpatnah, the Punjabi literary tradition is generally conceived to commence with Fariduddin Ganjshakar (1173-1266). Farid's mostly spiritual and devotional verse were compiled after his death in the *Adi Granth*.

Mughal and Sikh Periods

The *Janamsakhis*, stories on the the life and legend of Guru Nanak (1469-1539), are early examples of Punjabi prose literature. Nanak himself composed Punjabi verse incorporating vocabulary from Sanskrit, Arabic, Persian, and other Indic languages as characteristic of the Gurbani tradition. Sufi poetry developed under Shah Hussain (1538-1599), Sultan Bahu (1628-1691), Shah Sharaf (1640-1724), Ali Haider (1690-1785), and Bulleh Shah (1680-1757). In contrast to Persian poets who had preferred the *ghazal* for poetic expression, Punjabi Sufi poets tended to compose in the *Kafi*.

Punjabi Sufi poetry also influenced other Punjabi literary traditions particularly the Punjabi Qissa, a genre of romantic tragedy which also derived inspiration from Indic, Persian and Quranic sources. The Qissa of *Heer Ranjha* by Waris Shah (1706-1798) is among the most popular of Punjabi qisse. Other popular stories include *Sohni Mahiwal* by Fazal Shah, *Mirza Sahiba* by Hafiz Barkhudar (1658-1707), *Sassi Punnun* by Hashim Shah (1735?-1843?), and *Qissa Puran Bhagat* by Qadaryar (1802-1892).

Heroic ballads known as *Vaar* enjoy a rich oral tradition in Punjabi. Prominent examples of heroic or epic poetry include Guru Gobind Singh's in *Chandi di Var* (1666-1708). The semi-historical *Nadir Shah Di Vaar* by Najabat describes the invasion of India by Nadir Shah in 1739. The *Jangnama* of Shah Mohammad (1780-1862) recounts the First Anglo-Sikh War of 1854-56.

Modern Punjabi Literature

The Victorian novel, Elizabethean drama, free verse and Modernism entered Punjabi literature through the introduction of British education during colonial rule. The Punjabi novel developed through Nanak Singh (1897-1971) and Vir Singh. The novels, short stories and poetry of Amrita Pritam (1919-2005) highlighted, among other themes, the experience of women, and the Partition of India. Poetry began to explore more the experiences of the common man and the poor through the work of Puran Singh (1881-1931) whereas Dhani Ram Chatrik (1876-1957), Diwan Singh (1897-1944) and Ustad Daman (1911-1984) composed nationalist poetry during and after the Indian freedom movement. The Punjabi diaspora also produced poetry whose theme was revolt against British rule in *Ghadar di Gunj* ('Echoes of Mutiny'). Modernism was meanwhile introduced into Punjabi poetry through Prof. Mohan Singh (1905-78) and Shareef Kunjahi.

Post-Independence Literature

Among the more prominent Punjabi poets since 1947 are included Amrita Pritam, Shiv Kumar Batalvi (1936 –1973), Munir Niazi (1928–2006), Surjit Paatar (1944 -) and Pash (1950-1988). Punjabi fiction and drama has continued to explore modernist and post-modernist themes including sexuality, gender dynamics and the experience of the common man through the works of Balwant Gargi (1916-2003), Kartar Duggal (1917-), Ajit Cour (1934-) and Dalip Kaur Tiwana (1935 -). The rediscovery of Punjabi identity in Pakistan has been explored in the novels of Fakhar Zaman and Afzal Ahsan Randhawa. Literary criticism in Punjabi has also emerged through the writings of Shafqat Tanvir Mirza (b. 1932), Ahmad Salim, and Najm Hosain Syed (b. 1936).

Punjabi Diaspora literature has developed through writers in the United Kingdom, Canada, Australia, the United States as well as writers in Africa such as Ajaib Kamal (b. 1932) in Kenya. Some of the themes explored by diaspora writers include the cross-cultural experience of Punjabi migrants, racial discrimination, exclusion, and assimilation, the experience of women in the diaspora, and spirituality in the modern world.

Second generation writers of Punjabi ancestry such as Rupinderpal Singh Dhillon (b. 1969) have explored the relationship between British Punjabis and their immigrant parents as well as experiment with surrealism, science-fiction and crime-fiction.

15

Sindhi Literature

Sindhi language is ancient and rich in literature. Its writers have contributed extensively in various forms of literature both in poetry and prose. Sindhi literature is very rich and is generally considered one of the world's oldest.

The earliest reference to Sindhi literature is contained in the writings of Arab historians. It is established that Sindhi was the first and the earliest language of East in which the Quran was translated in the eighth or ninth century A.D. There is evidence of Sindhi poets reciting their verses before the Muslim Caliphs in Baghdad. It is also recorded that treatises were written in Sindhi on astronomy, medicine and history during the eighth and ninth centuries. Shortly afterwards, Pir Nooruddin, an Ismaili Missionary, wrote Sufis tic poetry in Sindhi language. His verses, known as "ginans", can be taken as the specimen of early Sindhi poetry. He came to Sindh during the year 1079 A.D. His poetry is an interesting record of the language which was spoken commonly at that time. He was a Sufi and a preacher of Islam. His verses are, therefore, full of mysticism and religion.

After him, Pir Shams Sabzwari Multani, Pir Shahabuddin and Pir Sadruddin are recognized as poets of Sindhi language. We even find some verses composed by Baba Farid Ganj Shakar, in Sindhi language. Pir Sadruddin (1290–1409 A.D.), was a great poet, saint and Sufi of his time. He composed his verses (ginans) in Lari and Katchi dialects of Sindhi. He also composed the "ginans" in the Punjabi, Seraiki, Hindi and Gujarati languages. He modified the old script of Sindhi language, which was commonly used by the lohana catse of Hindus of Sindh who embraced Islam under his teaching and were called by him 'Khuwajas' or 'Khojas'.

During the Sama dynasty (1010–1351 A.D.) who took over after Soomra,native Sindhi-speaking who ruled Sindh after the Arabs), and afterwards in the days of Arghuns, Tarkhans, Mughal governors (1521–1700 A.D.), Sindh produced may scholars and poets of Sindhi, Arabic and Persian languages. Qazi Qadan, Shah Karim of Bhulri (grand father of Shah Abdul Latif), Shah lutufullah Qadri, Shah Inayat Sufi Nasarpoori, Mir Masoom Shah, Makhdoom Nooh of Hala, lakho lutufullah, Mahamati Pirannath and many others are the renowned literary personalities of this period.

Bhagu Bhan, Sumang Charan, Shah Abdul Karim, Shah Inayat and many other poets of this period have enriched the language with mystic, romantic and epic poetry.

Many centers of learning (Madrasahs) (in Thatta) flourished during tenth to fifteenth centuries where celebrated scholars of Sindh used to teach religion, philosophy and rhetoric. The great scholars among them who earned high reputation even in the Muslim centres of Mecca and Madina were Makhdoom Abdul Hasan, Makhdoom Ziauddin, Makhdoom Muhammad Hashim Thattavi and Makhdoom Muhammad Muin Thattavi (that from Thatta). Their works are mostly in Arabic, Persian (Governing language of at that time) and Sindhi languages (language spoken by local peoples).

Shah Abdul Latif of Bhit (1690–1753) is the greatest thinker, Sufi, musician and poet of all time, produced by Sindh. Dr. Sorely, who compared the poetry of the great poets of all major languages of the world, including Greek, Latin and Arabic, in his book *Musa Pravaganus*, gives first place to Shah Latif for his language and thought. He invented a variant of Tanbura a musical instrument still used when his verses are sung by people who love his literature. He wrote Sassi Punnun, Umar Marvi in his famous book *Shah Jo Risalo*.

Bhittai gave new life, thought and content to the language and literature of Sindh. He traveled far and wide to the remotest corners of Sindh and saw for himself the simple and rustic people of his soil in love with life and its mysteries. He understood the ethos of the people and their deep attachment to the land, the culture, the music, the fine arts and crafts. He described Sindh and its people in the finest language, human mind can conceive of.

Through simple folk tales, Lateef has expressed profound ideas about universal brotherhood of mankind, patriotism, war against all kind of injustice and tyrannies, and above all the romance of human existence. He is in fact a pace maker and a catalyst for every generation and genre of Sindhi literature. He was a great musician also and he evolved fifteen new melodies (swaras). The great beauty of his poetry is that his every line or verse is sung till this day with a specific note or melody. His shadow is ever-lasting and all pervading he is sung not by the literature alone but even by the common people in the villages and towns of Sindh.

Sachal Sarmast, Saami and Khalifo Nabi Bux Laghari are celebrated poets of the Talpur period in Sindh (1783–1843 A.D.). Sachal Sarmast comes a galaxy of great names in literature. Khalifo Nabi Bux is by far the greatest epic poet of Sindh. His description of patriotic pathos and the art of war defies words. Rohal, Sami, Bedil, Bekas, Misri Shah, Hammal Faqir, Dalpat Sufi, Sabit Ali Shah, Khair Shah, Fateh Faqir and Manthar Faqir Rajar are some of the more noteworthy poets of the pre and early British era.

Modern Sindhi literature began with the conquest of Sindh by the British in 1843. The printing press was introduced. Magazines and newspapers brought about a revolution in Sindhi literature. Books were translated from various European languages and specially from English. People were hungry for knowledge and new forms of writing.

The pace of literature production can be judged from the example of Mirza Kalich Beg, who in the last two decades of the nineteenth century and the first two decades of the twentieth wrote more than four hundred books, including poetry, novels, short stories and essays. He also wrote on science, history, economics and politics. Thousands of books were turned out at that time on all forms and facets of literature. Hakim Fateh Mohammad Sewhani, Kauromal Khilnani, Dayaram Gidumal, Parmanand

Mewaram, Lalchand Amardinomal, Bheruamal Advani, Dr.Gurbuxani, Jhetmal Parsram, Sayaid Miran Mohammad Shah, Shamsuddin 'Bulbul' and Maulana Din Muhammad Wafai are some of the pioneers of modern literature in Sindhi language.

After World War I, the social and economic scene of the world underwent a tremendous change. The aftermath of the war and the socialist revolution of Russia affected the literature of every country. Sindhi literature too was influenced by these trends. Creating new awakening in the minds of the people working in the field of literature, they began to translate the new social consciousness into artistic forms of literature. They were now more objective and less romantic. Progressive thoughts opened the door for new trends in Sindhi literature.

Soon the struggle for freedom from the British also gathered momentum. This gave further momentum to literature. Consciousness about history and cultural heritage of Sindh served as a catalyst for research and intellectual upsurge. Great scholars like Allama I. I. Kazi his wife Elsa Kazi, Dr. Daudpota, Pir Ali Muhammad Shah Rashidi, Pir Husamuddin Shah Rashidi, Maulana Din Mohammad Wafai, Chetan Mariwala, Jairamdas Daulatram, Hashoo Kewal Ramani, Bherumal, Mehar Chand Advani, Muhammad Ibrahim Joyo, AllahDad Bohyo,Tirath Wasant and many others were producing learned treatises on various aspects of history, culture and other social subjects.

Mir Hasan Ali and Mir Abdul Hussain sangi, Khalifo Gul, Fazil Shah, Kasim, Hafiz Hamid, Mohammad Hashim, Mukhlis, Abojho, Surat Singh, Khaki, Mirza Qalich Baig, Zia and Aziz were the pioneers of poetry in Persian meter.

But the modern form and content of Sindhi poetry were given a new impetus by 'Bewas', Hyder Bux Jatoi and Dukhayal. There have been innumerable poets who have composed verses in the same vein.

The novel and short story became the main forms for prose. Hundreds of novel and short stories were translated from the European and modern. World War II saw the emergence of novelists and short storywriters like Narain Das Bhambhani, Gobind Malhi, Sundri Uttamchandani, Popti Hiranandani, Usman Deplai, Jamal Abro, Shaikh Ayaz, Rasheed Bhatti, Hafeez Akhund, Amar Jaleel, Naseem Kharal, Sirajul Haq Memon, Agha Saleem, Anis Ansari, Tariq Ashraf, Ali_Baba, Eshwar Chander, Manak, Ishtiaq Ansari, Kehar Shaukat, Mushtaq Shoro, Shaukat Shoro, Madad Ali Sindhi, Rasool Memon, Akhlaq Asnari, Reta Shahani, Rehmatullah Manjothi, Badal Jamali, Ishaque Ansari, Jan Khaskheli, Hasan Mansoor, Pervez, Shakoor Nizamani, Tariq Qureshi, Munawwar Siraj, Ismail Mangio, Fayaz Chand Kaleri, and many others.

For the last several decades, young writers experimented with new forms of prose as well as poetry. Free verses, sonnets and ballads have been written alongside the classical forms of poetry such as Kafi, Vaee, Bait, Geet and Dohira.

A few famous poets of today's Sindh are Makhdoom Talibul Mola, Ustaad Bukhari, Shaikh Ayaz, Darya Khan Rind, Makhdoom Amin Faheem, and Imdad Hussani.

In 1952, Noor-ud-din Sarki and Abdul Ghafoor Ansari restructured the literary forum of Sindhi language and called it Sindhi Adabi Sangat. Initially its activities were confined to the city of Karachi. Inspired by the success of its activities in Karachi, interest developed over the rest of Sindh. This led to the launch of other branches in other parts of Sindh as well. Such that it now attracts most of the Sindhi literary figures all over the world; besides branches in Pakistan, there are now chapters overseas as well.

16

Tamil Literature

Tamil literature refers to the literature in the Tamil language. Tamil literature has a rich and long literary tradition spanning more than two thousand years. The oldest extant works show signs of maturity indicating an even longer period of evolution. Contributors to the Tamil literature are mainly from Tamil people from Tamil Nadu, Sri Lankan Tamils from Sri Lanka, and from Tamil diaspora. Also, there have been notable contributions from European authors. The history of Tamil literature follows the history of Tamil Nadu, closely following the social and political trends of various periods. The secular nature of the early Sangam poetry gave way to works of religious and didactic nature during the Middle Ages. Jain and Buddhist authors during the medieval period and Muslim and European authors later, contributed to the growth of Tamil literature.

A revival of Tamil literature took place from the late nineteenth century when works of religious and philosophical nature were written in a style that made it easier for the common people to enjoy. Nationalist poets began to utilize the power of poetry in influencing the masses. With growth of literacy, Tamil prose began to blossom and mature. Short stories and novels began to appear. The popularity of Tamil Cinema has also provided opportunities for modern Tamil poets to emerge.

Sangam Age

Sangam literature comprises some of the oldest extant Tamil literature, and deals with love, war, governance, trade and bereavement. Unfortunately much of the Tamil literature belonging to the Sangam period had been lost. The literature currently available from this period is perhaps just a fraction of the wealth of material produced during this golden age of Tamil civilization. The available literature from this period has been broadly divided in antiquity into three categories based roughly chronology. These are: the Major Eighteen Anthology Series comprising the Eight Anthologies and the Ten Idylls and the Five Great Epics. *Tolkaappiyam,* a commentary on grammar, phonetics, rhetoric and poetics is dated from this period.

Tamil legends hold that these were composed in three successive poetic assemblies (*Sangam*) that were held in ancient times on a now vanished continent far to the south of India. A significant amount of literature could have preceded *Tolkappiyam* as grammar books are usually written after the existence of literature over long periods. Tamil tradition holds the earliest *Sangam* poetry to be over twelve millennial old. Modern linguistic scholarship places the poems between the first century BC and the third century AD.

Sangam age is considered by the Tamil people as the golden era of Tamil language. This was the period when the Tamil country was ruled by the three crowned kings' the Cheras, Pandyas and the Cholas. The land was at peace with no major external threats. Asoka's conquests did not impact on the Tamil land and the people were able to indulge in literary pursuits. The poets had a much casual relationship with their rulers than can be imagined in later times. They could chide them when they are perceived to wander from the straight and narrow. The greatness of the Sangam age poetry may be ascribed not so much to its antiquity, but due to the fact that their ancestors were indulging in literary pursuits and logical classification of the habitats and society in a systematic manner with little to draw from precedents domestically or elsewhere. The fact that these classifications were documented at a very early date in the grammatical treatise *Tolkappiyam*, demonstrates the organized manner in which the Tamil language has evolved. *Tolkappiyam* is not merely a textbook on Tamil grammar giving the inflection and syntax of words and sentences but also includes classification of habitats, animals, plants and human beings. The discussion on human emotions and interactions is particularly significant. Tolkappiyam divided into three chapters: orthography, etymology and subject matter (*Porul*). While the first two chapters of Tolkappiyam help codify the language, the last part, *Porul* refers to the people and their behavior. The grammar helps to convey the literary message on human behavior and conduct, and uniquely merges the language with its people.

The literature was classified in to the broad categories of 'subjective' (*akam*) and 'objective' (*puram*) topics to enable the poetic minds to discuss any topic under the sun, from grammar to love, within the framework of well prescribed, socially accepted conventions. Subjective topics refer to the personal or human aspect of emotions that cannot be verbalized adequately or explained fully. It can only be experienced by the individuals and includes love and sexual relationship.

Recognizing that human activities cannot take place in vacuum and are constantly influenced by environmental factors, human experiences, in general, and subjective topics in particular, are assigned to specific habitats. Accordingly land was classified into five genres (*thinai*): *kurinji* (mountainous regions), *mullai* (forests), *marutham* (agricultural lands), *neithal* (seashore), *paalai* (wasteland). The images associated with these landscapes – birds, beasts, flowers, gods, music, people, weather, seasons – were used to subtly convey a mood, associated with an aspect of life. *Kuruntokai*, a collection of poems belonging to the *Ettuthokai* anthology demonstrates an early treatment of the Sangam landscape. Such treatments are found to be much refined in the later works of *Akananuru* and *Paripaatal*. *Paripaatal* takes its name from the musical *Paripaatal meter* meter utilised in these poems. This is the first instance of a work set to music. *Akaval* and *kalippa* were the other popular meters used by poets during the Sangam age.

Post-Sangam Period

Didactic Age

The three centuries after the Sangam age witnessed an increase in the mutual interaction of Sanskrit and Tamil. A number of words and concepts relating to ethics, philosophy and religion were mutually borrowed and exchanged between the languages. Around 300 CE, the Tamil land was under the influence of a group of people known as the Kalabhras. The Kalabhras were Buddhist and a number of Buddhist authors flourished during this period. Jainism and Buddhism saw rapid growth. These authors, perhaps reflecting the austere nature of their faiths, created works mainly on morality and ethics. A number of Jain and Buddhist poets contributed to the creation of these didactic works as well as grammar and lexicography. The collection the minor eighteen anthology was of this period.

The best known of these works on ethics is the *Tirukkural* by Thiruvalluvar. The book is a comprehensive manual of ethics, polity and love, containing 1,330 distichs or *kural* divided into chapters of ten distichs each: the first thirty-eight on ethics, the next seventy on polity and the remainder on love.

Other famous works of this period are *Kalavali, Nalatiyar, Inna Narpathu* and *Iniyavai Narpathu*. The Jain texts *Nalatiyar* and *Pazhamozhi Nanuru* each consist of four hundred poems, each of which cites a proverb and then illustrates it with a story.

Hindu Devotional Period

After the fall of the Kalabhras around 600 CE saw a reaction from the thus far suppressed Hindus. The Kalabhras were replaced by the Pandyas in the south and by the Pallavas in the north. Even with the exit of the Kalabhras, the Jain and Buddhist influence still remained in Tamil Nadu. The early Pandya and the Pallava kings were followers of these faiths. The Hindu reaction to this apparent decline of their religion was growing and reached its peak during the later part of the seventh century. There was a widespread Hindu revival during which a huge body of Saiva and

Vaishnava literature was created. Many Saiva Nayanmars and Vaishnava Alvars provided a great stimulus to the growth of popular devotional literature. Karaikkal Ammaiyar who lived in the sixth century CE was the earliest of these Nayanmars. The celebrated Saiva hymnists Sundaramurthi, Thirugnana Sambanthar and Thirunavukkarasar (also known as *Appar*) were of this period. Of Appar's verses 3066 have survived. Sambandar sang 4169 verses. Together these form the first six books of the Saiva canon, collected by Nambi Andar Nambi in the tenth century. Sundarar wrote *Tiruttondartokai* which gives the list of sixty-two Nayanmars. This was later elaborated by Sekkilar in his *Periyapuranam* (4272 verses). Manikkavasagar, who lived around the eight century CE was a minister in the Pandya court. His *Tiruvasakam* consisting of over 600 verses is noted for its passionate devotion.

Along with the Saiva Nayanmars, Vaishnava Alvars were also producing devotional hymns and their songs were collected later into the Four Thousand Sacred Hymns (*Naalayira Divyap Prabhandham*). The three earliest Alvars were Poygai, Pudam and Pey. Each of these wrote one hundred *Venpas*. Tirumalisai Alwar who was a contemporary of the Pallava Mahendravarman I wrote such works as *Naanmugantiruvadiandadi*. Tirumangai Alvar who lived in the eighth century CE was a more prolific writer and his works constitute about a third of the Diyaprabhandam. Periyalvar and his adopted daughter Andal contributed nearly 650 hymns to the Vaishnava canon. Andal symbolised purity and love for the God and wrote her hymns addressing Vishnu as a lover. The hymn of Andal which starts with *Vaaranam*

Aayiram (One Thousand Elephants) tells of her dream wedding to Vishnu and is sung even today at Tamil Vaishnava weddings. Nammalvar, who lived in the ninth century, wrote *Tiruvaimoli*. It comprises 1,101 stanzas and is held in great esteem for its elucidation of the Upanishads. This corpus was collected by Nathamuni, around 950 CE and formed the classical and vernacular basis for Sri Vaishnavism.

Narrative Epics

Cilappatikaram is one of the outstanding works of general literature of this period. The authorship and exact date of the classic *Cilappatikaram* are not definitely known. Ilango Adigal, who is credited with this work was reputed to be the brother of the Sangam age Chera king Senguttuvan. However we have no information of such a brother in the numerous poems sung on the Chera king. The *Cilappatikaram* is unique in its vivid portrayal of the ancient Tamil land. This is unknown in other works of this period. *Cilappatikaram* and its companion epic *Manimekalai* are Buddhist in philosophy. *Manimekalai* was written by Sattanar who was a contemporary of Ilango Adigal. Manimekalai contains a long exposition of fallacies of logic which is considered to be based on the fifth century Sanskrit work *Nyayapravesa* by Dinnag. Kongu Velir, a Jain author wrote *Perunkathai* based on the Sanskrit *Brihatkatha*. *Valayapathi* and *Kundalakesi* are the names of two other narrative poems of this period written by a Jain and a Buddhist author respectively.

Medieval Literature

Imperial Cholas when the entire south India was under a single administration. The period between the eleventh and the thirteenth centuries, during which the Chola power was at its peak, there were relatively few foreign incursions and the life for the Tamil people was one of peace and prosperity. It also provided the opportunity for the people to interact with cultures beyond their own, as the Cholas ruled over most of the South India, Sri Lanka and traded with the kingdoms in southeast Asia. The Cholas built numerous temples, mainly for their favourite god Siva, and these were celebrated in numerous hymns.

The *Prabhanda* became the dominant form of poetry. The religious canons of Saiva and Vaishnava sects were beginning to be systematically collected and categorised. Nambi Andar Nambi, who was a contemporary of Rajaraja Chola I, collected and arranged the books on Saivism into eleven books called *Tirumurais*. The hagiology of Saivism was standardised in *Periyapuranam* (also known as *Tiruttondar Puranam*) by Sekkilar, who lived during the reign of Kulothunga Chola II (1133 – 1150 CE). Religious books on the Vaishnava sect were mostly composed in Sanskrit during this period.

The great Vaishnava leader Ramanuja lived during the reigns of Athirajendra Chola and Kulothunga Chola I, and had to face religious persecution from the Cholas who belonged to the Saiva sect. One of the best know Tamil work of this period is the *Ramavatharam* by Kamban who flourished during the reign of Kulottunga III. *Ramavatharam* is the greatest epic in Tamil Literature, and although the author states that he followed Valmiki, his work is not a mere translation or even an adaptation of the Sanskrit epic. Kamban imports into his narration the colour and landscape of his own time. A contemporary of Kamban was the famous poetess Auvaiyar who found great happiness in writing for young children. Her works, *Athichoodi* and *Konraiventhan* are even now generally read and taught in schools in Tamil Nadu. Her two other works, *Mooturai* and *Nalvali* were written for slightly older children. All the four works are didactic in character. They explain the basic wisdom that should govern mundane life.

Of the books on the Buddhist and the Jain faiths, the most noteworthy is the *Jivaka-chintamani* by the Jain ascetic Thirutakkadevar composed in the tenth century. *Viruttam* style of poetry was used for the first time for the verses in this book. The five Tamil epics *Jivaka-chintamani, Cilappatikaram, Manimekalai, Kundalakesi* and *Valayapathi* are collectively known as the The Five Great Epics of Tamil Literature. There were a number of books written on Tamil grammar. *Yapperungalam* and *Yapperungalakkarigai* were two works on prosody by the Jain ascetic Amirtasagara. Buddamitra wrote *Virasoliyam,* another work on Tamil grammar, during the reign of Virarajendra Chola. *Virasoliyam* attempts to find synthesis between Sanskrit and Tamil grammar. Other grammatical works of this period are *Nannul* by Pavanandi, *Vaccanandi Malai* by Neminatha, and the annotations on the puram theme, *Purapporul Venpamalai* by Aiyanaridanar.

There were biographical and political works such as Jayamkondar's *Kalingattupparani,* a semi-historical account on the two invasion of Kalinga by Kulothunga Chola I. Jayamkondar was a poet-laureate in the Chola court and his work is a fine example of the balance between fact and fiction the poets had to tread. Ottakuttan, a close contemporary of Kambar, wrote three *Ulas* on Vikrama Chola, Kulothunga Chola II and Rajaraja Chola II.

Vijayanagar and Nayak Period

The period from 1300 CE to 1650 was a period of constant change in the political situation of Tamil Nadu. The Tamil country was invaded by the armies of the Delhi Sultanate and defeated the Pandya kingdom. The collapse of the Delhi Sultanate triggered the rise of the Bahmani Sultans in the Deccan. Vijayanagar empire rose from the ashes of the kingdoms of Hoysalas and Chalukyas and eventually conquered the entire south India. The Vijayanagar kings appointed regional governors to rule various territories of their kingdom and Tamil Nadu was ruled by the Madurai Nayaks, Thanjavur Nayaks and Gingee Nayaks. This period saw a large output of philosophical works, commentaries, epics and devotional poems. A number of monasteries (*Mathas*) were established by the various Hindu sects and these began to play a prominent role in educating the people. Numerous authors were of either the Saiva or the Vaishnava sects. The Vijayanagar kings and their Nayak governors were ardent Hindus and they patronised these *mathas*. Although the kings and the governors of the Vijayanagar empire spoke Kannada and Telugu they encouraged the growth of Tamil literature as we find no slowing down in the literary output during this period.

There was a large output of works of philosophical and religious in nature, such as the *Sivananabodam* by Meykandar. At the end of the fourteenth century Svarupananda Desikar worte two anthologies on the philosophy os *Advaita*, the *Sivaprakasapperundirattu*. Arunagirinatha who lived in Tiruvannamalai in the fourteenth century wrote *Tiruppugal*. Around 1,360 verses of unique lilt and set to unique metres these poems are on the god Muruga. Madai Tiruvengadunathar, an official in the court of the Madurai Nayak, wrote *Meynanavilakkam* on the Advaita Vedanta. Sivaprakasar, in the early seventeenth century wrote a number of works on the Saiva philosophy. Notable among these is the *Nanneri* which deals with moral instructions. A considerable par to the religious and philosophical literature of the age took the form of *Puranas* or narrative epics. A number of these were written on the various deities of the temples in Tamil Nadu and are known as Sthala Puranas, based on legend and folklore. One of the most important of the epics was the Mahabharatam by Villiputturar. He translated Vyasa's epic into Tamil and named it *Villibharatam*. *Kanthapuranam* on the god Murugan was written by Kacchiappa Sivachariyar who lived in the fifteenth century. This work was based broadly on the Sanskrit *Skandapurana*. Varatungarama Pandya, a Pandya king of the period was a littérateur of merit and wrote *Paditrruppattanthathi*. He also translated into Tamil the erotic book known as *Kokkoha* from Sanskrit.

This period also an age of many commentaries of ancient Tamil works. Adiyarkunallar wrote an annotation on Cilappatikaram. Senavaraiyar wrote a commentary on the Tolkappiyam. Then came the famous Parimelalagar whose commentary on the Tirukural is still considered one of the best available. Other famous annotators such as Perasiriyar and Naccinarikiniyar wrote commentaries on the various work of Sangam literature. The first Tamil dictionary was attempted by Mandalapurusha who compiled the lexicon *Nigandu Cudamani*. Thayumanavar, who lived in the early eighteenth century, is famous for a number of short poems of philosophical nature.

The seventeenth century also saw for the first time literary works by Muslim and Christian authors. The population of Muslims and Christians were growing in Tamil Nadu with the influences of the Delhi Sultanate and the growing European missionaries. Syed Khader known in Tamil as Sithaakkathi, lived in the seventeenth century and was a great patron of all Tamil poets. He commissioned the creation of a biography on the Islamic prophet Muhammad. Omar known in Tamil as Umarupulavar, wrote *Seerapuranam* on the life of Muhammad. Costanzo Giuseppe Beschi (1680-1746), better known as Veeramamunivar, compiled the first dictionary in Tamil. His *Chathurakarathi* was the first to list the Tamil words in alphabetical order. Veeramamunivar is also remembered for his Christian theological epic *Thembavani* on the life and teaching of Jesus Christ.

Modern Era

During the eighteenth and the nineteenth century Tamil Nadu witnessed some of the most profound changes in the political scene. The traditional Tamil ruling clans were superseded by European colonists and their sympathisers. The Tamil society underwent a deep cultural shock with the imposition of western cultural influences. The Hindu religious establishments attempted to stem the tide of change and to safeguard the Tamil cultural values. Notable among these were the Saiva monasteries at Tiruvavaduthurai, Dharmapuram, Thiruppananthal and Kundrakudi. Meenakshisundaram Pillai (1815-1876) was a Tamil scholar who taught Tamil at one of these monasteries. He wrote more than eighty books consisting of over 200,000 poems. He is more famous however for encouraging U.V.Swaminatha Iyer to go search for

Tamil books that have been lost for centuries. Gopalakrishna Bharathi lived during the early nineteenth century. He wrote numerous poems and lyrics set to tune in Carnatic music. His most famous work is the *Nandan Charitam* on the life of Nandanar who having been born in a sociologically lower caste, faces and overcomes the social obstacles in achieving his dream of visiting the Chidambaram temple. This work is a revolutionary social commentary considering the period in which it was written, although Gopalakrishna Bharati expanded on the story in *Periyapuranam*. Ramalinga Adigal (Vallalar) (1823-1874) wrote the devotional poem *Tiruvarutpa* is considered to be a work of great beauty and simplicity.

Maraimalai Adigal (1876-1950) advocated for the purity of Tamil and wanted to clean it of words with Sanskrit influences. One of the great Tamil poets of this period was Subramanya Bharathi. His works are stimulating in their progressive themes like freedom and feminism. Bharathy introduced a new poetic style into the somewhat rigid style of Tamil poetry writing, which had followed the rules set down in the *Tolkaappiyam*. His *puthukkavithai* (Lit.:new poetry) broke the rules and gave poets the freedom to express themselves. He also wrote Tamil prose in the form of commentaries, editorials, short stories and novels. Some of these were published in the Tamil daily *Swadesamitran* and in his Tamil weekly *India*. Inspired by Bharathi, many poets resorted to poetry as a means of reform. Bharathidasan was one such poet. U.V.Swaminatha Iyer, was instrumental in the revival of interest in the Sangam age literature in Tamil Nadu. He travelled all over the Tamil country, collecting, deciphering and publishing ancient books such as

Cilappatikaram, Kuruntokai, etc. He published over 90 books and wrote *En caritham,* an autobiography.

Tamil Novel

The novel as a genre of literature arrived in Tamil in the third quarter of nineteenth century, more than a century after it became popular with English writers. Its emergence was perhaps facilitated by the growing population of Tamils with a western education and exposure to popular English fiction. Mayuram Vedanayagam Pillai wrote the first Tamil novel *Prathapa Mudaliar Charithram* in 1879. This was a romance with an assortment of fables, folk tales and even Greek and Roman stories, written with the entertainment of the reader as the principal motive. It was followed by *Kamalambal Charitram* by B.R. Rajam Iyer in 1893 and *Padmavathi Charitram* by A. Madhaviah in 1898. These two portray the life of Brahmins in 19th century rural Tamil Nadu, capturing their customs and habits, beliefs and rituals.

Although it was primarily a powerful narration of the common man's life in a realistic style spiced with natural humour, Rajam Iyer's novel has a spiritual and philosophical undertone. Madhaviah tells the story in a more realistic way with a searching criticism of the upper caste society, particularly the sexual exploitation of girls by older men. Mr. D. Jayakanthan - the real trend setter in modern day Tamil novels.He has not only enriched the high traditions of literary traditions of Tamil language but has also made outstanding contribution towards the shaping of Indian literature. His literature presents a deep and sensitive understanding of complex human nature and is an authentic and vivid index of Indian reality. His famous novel Sila Nerangalil Sila Manithargal notable one.

Since the 1990s, a number of experimental and avant-garde Tamil writers have emerged as major figures, including Charu Nivedita, whose fractured narratives are often full of graphic sex and violence, and Konangi, who mixes classical Tamil inflections with experimental sound poetry.

Popular Fiction

Crime and detective fiction has enjoyed wide popularity in Tamil Nadu since the 1930s. Popular authors in the years before independence included Kurumbur Kuppusami and Vaduvur Duraisami Iyengar.

In the 1950s and 60s, Tamilvanan's detective hero Shankarlal carried readers to a variety of foreign locales, while using a pure Tamil with very few Hindi or English loan words. From the 1980s to the present, leading authors include Subha, Pattukkottai Prabakar and Rajesh Kumar (who also writes science fiction and other genres). These writers are often extremely prolific, with hundreds or even thousands of short novels to their credit, and one or more short novel published in a monthly periodical. Indra Soundar Rajan, another popular modern author, writes supernatural crime thrillers usually based around Hindu mythology.

In the 1950s and 60s, Chandilyan wrote a number of very popular historical romance novels set in medieval India or on medieval trade routes with Malaysia, Indonesia and Europe.

Modern romance novels are represented by the current bestselling author in the Tamil language, Ramanichandran.

Though sales of Tamil pulp fiction have declined since the hey-day of the mid-1990s, and many writers have turned to the more lucrative television serial market, there remains a thriving scene.

The rise of the Internet has triggered a dramatic growth in the number of Tamil blogs and specialist portals catering to political and social issues.

17

Telugu Literature

Telugu literature flowered in the early 16th century under the Vijayanagar empire, of which Telugu was the court language. Telugu is Vikriti, that is a language formed by modification of sanskrit and prakrit. It would appear that Andhras adopted a form of Prakrit which, in course of development, became the immediate ancestor of Telugu. Every Telugu grammatical rule is laboriously deduced from a Sanskrit canon.

Early Telugu Literature

Nannaya Bhattarakudu's *Andhra Mahabharatamu* produced around the 11th century is commonly referred to as the first Telugu literary composition (Aadi kaavyam). Although there is evidence of Telugu literature before Nannaya, he is still referred to as *Aadi Kavi* (the first poet) because he was the first poet to establish a formal grammar for written Telugu. Nannaya meticulously laid down the ground rules and semantics of writing in Telugu by borrowing from Sanskrit grammar and inventing original rules. Telugu literature until then was Prakrit based and devoid of a grammar. Nannaya was only able to finish the first two chapters and a part of the third chapter of the *Mahabharata.*

It is also believed that the pre-Nannaya Literature probably Jain was destroyed by the Kakateeya rulers who were primarily Kapu and Kamma rulers and fanatically anti-Sanskrit. While some believe Nanne Choadudu's famous work Kumara Sambhavam was composed in 10th century before Nannaya's Mahabaratha, others place Nanne Choadudu between the period of Nannaya and Tikkana.

Andhra Mahabharatamu was later furthered by Tikanna Somayaji (1205–1288) who wrote all the remaining chapters (4-18). Yerrapragada (fourteenth century) finished the epic by completing the remaining part of third chapter. He masterfully mimics Nannaya's style in the beginning, slowly changes tempo and finishes the chapter in the writing style of Tikkana. Nannaya, Tikanna and Yerrapragada are known as the *Kavitraya* or the three great poets of Telugu for this mammoth effort. Other such translations like Marana's *Markandeya Puranam,* Ketana's *Dasakumara Charita,* Yerrapragada's *Harivamsam* followed. Many scientific works like *Ganitasarasangrahamu* by Pavuluri Mallana and *Prakirnaganitamu* by Eluganti Peddana are written in 12th century in Telugu.

Some of the early landmarks are Srinathudu's *Sringara Naishadham,* Potana's *Dasamaskandham,* Jakkana's *Vikramarka Charitra* and Talapaka Timmakka's *Subhadra Kalyanam.* Literary activities flourished, during the rule of Vijayanagara dynasty. Krishnadevaraya' s time (sixteenth century) is considered the golden age in the history of Telugu literature. The king, a poet himself, introduced the *Prabandha* (a kind of love poetry) in Telugu literature with his *Amukta Malyada.* His court had the *Ashtadiggajas* (literally "eight elephants") who were the known to be the greatest of poets of that time.

Some critics dismiss the following period, dominated by prabandhas, as a decadent age. Of the dozens of works of the eighteenth to mid nineteenth century, Kankanti Paparaju's *Uttara Ramayana* in *campu* style and the play *Vishnumayavilasa* stand out. Other genres bloomed at the same time. Innumerable Yakshaganas or indigenous dramas of song and prose works were also produced. Tyagaraja (1767–1847) of Tanjore composed devotional songs in Telugu, which form a big part of the repertoire of Carnatic music.

Modern Telugu Literature

Charles Philip Brown (1798-1884), was an employee of East India Company whose quest to understand the basic structure of Telugu language made him embark upon an exploration of Telugu literature. His pursuit is said to be the only present day source of the many classics in Telugu literature.

Although the first printed Telugu book was out in 1796, it was a while before the modern period in Telugu literature set in. Young men acquainted with English literature were influenced by Shelley, Keats and Wordsworth, and a new type of romantic poetry called the *Bhavakavithwam* was born.

The father of modern Telugu literature is Kandukuri Viresalingam Pantulu (1848—1919), who wrote a novel, Rajasekhara Charitamu, inspired by the Vicar of Wakefield. He was the first person in modern times to use literature to eradicate social evils. He was followed by Rayaprolu Subba Rao, Gurazada Appa Rao, Viswanatha Satyanarayana, Katuri Venkateswara Rao, Jashuva, Devulapalli Venkata Krishna Sastry, Sri

Sri, Puttaparty Narayana Charyulu and others in the sphere of poetry. Viswanatha Satyanarayana had won the coveted Jnanapith Award. "Kanyasulkam" (Bride-Money), the first social play in Telugu by Gurazada Appa Rao was a thumping success. We also find the progressive movement, free verse movement and Digambara style finding expression in Telugu verse. The well-known modern Telugu novelists were Unnava Lakshminarayana (of Malapalli fame), Viswanatha Satyanarayana (Veyi Padagalu), Kutumba Rao and Buchchi Babu. Telugu is specially known for its daring experiments in the field of poetry and drama.

Poetry

Towards the end of the 19th century there was a sea change in the social, cultural and literary outlook of the Telugus. Kandukuri Veeresalingam Pantulu (1848-1919) was the first to make literature an effective instrument of social change. Gidugu Rama Murthy Pantulu (1863-1940) was a great scholar and an authority on grammar and usage. He advocated a radical change in the use of Telugu in the journals and literary works.

Gurajada Appa Rao Pantulu (1861-1915) a contemporary of both the poets chose to break away from the traditional learned diction and paved way for new trends. The influence of English and Englishman was confined to literary modes and an inspiration for democratic ideals.

The romantic poetry of three decades starting from 1910 is called *bhava kavita*. It was against *Prabhanda* School of poetry in diction, technique and theme. The influence of English Romantic poets was profound. D.V. Krishna Sastri was by far the most romantic of the romantic school of poets. His *Krishna Paksham, Prayasam* and *Urvashi* epitomized the new trend in Telugu poetry.

Yenki Patalu by Nanduri Venkata Subbarao (1895-1957) centered around *Yenki* written in the accent of the rustics, and to admit them to poetry appeared to be a sacrilege. Kavikondala Venkata Rao (1892-1969) was a nature poet. Grass flowers, an old woman who collects the left over grain in the fields after the crop is reaped, and a little girl on a country boat are subjects for his poems. Duvvuri Rami Reddy's *Krishivaludu* describes the life of a farmer and his family in all seasons. Kodali Subba Rao's *Kshetram* is one of the most moving collections of poems, highlighting the glory of Andhras during the period of Reddy and Vijayanagar rulers.

Tirupati Venkata kavulu—Divakarla Tirupati Satri and Chellapilla Venkata Sastri dominated the literary scene. Experts in *Satavadhanam,* they popularized poetry. Pingali (1894-19723) and Katuri(1895-1962) showed interest in rural life. *Tolakari, Soundara Nandam, Gudigantalu Hridayam* are their popular works.

Viswanatha Satyanarayana (1895-1976) strode the literary world like a colossus. His *Veyi Padagalu* brilliantly records the agony of change the country was experiencing in contemporary times. *Andhra Paurusham* and *Andhra aprasasti* were written with patriotic fervour. *Ritusamharam* has a romantic touch and *KInnerasani* is about a lovely rivulet joining river Godavari. *Sringara Veed, Sri Krishna Sangeetham, Maa Swami* and *Madhyakkaralu* are some of his well known works.

Sistla Uma Maheshwara Rao experimented with the metre and paved way for a proletarian revolution. In *Vishnu Dhanuvu* he used traditional ideas and expression, but it structure was novel. Pattabhi (1914 - 2006) in *Fidelu Ragala Dozen* took the readers by surprise breaking the grammatical, semantic and syntactic rules. *Kaita Naa Dayita, Pranayabhishekam* gave anew dimension with his experiments in versification and rhyme scheme.

In 1943 Abhyudaya Rachayitala Sangham was conducted at Tenali with Tapi Dharma Rao as president. Marxist thinking and Unnava Lakshminarayana's *maala pilla* influenced young poets like Sri Sri. His *Mahaprasthanam, MaroPrasthanam* was forerunner of ARASAM POETRY. He was influenced by surrealism. His other works include *Siri Siri Muvva Satakam, Praasa kreedalu* and *Limericks*.

Bellamkonda Ramdas, Yelchuri Subrahmanyam and Kundurti Anjaneyaulu published a book of poems entitled *Niagara*. It is about the ultimate victory of the revolutionary forces and the revolt of the downtrodden.Kundurti published *Nagaram lo Vaana, Asha, Megha mala and Idhi na Janda*. Rentala Goplakrishna was very close to Niagara poets. His *Akali patalu, Sangharshana* are soul stirring. A. Soma Sunder's Vajrayudham, *Okka Kondalo Veyi Silpalu, Godavari Jala Pralayam* are very reflective. ogineni Venkateshwara rao's *Death in the palm of the Hand, Letter from Mother to her Son* are poignant tales of atrocity in the hands of police. Anisetty SubbaRao's *Agni Veena* and Gangineni's *Idayani* are examples of progressive poetry.

Dasarathi Krishnamacharya (1926-87) voiced inpowerful classical verse the resentment and anger of

Telangana against the autocratic rule of the Nizam. He will be remembered for his *Rudraveenai* and *Mahaandhrodayami*. Sri Kaloji Narayana Rao's (1914) *Naa Godava* is ironic in tone.C. VijayaLakshmi's *Karu chikati lo Kanti Rekah* castigates corruption, institutionalized prostitution and other social evils.

Arudhra (Bhagavathula Sadasiva Sankara Sastry 1925-98) is a man of great repute. *Twame Vaaham, CineVaali* are his technically innovative works. Narla Chiranjeevi, Narapa Reddy, Tummala Venkata Ramayya etc were a part of the progressive writers' movement. By 1955 the Progressive Writer's Movement had stagnated.

Devarakonda Bala Gangadhara Tilak (1921-66) was a lover of words, of flowers and singing birds. He knew the horrors of war and was moved by the sufferings of the poor. His *Amrutham Kurisina Rathri* shows him as a dreamer and a romantic. Tilak's poetry became an enigma for the progressive group. Kundurthi called him Bhavabhyudhaya poet. Tilak gave fillip to a new kind of poetry called *Anubhuti* poetry.

By mid- sixties the progressive group was groping in darkness. Six young men, Nagna Muni (M.H.Kesava Rao), Nikhileshwar (Yadava Reddy), Jwala Mukhi (Veera Raghavacharyulu), Cherabanda Raju (Baddam Bhaskara Reddy), Bhairavayya (Man Mohan Sahay) and Maha Swapna (Kammisetti Venkateshwara Rao) stormed into the literary field and called themselves *Digambara* poets. They found hypocrisy all around an dman was getting crushed under the iron heels of money power. He should throw off his mask and pretensions, and see himself in true colors. They rejected all traditional literature and with it religion, Sahitya Academies and cinema culture.

They led the formation of VIRASAM poets (Viplava Rachayitala Sangham). *Thudi Payanam, Tholi Vijayam, Bhummyakasalu, Jatkavala* became popular during this period. K.G. Satya Murthy popularly known as Sivudu wrote *Narudo- Bhaskaruda* and is considered to be the first revolutionary song. The songs Naa Chelli Chandramma, Amma are very moving poems. Nagna Muni's *Paalu Erra Baddayi, Koyya Gurram* are some of his best poems. Cherabanda Raju's *Gamyam,Kanthiyudham, Gowramma Kalalu, Paleru patalu* are very effective. Vara Vara Rao, K.V. Ramana Reddy, Gaddar, Vangapandu Prasada Rao, K.Siva Reddy, C.V. Krishna Rao are influenced by this movement. Seela Veeraraju's *Adde Gadi, Hridayam,Malli Velugu, Kitiki Kannu, Yeti Valuku Yeduru Yerra Dabba Railu* were well received. Jugganti Jagannadham's *Pathala Garige* and *Indian Private Limited* are experiences of the village. Sasanka's *Naya Jamana* projects the poet's dream of a new world where inequalities are banned. Seela Subhadra Devi produced *Akali Nrutyaṁ*.

Gunturu Seshendra Sarma (b 1927 -) started Kavi Sena Movement and published its manifesto in 1978 - he called it the manifesto of modern science of aesthetics. He produced several volumes of poetry- *Naa Desam- Na Prajalu, Sesha Jyothsna, Munday Suryudu, Neerai Parai Poindi* etc. His works have been translated into several Indian languages. Profile and a few poems of Seshendra Sharma are included in the section *'Masters.'*

Ismail was an *Anubhuti* poet. He proclaimed that bhava Kavi's preoccupation is with subjective experiences and feelings. He has poems on Bull's eye, A donkey, A well, A wood pecker and A window. His poem *Chilukalu Vaalina Chettu* is a fine poem. *Mritya Vriksham, Chettu Naa Adarsam, Raatri Vachina Rahasyapu Vaana, Baalchi lo Chandrodayam* is abounding with beauty and goodness.

Indraganti Srikanth Sarma's *Anubhuti Geetalu* published in 1976 wherein the poet is intent on communicating an experience, which by its very nature is abstract, poetry can not resort to an intellectual exercise, rather the poet translates it into images and symbols.

Vegunta Mohan Prasad popularly known as MO is a difficult poet because of his surrealistic leanings, his personal symbols and the range of his allusions.

Kothapally Satya Srimannarayana is an Anubhuti poet and a keen observer of nature and human feelings. Godavari Sarma's *Godavari Gala Galalu* presents humanistic values. Raju is also an anubhuti poet at a different level.

Ajanta (Penumarthi Viswanatha Sastri)'s *Chetlu Kooluthunna Drisyam* portrays modern man's despair, his loneliness and helplessness.*Mrityuvu Hasya Priyatvam* telescopes birth, growth and death of a poem and a human into a unified experience of agony, strife, uncertainty and ultimately death. The word is the strategic unit in the poem the meaning of which forever eludes the reader's grasp.

Short Story

After the '50s in the last century of the previous millennium the print media began playing the biggest ever role in promoting enthusiastic new comers in fiction, long and short. Films needed good themes and stories. Many novels were made into films and very successful ones at that. A number of journals and even some daily newspapers serialized long fiction. Telugu did not lag behind. The realization of the inadequacy of the vote as an equalizing force resulted in powerful voices demanding an opportunity for power sharing, hungering for social equality in real life situation. Reservations have been found to be inadequate and for that reason not the complete answer for social justice. Short story thrived. There was a boom of long fiction, especially by the fair sex, who instinctively know how to drive home their point in a myriad ways. They won their point and the hearts of the readers. Their voice was persuasive, convincing and logical: they came to be heard.

The brightest side of the picture showed the emerging trend of following the basic trend of Nativism ('our' tribulations, 'our' problems, 'our' professions, 'our' people, and 'our' own spoken language) as seen in the brand new writers. Though it remains to be seen as to how long it continues with verve to crystallize into a movement, there has been a prolific production of short fiction along with free verse. Register-wise, profession-wise, even caste-wise writing to highlight social problems faithfully and realistically acquired a good 'space'. Telangana writing, Rayalaseema writing, came to attract wide reader attention. Fiction like *Khakee Batukulu* dealing with experiences of working in the police dept, or *Ramesam Revenue Udyogam* describing the experiences of working in the revenue department too, have come up.

Things have come to such a pass that some saw 'fragmentation' of literature. Seminars were conducted on the subject. "Fragmentation of Literature" is possibly an attitudinal misnomer for 'diversification' and 'democratization' of creative writing. It is a fear that literature is being broken to cater to particular peoples in a language community. In the Indian context, the depressed classes, the hitherto neglected, are writing for a clientele, which is very limited. Yearning for identity, personal or group related and individual insights are basic to creative expression. Diversity is not fragmentation.

With the perceptions of literature undergoing some kind of expansion, new perspectives opened up. Earlier the target readers for the writers have been all Telugu-speaking people. The attention and the purview of the writer is focussed sharply on people speaking a particular regional variety and describing a particular strata or class of people with a sense of social reality tempered with sociological consciousness, *saamajika spruha*. With this the short story began coming up powerfully in regional varieties of expression, focussing on the downtrodden, the oppressed and the neglected and those from the lowest of the low occupations.

In the hands of some writers, as a genre, short story went on expanding the techniques in narration, description and the handling of dialogue, exploring the charm of 'categories' and 'labels' from other languages and cultures. The influences have not been only from other countries but also from other regions in our own country. There has been a slowly growing demand for fiction translated from our *bhasha* (Indian languages) short stories. KATHA has come up as a hard working non-commercial voluntary organization. The attitudes of writers from *bhashas*, the points of their focus, their empathy for the weak are shaping the story in Telugu. The enormous popularity of a monthly like VIPULA is a case in point. Even other Telugu periodicals are including translated stories in their wares.

For the last two decades, Telugu short story has been forging ahead with rapid strides. Writers writing in a 'variety' of regional languages have come into deserved prominence. Among the many a few could be easily cited readily: besides the already prominent like Naveen, Mudiganti Sujata Reddy, Yashoda Reddy and Kasila Pratapa Reddy, several others made very singificant contributions. They are Dr Chandrasekhara Rao, Kaluva Mallayya, Peddinti Ashok Kumar, Aitha Chandrayya to name some. These have brought into the fore the agony of the neglected region and the neglected among the pitiably poor in the rural areas of Telangana. The media justifiably promoted the new writers with zeal and verve. Some writers went beyond writing stories, which riveted the attention of the complacent rest of the Andhra Pradesh. There was a demand to recognize their language as Telanganam with status equivalent to that of Telugu.

A Telugu story should have telugudanam, the quality of being Telugu." It is relevant to recall here that in the good old world *Andhra Patrika,* while announcing the Deepavali Story Contest would lay down that the entries of the stories should reflect this telugudanam in character, incident as well as the culture , life style etc. This is fair enough.

But what if the language 'deliberately' and 'thoughtlessly' becomes incomprehensible when used for all characters and descriptions just to make it correspond to a particular variety if language? Writing offered like this, readers would not be able to understand and there would be near breakdown of communication.

Against the background of a demand for a separate state for the people of Telangana, the vociferous demands of people are understandable. A newspaper item written by one from Telangana was: "Are language battles inevitable?" Telugu has only one word yuddham for both war and battle, said Choppadandi Sudhakar. S. Shoba Devi pleaded for a language movement. These ideas are really irrelevant in the discussion of short story in Telugu. People began to point out that Telugu story began with Gunadhya and Hala and the modern short story began with Madapati Hanumantha Rao and Suravarapu Pratapa Reddy. One vociferously held that it was sheer injustice that Gurajada and his Vizianagaram should be given the credit or somebody else, since it was Karimnagar, which produced the first short story. Another wrote that Siddipuram (today's Siddipet) as the birthplace and location of a mine of stories.

Regional and even varieties of social class levels have come up in recent years. This is widening the horizons of the short story from the point of language and expression and different styles and preoccupations. 'Chaurasta,' already referred to, 'Ootabaayi' (Peddinti Ashok Kumar) and 'Jeevani' (Dr V.Chandrasekhara Rao) hold the mirror upto a specific regional reality. *'Mittoorodikathalu'* (Naamini Subrahmanyam Naidu) written in a variety of the language of Rayalaseema is a class by itself. Munipalle Raju's *'Astitwaaniki aavala'* (purported to be in the genre of Magical Realism), drew praise as well as hard criticism. There is evidently a risk of labelling one's own writing with terms and categories perfected by outsiders. If labels are a must we have to evolve them ourselves with enough theoretical buttressing. Somasunder, the reputed poet provocatively titled his critique on Munipalle's book *'Rokali thalaku chuttukunna kathakudu,'* the storywriter who tied the tall wooden pestle round his head.

These stories are philosophical in a sense but surely readable for the complexity and newness they have. Somaraju Suseela's *'Illeramma kathalu'* (Brahmin, 'Familectic") are replete with fresh insights, observation and the truth of life. These opened up a new vista of life.

There is more to short story than mere reform or search for identity after fifty and odd years of self-government. To say this is no denigration of either *samajika spruha* or *astitwa aakaanksha*. As a genre of imaginative literature and creative self-expression, it has other functions too – like charting the unmapped regions of the mind with insight and imagination. Social realism is fine but there is a more vital kind of realism, the psychological. With the same Nativist touch and social awareness individual psyches too could be explored against the Telugu background in a suitable artistic form. When this is accomplished, Telugu story can aspire to reach a wider readership enlarging its clientele by exploring fresh regions of the mind and new areas hitherto unnoticed.

18

Urdu Literature

Urdu literature has a long and colorful history that is inextricably tied to the development of that very language, Urdu, in which it is written. While it tends to be heavily dominated by poetry, the range of expression achieved in the voluminous library of a few major verse forms, especially the ghazal and nazm, has led to its continued development and expansion into other styles of writing, including that of the short story, or afsana. It is today most popular in the countries of India and Pakistan and is finding interest in foreign countries primarily through South Asians.

Beginnings

Urdu literature may be said to find its provenance some time around the 14th century in India amongst the sophisticated gentry of Persian courts. The presence of the Muslim gentry in a largely Hindu India, while clearly acknowledged, did not so nearly dominate the consciousness of the Urdu poet as much as did the continuing traditions of Islam and Persia. The very color of the Urdu language, with a vocabulary almost evenly split between Sanskrit-derived Prakrit and Arabo-Persian words, was a reflection of the newness of cultural amalgamation and yet the insistence on retaining what was best and most beautiful about the lands of Afghanistan and Persia.

A man who exercised great influence on the initial growth of not only Urdu literature, but the language itself (which only truly took shape as distinguished from both Persian and proto-Hindi around the 14th century) was the famous Amir Khusro. Credited, indeed, with the very systematization of northern Indian classical music, known as Hindustani, he wrote works in both Persian and Hindavi, frequently engaging in ingenious mixes of the two. While the couplets that come down from him in are representative of a latter-Prakrit Hindi bereft of Arabo-Persian vocabulary, his influence on court viziers and writers must have been mighty, for but a century after his passing Quli Qutub Shah was seen to take to a language that may be safely said to be Urdu.

Poetry and Prose

Urdu literature was generally composed more of poetry than of prose. The prose component of Urdu literature was mainly restricted to the ancient form of long-epic stories called Daastaan. These long-epic stories would deal with magical and otherwise fantastic creatures and events in a very complicated plot.

Urdu poetry started after the period mentioned earlier in the Deccan (South India). With time the usage of Urdu for poetry spread to Northern India. The most well developed vessel of poetry has turned out to be the Ghazal which has by far exceeded all other forms of Urdu poetry by its quality and quantity within the cosmos of Urdu.

18th-century literature

Well known Urdu poets from this era include:

- Faaiz Dehlvi
- Khan Arzu
- Mubarak Abru
- Mir Taqi Mir
- Mirza Sauda
- Mir Dard
- Mirza Ghalib

Later writers have come to identify this period as one of comparative political instability, economic depression and social devolution. Hence the literature of this period is either generally in keeping with the epicurian attitude of people trying to find solace in the arms of literature; or of those horrified by the inertia of the changes, and their inability to effect change

Short Fiction

Wellknown Urdu Short Fiction (AFSANA) writers of the century are:

1) Premchand
2) Dr. Rafiq Hussain
3) Rajinder Singh Bedi
4) Saadat Hassan Manto
5) Ahmad Nadeem Qasmi
6) Ashfaq Ahmed
7) Bano Qudsia
8) Bhupendra nath Kaushik "fikr"
9) Ghulam Abbas

Forms of Urdu writing

Urdu writing in its various primitive forms can be traced to Muhammad Urfi (Tadhkirah - 1228 AD), Amir Khusro (1259-1325 AD) and Kwaja Muhammad Husaini (1318-1422 AD). As Urdu started flourishing in the kingdoms of Golconda and Bijapur, the earliest writings in Urdu are in the Dakhni (Deccani) dialect. The Sufi saints were the earliest promoters of the Dakhni Urdu. The Sufi-saint Hazrat Khwaja Banda Nawaz Gesudaraz is considered to be the first prose writer of Dakhni Urdu and some treatises like Merajul Ashiqin and Tilawatul Wajud are attributed to him but his authorship is open to doubt. The first literary work in Urdu is that of Bidar poet Fakhruddin Nizami's mathnavi 'Kadam Rao Padam Rao' written between 1421 and 1434 A.D. Kamal Khan Rustami (Khawar Nama) and Nusrati (Gulshan-e-Ishq, Ali Nama and Tarikh-e-Iskandari) were two great poets of Bijapur. Muhammed Quli Qutb Shah, the greatest of Golconda Kings who was a distinguished poet, is credited with introducing a secular content to otherwise predominantly religious Urdu poetry. His poetry focused on love, nature and social life of the day.

Among the other important writers of Dakhni Urdu were Shah Miranji Shamsul Ushaq (Khush Nama and Khush Naghz), Shah Burhanuddin Janam, Mullah Wajhi (Qutb Mushtari and Sabras), Ghawasi (Saiful Mulook-O-Badi-Ul-Jamal and Tuti Nama), Ibn-e-Nishati (Phul Ban) and Tabai (Bhahram-O-Guldandam). Wajhi's Sabras is considered to be a masterpiece of great literary and philosophical merit. Vali Mohammed or Vali Dakhni (Diwan) was one of the most prolific Dakhni poets of the medieval period. He developed the form of the ghazal. When his Diwan

(Collection of Ghazals and other poetic genres) reached Delhi, the poets of Delhi who were engaged in composing poetry in Persian language, were much impressed and they also started writing poetry in Urdu, which they named Rekhta.

The medieval Urdu poetry grew under the shadow of Persian poetry. Unlike the Hindi poetry, which grew out of the Indian soil, Urdu poetry was initially fed with Persian words and imagery. Sirajuddin Ali Khan Arzu and Shaikh Sadullah Gulshan were the earliest promoters of Urdu language in North India. By the beginning of the 18th century a more sophisticated North Indian variation of the Urdu language began to evolve through the writings of Shaikh Zahooruddin Hatim (1699-1781 AD), Mirza Mazhar Jan-e-Janan (1699-1781 AD) Khwaja Mir Dard (1719- 1785 AD), Mir Taqi Mir (1722-1810 AD), Mir Hasan (1727-1786 AD) and Mohammed Rafi Sauda (1713-1780 AD). Sauda has been described as the foremost satirist of Urdu literature during the 18th Century. His Shahr Ashob and Qasida Tazheek-e-Rozgar are considered as masterpieces of Urdu literature. Mir Hassan's mathnavi Sihr-ul-Bayan and Mir Taqi Mir's mathnavies provided a distinct Indian touch to the language. Mir's works, apart from his six Diwans, include Nikat-ush-Shora (Tazkira) and Zikr-se-Mir (Autobiography).

Shaik Ghulam Hamdani Mushafi (1750-1824), Insha Allah Khan (Darya-e-Latafat and Rani Ketaki), Khwaja Haider Ali Atish, Daya Shankar Naseem (mathnavi: Gulzare-e-Naseem), Nawab Mirza Shauq (Bahr-e-Ishq, Zahr-e-Ishq and Lazzat-e-Ishq) and Shaik Imam Bakhsh Nasikh were the early poets of Lucknow. Mir Babar Ali Anees (1802-1874) excelled in the art of writing marsiyas.

The last Mughal emperor Bahadur Shah Zafar was a poet with unique style, typified by difficult rhymes, excessive word play and use of idiomatic language. He has authored four voluminous Diwans. Before the national uprising of 1857 the reign of Bahadur Shah Zafar witnessed the luxurious spring of Urdu poetry immediately followed by the chilly winds of autumn. Shaik Ibrahim Zauq was the Shah's mentor in poetry. Next to Sauda he is considered to be the most outstanding composer of qasidas (panegyrics). Hakim Momin Khan Momin wrote ghazals in a style peculiar to him. He used ghazal exclusively for expressing emotions of love. Any description of Urdu literature can never be complete without the mention of Mirza Asadullah Khan Ghalib (1797-1869), who is considered as the greatest of all the Urdu poets. With his passion for originality, Ghalib brought in a renaissance in Urdu poetry. In the post - Ghalib period, Dagh (b. 1831) emerged as a distinct poet, whose poetry was distinguished by its purity of idiom and simplicity of language and thought.

Modern Urdu literature covers the time from the last quarter of the 19th century till the present day and can be divided into two periods: the period of the Aligarh Movement started by Sir Sayyid Ahmed Khan and the period influenced by Sir Mohammed Iqbal followed by the Progressive movement and movements of Halqa-e-Arbab-e-Zouq, Modernism and Post modernism. However, Altaf Hussain Hali (1837-1914) is the actual innovator of the modern spirit in Urdu poetry. Hali's works include Diwan-e-Hali, Madd-o-Jazr-e-Islam or Musaddas-e-Hali (1879), Shakwa-e-Hind (1887), Munajat-e-Beva (1886) and Chup ki Dad (1905). Hali showered the art of writing biographies with a critical approach in his biographies

Hayat-e-Sadi and Hayat-e-Jaweed. Hali was the pioneer of modern criticism.

His Muqaddama-e-Sher-o-Shaeri is the foundation stone of Urdu criticism. Shibli Nomani (b.1857) is considered as the father of modern history in Urdu. He has produced several works based on historical research, especially on Islamic history, like Seerat-un-Noman (1892) and Al Faruq (1899). Shibli also produced important works like Swanih Umari Moulana Rum, Ilmul Kalam (1903), Muvazina-e-Anis-o-Dabir (1907) and Sher-ul-Ajam (1899). Mohammed Hussain Azad was an important writer and poet of this period. He laid the foundation of modern poem in Urdu. Ab-e-Hayat, Sukhandan-e-Pars, Darbar-e-Akbari and Nazm-e-Azad are some of his outstanding literary works.

Other leading poets of modern period include Syyid Akbar Husain Akbar Allahabadi (1846-1921), who had a flair for extempore composition of satiric and comic verses, Khushi Mohammed Nazir (1872-1944), who composed Jogi and Pani Mein, Mohammed Iqbal (1873-1938), Durga Sahai Suroor (d.1910), Mohammed Ali Jauhar (d.1931) and Hasrat Mohani (d.1951). Iqbal's poetry underwent several phases of evolution from Romanticism (Nala-e-Yateem and Abr-e-Guhar Bar) to Indian Nationalism (Tasvir-e-Dard, Naya Shivala and Tarana-e-Hindi) and finally to Pan-Islamism (Shakva, Sham-o-Shair, Jawab-e-Shakva, Khizr-e-Rah and Tulu-e-Islam).

Fani Badayuni (1879-1941), Shad Azimabadi (1846-1927), Yagana Changezi (1884-1956), Asghar Gondavi (1884-1936), Jigar Moradabadi (1896-1982), Akhtar Shirani, Faiz Ahmed Faiz (1912-1985), Miraji (1912-1950), N.M.Rashid (1910-1976), Akhtarul-Iman (b.1915),

Ali Sardar Jafri (b.1913), Makhdoom Mohiuddin (1908 -1969), Kaifi Azmi (b.1918), Jan Nisar Akhtar (1914-1979), Sahir Ludhianvi (1922-1980), Majrooh Sultanpuri (1919-2000), Asrarul Haq Majaz (1911-1955), Nasir Kazmi, Ibn-e-Insha and Dr Kalim Ajiz have taken the Urdu poetry to new heights.

A new generation of poets emerged around the sixth decade of twentieth century. The leading poets of this generation include Khaleelur Rahman Aazmi, Himyat Ali Shair, Balraj Komal, Ameeq Hanafi, Kumar Pashi, Makhmoor Saidi, Mazhar Imam, Dr Mughni Tabassum, Bani, Munir Niyazi, Suleman Areeb, Aziz Qaisi, Saqi Faruqi, lftekhar Arif, Saleem Ahmed, Qazi Saleem, Shafiq Fatima Shera, Bashar Nawaz, Akbar Hyderabadi, Waheed Akhter, Shaz Tamkanat, Zubair Razvi, Muztar Majaz, Mushaf Iqbal Tausifi, Zohra Nigah, Kishwar Naheed, Zahida Zaidi, Siddiqua Shabnam and others.

The short story in Urdu began with Munshi Premchand's Soz-e-Vatan (1908). Premchand's short stories cover nearly a dozen volumes including Prem Pachisi, Prem Battisi, Prem Chalisi, Zad-e-Rah, Vardaat, Akhri Tuhfa and Khak-e-Parvana. Mohammed Hussan Askari and Khwaja Ahmed Abbas are counted among the leading lights of the Urdu Short story. The Progressive Movement in Urdu fiction gained momentum under Sajjad Zaheer (1905-1976), Ahmed Ali (1912-1994), Mahmood-uz-Zafar (1908-1994) and Rasheed Jahan (1905-1952). Urdu writers like Rajender Singh Bedi and Krishn Chander (1914-1977) showed commitment to the Marxist philosophy in their writings. Krishn Chander's Adhe Ghante Ka Khuda is one of the most memorable stories in Urdu literature. His other renowned short stories include

Zindagi Ke Mor Par, Kalu Bhangi and Mahalaxmi Ka Pul. Bedi's Garm Kot and Lajvanti are among the masterpieces of Urdu short story. Bedi's important works include collections of short stories, Dana-o-Daam Girhen, Kokh Jali and Apne Dukh Mujhe Dedo etc., collection of plays "Saat Khel" and a novel Ek Chadar Maili Si (1972). Manto, Ismat Chughtai and Mumtaz Mufti form a different brand of Urdu writers who concentrated on the "psychological story" in contrast to the "sociological story" of Bedi and Krishn Chander. Some of Ismat Chughtai's leading short stories are Chauthi Ka Jora, Do Hath, Lehren and Lihaf. Manto dealt in an artistic way with many unconventional subjects, like sex, which were considered taboo by the Middle-class. His Thanda Gosht, which dealt with the subject of necrophilia, shocked the readers. Another of Manto's praise-worthy works was Khol Do, which tackled the horrors of partition. Ahmad Nadeem Qasmi (b.1915) is another leading name in Urdu short story. His important short stories include Alhamd-o-Lillah, Savab, Nasib and others. In the post-1936 period, the writers belonging to the Halqa-e-Arbab-e-Zauq produced several good stories in Urdu. Upender Nath Ashk (Dachi), Ghulam Abbas (Anandi). Intezar Hussain, Anwar Sajjad, Balraj Mainra, Surender Parkash and Qurratul-ain Haider (Sitaroun Se Aage, Mere Sanam Khane) are the other leading lights of Urdu short story. Several leading fiction writers emerged from the city of Hyderabad in the contemporary times, which include Jeelani Bano, Iqbal Mateen, Awaz Sayeed, Kadeer Zaman, Mazhr-uz-Zaman and others.

Novel writing in Urdu can be traced to Nazir Ahmed (1836 - 1912) who composed several novels like Mirat-ul-Urus (1869), Banat-un-Nash (1873),

Taubat-un-Nasuh (1877), Fasana-e-Mubtala (1885), Ibn-ul-Waqt (1888), Ayama (1891) and others. Pandit Ratan Nath Sarshar (1845 - 1903)'s Fasana-e-Azad, Abdul Halim Sharar (1860 - 1920)'s Badr-un-Nisa Ki Musibat and Agha Sadiq ki Shadi, Mirza Muhammed Hadi Ruswa's Umrao Jan Ada (1899) are some of the great novels and novelettes written during the period. Niaz Fatehpuri (1887 - 1966) and Qazi Abdul Gaffar (1862-1956) were the other eminent early romantic novelists in the language. However, it was Premchand (1880-1936) who tried to introduce the trend of realism in Urdu novel. Premchand was a prolific writer who produced several books. His important novels include Bazare-e-Husn (1917), Gosha-e-Afiat, Chaugan-e-Hasti, Maidan-e-Amal and Godan. Premchand's realism was further strengthened by the writers of the Indian Progressive Writers' Association like Sajjad Zaheer, Krishn Chander and Ismat Chughtai. Krishn Chander's Jab Khet Jage (1952), Ek Gadhe Ki Sarguzasht (1957) and Shikast are considered among the outstanding novels in Urdu literature. Ismat Chughtai's novel Terhi Lakir (1947) and Qurratul-ain Haider's novel Aag Ka Darya are considered as important works in the history of Urdu novel. Khwaja Ahmed Abbas, Aziz Ahmed, Balwant Singh, Khadija Mastur, Intezar Hussain are the other important writers in Urdu in the contemporary times.

Urdu was not confined to only the Muslim writers. Several writers from other religions also wrote in Urdu. Prominent among them are Munshi Premchand, Firaq Gorakhpuri, Pandit Ratan Nath Sarshar (Fasana-e-Azad) and Brij Narain Chakbast (1882 - 1926), who composed Subh-e-Watan and Tilok Chand Mahrum (1887-1966), who composed Andhi and Utra Hua Darya, Krishn Chander, Rajindar Singh

Bedi, Kanhaiyalal Kapur, Upendar Nath Ashk, Jagan Nath Azad, Jogender Pal, Balraj Komal and Kumar Pashi.

Akbar Allahabadi (1846-1921) was the pioneer among the Urdu humorists and satirists. Majeed Lahori, Mehdi Ali Khan, Patras Bokhari (1898-1958), Mirza Farhatullah Beg, Shafiq-ur-Rahman, Azim Baig Chughtai, Ibn-e-Insha, Mushfiq Khwaja, Mushtaq Ahmed Yousifi, K.L.Kapur, Amjad Hussain, Mujtaba Hussain, Himayatullah and Talib Khundmeri are the other leading names in the field of humour.

Prof. Hafiz Mohammed Sheerani (1888-1945) devoted long years to the field of literary criticism. Others in this field include Shaikh Mohammed Ikram (1907-1976), Sayyid Ihtesham Hussain (1912 - 1976), Mohammed Hasan Askari, Ale-Ahmed Suroor, Mumtaz Husain, Masud Husain, Shams-ur-Rahman Faruqi, Gopichand Narang, Mughni Tabassum (b.1930) and others.

19

Indian English Literature

Indian English Literature (IEL) refers to the body of work by writers in India who write in the English language and whose native or co-native language could be one of the numerous languages of India. It is also associated with the works of members of the Indian diaspora, such as writer Salman Rushdie, who was born in India.

It is frequently referred to as Indo-Anglian literature. (*Indo-Anglian* is a specific term in the sole context of writing that should not be confused with the term *Anglo-Indian*). As a category, this production comes under the broader realm of postcolonial literature- the production from previously colonised countries such as India.

IEL has a relatively recent history; it is only one and a half centuries old. The first book written by an Indian in English was by Sake Dean Mahomet, titled *Travels of Dean Mahomet*; Mahomet's travel narrative was published in 1793 in England. In its early stages it was influenced by the Western art form of the novel. Early Indian writers used English unadulterated by Indian words to convey an experience which was essentially Indian. Raja Rao's *Kanthapura* is Indian in terms of its storytelling qualities. Rabindranath Tagore wrote in Bengali and English and was responsible for the translations of his own work into English. Dhan Gopal Mukerji was the first Indian author to win a literary award in the United States. Nirad C. Chaudhuri, a writer of non-fiction, is best known for his *The Autobiography of an Unknown Indian* where he relates his life experiences and influences. P. Lal, a poet, translator, publisher and essayist, founded a press in the 1950s for Indian English writing, Writers Workshop.

R.K. Narayan is a writer who contributed over many decades and who continued to write till his death recently. He was discovered by Graham Greene in the sense that the latter helped him find a publisher in England. Graham Greene and Narayan remained close friends till the end. Similar to Thomas Hardy's Wessex, Narayan created the fictitious town of Malgudi where he set his novels.

Some criticise Narayan for the parochial, detached and closed world that he created in the face of the changing conditions in India at the times in which the stories are set. Others, such as Graham Greene, however, feel that through Malgudi they could vividly understand the Indian experience. Narayan's evocation of small town life and its experiences through the eyes of the endearing child protagonist Swaminathan in *Swami and Friends* is a good sample of his writing style.

Simultaneous with Narayan's pastoral idylls, a very different writer, Mulk Raj Anand, was similarly gaining recognition for his writing set in rural India; but his stories were harsher, and engaged, sometimes brutally, with divisions of caste, class and religion.

Later History

Among the later writers, the most notable is Salman Rushdie, born in India, now living in the United Kingdom. Rushdie with his famous work *Midnight's Children* (Booker Prize 1981, Booker of Bookers 1992, and Best of the Bookers 2008) ushered in a new trend of writing. He used a hybrid language - English generously peppered with Indian terms - to convey a theme that could be seen as representing the vast canvas of India. He is usually categorised under the magic realism mode of writing most famously associated with Gabriel García Márquez.

Bharati Mukherjee, author of *Jasmine* (1989), has spent much of her career exploring issues involving immigration and identity with a particular focus upon the United States and Canada.

Vikram Seth, author of *A Suitable Boy* (1994) is a writer who uses a purer English and more realistic themes. Being a self-confessed fan of Jane Austen, his attention is on the story, its details and its twists and turns.

Shashi Tharoor, in his *The Great Indian Novel* (1989), follows a story-telling (though in a satirical) mode as in the Mahabharata drawing his ideas by going back and forth in time. His work as UN official living outside India has given him a vantage point that helps construct an objective Indianness.

Mysore N. Prakash, author of *The Courtesan and the Sadhu* (2008) is a Texas based writer who uses historical themes to address spiritual concepts.

Other authors include Vikram Chandra, Anita Desai, Kiran Desai, Arundhati Roy, Gita Mehta, Chitra Banerjee Divakaruni, Raj Kamal Jha, Jhumpa Lahiri,

Bharti Kirchner, Khushwant Singh, Vijay Singh, Tarun Tejpal, Amit Chaudhuri, Amitav Ghosh, Vikas Swarup, Rohinton Mistry, Suketu Mehta, Kiran Nagarkar, Dr Birbal Jha,and C R Krishnan.

Recent Trends

One of the key issues raised in modern context is the superiority/inferiority of IWE as opposed to the literary production in the various languages of India. Key polar concepts bandied in this context are superficial/ authentic, imitative/creative, shallow/deep, critical/ uncritical, elitist/parochial and so on.

The views of Rushdie and Amit Chaudhuri expressed through their books *The Vintage Book of Indian Writing* and *The Picador Book of Modern Indian Literature* respectively essentialise this battle.

Rushdie's statement in his book – "the ironic proposition that India's best writing since independence may have been done in the language of the departed imperialists is simply too much for some folks to bear" – created a lot of resentment among many writers, including writers in English. In his book, Amit Chaudhuri questions – "Can it be true that Indian writing, that endlessly rich, complex and problematic entity, is to be represented by a handful of writers who write in English, who live in England or America and whom one might have met at a party?"

Chaudhuri feels that after Rushdie, IWE started employing magical realism, bagginess, non-linear narrative and hybrid language to sustain themes seen as microcosms of India and supposedly reflecting Indian conditions. He contrasts this with the works of earlier writers such as Narayan where the use of

English is pure, but the deciphering of meaning needs cultural familiarity. He also feels that Indianness is a theme constructed only in IWE and does not articulate itself in the vernacular literatures. He further adds "the post-colonial novel, becomes a trope for an ideal hybridity by which the West celebrates not so much Indianness, whatever that infinitely complex thing is, but its own historical quest, its reinterpretation of itself".

Some of these arguments form an integral part of what is called postcolonial theory. The very categorisation of IWE – as IWE or under post-colonial literature – is seen by some as limiting. Amitav Ghosh made his views on this very clear by refusing to accept the Eurasian Commonwealth Writers Prize for his book *The Glass Palace* in 2001 and withdrawing it from the subsequent stage.

The renowned writer V. S. Naipaul, a third generation Indian from Trinidad and Tobago and a Nobel prize laureate, is a person who belongs to the world and usually not classified under IWE. Naipaul evokes ideas of homeland, rootlessness and his own personal feelings towards India in many of his books.

Jhumpa Lahiri, a Pulitzer prize winner from the U.S., is a writer uncomfortable under the label of IWE.

Recent writers in India such as Arundhati Roy and David Davidar show a direction towards contextuality and rootedness in their works. Arundhati Roy, a trained architect and the 1997 Booker prize winner for her *The God of Small Things*, calls herself a "home grown" writer. Her award winning book is set in the immensely physical landscape of Kerala. Davidar sets his *The House of Blue Mangoes* in Southern Tamil Nadu. In both the books, geography and politics are integral to the narrative. In his novel Lament of Mohini (2000), Shreekumar Varma touches upon the unique matriarchal system and the *sammandham* system of marriage as he writes about the Namboodiris and the aristocrats of Kerala.

Poetry

A much over-looked category of Indian writing in English is poetry. As stated above, Rabindranath Tagore wrote in Bengali and English and was responsible for the translations of his own work into English. Other early notable poets in English include Derozio, Michael Madhusudan Dutt, Joseph Furtado, Armando Menezes, Toru Dutt, Romesh Chandra Dutt, Sri Aurobindo, Sarojini Naidu, and her brother Harendranath Chattopadhyaya.

In modern times, Indian poetry in English was typified by two very different poets. Dom Moraes, winner of the Hawthornden Prize at the precocious age of 19 for his first book of poems "A Beginning" went on to occupy a pre-eminent position among Indian poets writing in English. Nissim Ezekiel, who came from India's tiny Bene Israel Jewish community, created a voice and place for Indian poets writing in English and championed their work.

Their contemporaries in English poetry in India were Jayanta Mahapatra, Gieve Patel, A. K. Ramanujan, Rajagopal Parthasarathy, Keki Daruwala, Adil Jussawala, Arun Kolatkar, Dilip Chitre, Eunice De Souza, Kersi Katrak, P. Lal and Kamala Das among several others.

A generation of exiles also sprang from the Indian diaspora. Among these are names like Agha Shahid Ali, Sujata Bhatt, Melanie Silgardo and Vikram Seth.

Indo-Nostalgic Writing

Indo-Nostalgic writing is a somewhat loosely defined term encompassing writings, in the English language, wherein nostalgia regarding the Indian subcontinent, typically regarding India, represent a dominant theme or strong undercurrent. The writings may be memoirs, or quasi-fictionalized memoirs, travelogues, or inspired in part by real-life experiences and in part by the writer's imagination. This would include both mass-distributed "Indo-Anglian" literature put out by major publishing houses and also much shorter articles (e.g. feature pieces in mainstream or literary magazines) or poetry, including material published initially or solely in webzines.

Certainly, Indo-Nostalgic writings have much overlap with post-colonial literature but are generally not about 'heavy' topics such as cultural identity, conflicted identities, multilingualism or rootlessness. The writings are often less self-conscious and more light-hearted, perhaps dealing with impressionistic memories of places, people, cuisines, Only-in-India situations, or simply vignettes of "the way things were". Of late, a few Indo-nostalgic writers are beginning to show signs of "long-distance nationalism", concomitant with the rise of nationalism within India against the backdrop of a booming economy.

Typically, the authors are either Western-based writers of Indian origin (e.g. Salman Rushdie, Rohinton Mistry, Vijay Singh, Suketu Mehta), or Western writers who have spent long periods of time in the subcontinent, possibly having been born or raised in India, perhaps as the children of British Raj-era European expatriates or missionaries (e.g. Jim Corbett,

Stephen Alter). Or, they may even be Anglo-Indians who have emigrated from the subcontinent to the West. Third Culture Kids (TCKs) often grow up to produce Indo-Nostalgic writings that exhibit palpably deep (and perhaps somewhat romanticized) feelings for their childhoods in the subcontinent. Accordingly, another common theme in Indo-Nostalgic writing is "rediscovery" or its cousin, "reconnection".

Of course, for mass-distributed authors, Indo-Nostalgic writings may not necessarily represent *all* of their literary output, but certainly would represent a high percentage; it is their sweet spot, after all. Finally, it is worth noting that the markets for such writers are almost entirely in the West; despite the rapid growth in the incomes of urban Indians, the sales of English-language literature within India (other than books required for educational degrees or professional purposes) are minuscule compared to sales in the West, even if one includes pirated copies.

Bibliography

Aurobindo, Sri, *The Future Poetry,* Sri Aurobindo Ashram, Pondicherry, 1994.

Chitre, Dilip, Vague Targets; Some Thoughts on Indian English Poetry and (of course) poetry in General', *The Bombay Literary Review,* No.1. 1991.

Das, Kamala, *Alphabet of Lust,* Orient Paper Backs, New Delhi, 1976.

Dwivedi, A.N. *Kamala Das and Her Poetry,* Doab's House Book Sellers and Publishers, Delhi, 1983.

Gokak, V.K., *The Golden Treasury of Indo-Anglian Poetry: 1828-1965,* New Delhi, Sahitya Academy, 1970.

Gupta, Ramesh K., A Feminist Voice - A Study of Kamala Das's Poems, in *Indian English Literature,* New Delhi: Atlantic Publishers and Distributers, 2002, p. 45.

Heinemann, William, *Broken Wing: The Songs of Love, Death and Destiny,* John Lane Co, NewYork, 1917.

Iyengar, K.R., Srinivasa, *Indian Writing in English,* Bombay, Asia Publishing House, 1973.

Jain, Sushil Kumar. *Indian literature in English : a bibliography* Regina Campus Library, University of Saskatchewan Regina, Sask. 1965.

King, Bruce, *Modern Indian Poetry in English,* Oxford University Press, New Delhi, 2001.

Kohli, Devindra, *Kamala Das,* Arnold Heinemann Publishers Pvt. Ltd, New Delhi, 1975.

Naidu, Sarojini, *Select Poems,* Oxford University Press, London, 1930.

Naik M. K. (ed.), *Perspectives on Indian Poetry in English*, Delhi: Abhinay Publication, 1984, p. 219.

Narasimhaiah, C.D., (ed.), *East West Poetics at Work*, Sahitya Akademi, New Delhi, 1994. (ed.), *An Inquiry into the Indianness of Indian English Literature*, Sahitya Akademi, New Delhi, 2001.

Narasimhaiah, C.D., Indian Writers of English: Sarojini Naidu, *The Literary Criterion*, II No.2 Summer 1955.

Nayar, K.Pramod, The Persistence of Memory, New Poetry, *Chandrabhaga*, No.3 (summer), 2001.

Plimpton, George (ed.), Paris Review Interviews, *Women Writers at Work*, Harville Publications, Great Britain, 1999.

Rayan, Krishna, *The Lamp and The Jar*, Sahitya Akademi, New Delhi, 2002.

Samson,George. *The Concise Cambridge History of English Literature*, The University Press, Cambridge, 1945.

Sharma, I.K., (ed.), *New Indian English Poetry: An Alternative Voice*, Book Enclave, Jaipur, 2004.

Srinivasa Iyengar K.R., *Indian Writing in English*, New Delhi: Sterling Publishers, 1983, p.677.

Toru Dutt and Sarojini Naidu, *Commonwealth Quarterly*, 3, No.9, Dec. 1978.

Woolf, Virginia, *A Room of One's Own*, London: Granada Publishers, 1979, p.43.

Index